Members
of the Tribe

Members of the Tribe

NATIVE AMERICA IN THE JEWISH IMAGINATION

Rachel Rubinstein

WAYNE STATE UNIVERSITY PRESS

DETROIT

14   13   12   11   10   5   4   3   2   1

LIBRARY OF CONGRESS CATALOGING-IN-PUBLICATION DATA
Rubinstein, Rachel, 1972–
Members of the tribe : native America in the Jewish imagination / Rachel Rubinstein.
p. cm.
Includes bibliographical references and index.
ISBN 978-0-8143-3434-8 (pbk. : alk. paper)
1. American fiction—Jewish authors—History and criticism. 2. Indians in literature. I. Title.
PS153.J4R83 2010
813'.509352997073—dc22
2009028349

Designed and typeset by Charlie Sharp, Sharp Des!gns, Lansing, Michigan
Composed in Adobe Sabon

Contents

Acknowledgments

This project began as a dissertation in the Department of English and American Literature and Language at Harvard University, and I thank those who saw it into and through its first incarnation: teachers Lawrence Buell, Marcus Moseley, David Roskies, and Marc Shell and mentors and advisors Sacvan Bercovitch, Elisa New, Werner Sollors, and Ruth Wisse. I also thank members of the American literature graduate student colloquium for their careful and generous responses to early chapters. I am deeply grateful to colleagues who read and responded to the project in its later phases and who gave so very generously of their time and advice: Jonathan Freedman, Daniel Itzkovitz, Olga Litvak, Alyssa Quint, Lise Sanders, Marita Sturken, Alan Trachtenberg, Donald Weber, and my readers and editors at Wayne State University Press, whose careful, insightful comments were invaluable. For the past six years, I have had the good fortune to teach at Hampshire College, and I am grateful to students and colleagues here for their insights, interest, and support. I thank my colleagues in the Schools of Humanities, Arts, and Cultural Studies, and in Social Science, especially Aaron Berman, Michele Hardesty, Alan Hodder, L. Brown Kennedy, Karen Koehler, Rebecca Miller, Lise Sanders, Eric Schocket (still sorely missed), Susan Tracy, James Wald, as well as the organizers and participants in our faculty seminars in which I have had the opportunity to present and talk about my work. I would like to thank students and research assistants Debra Caplan, Kari Collins, and Evan Silberman. I would also like to thank my Five College colleagues in CISA: Center for Crossroads in the Study of the Americas, where I first presented my work as a new fellow several years ago. For their attention and interest in my work and for so many enormously helpful conversations, I thank colleagues in the wider academic community: Aviva Ben-Ur, David Biale, Jules Chametzky, Judith Friedlander, Janet Hadda, Daniel Horowitz, Stephen Katz, Rebecca Kobrin, Arnold Krupat, Jack Kugelmass, Julian Levinson, Ezra Mendelsohn, Alan Mintz, Yaron Peleg (he may not remember, but a casual comment from him at a conference was what started everything), Gabriella Safran, Jonathan Schorsch, Jeffrey Shandler, David Shneer, Eliza Slavet, Eric Sundquist, and Hana Wirth-Nesher. This list could go on, and I apologize if I have neglected to mention everyone by name.

An earlier version of chapter 3 appeared in *American Quarterly,* and an earlier version of chapter 4 appeared in *Shofar: An Interdisciplinary Journal of Jewish Studies*. In addition, a number of institutions have provided support, materials, and resources for my research. The Mellon Foundation, Memorial Foundation for Jewish Culture, and National Foundation for Jewish Culture all provided support for the project in its dissertation phase. I am grateful to Widener and Houghton libraries, the New York Public Library, YIVO Institute for Jewish Research, the American Jewish Historical Society, the Jewish National and University Library in Jerusalem, the libraries of the Five Colleges, and the National Yiddish Book Center, where I gathered materials for this work. I am grateful for the generous support of the Littauer Foundation and Hampshire College's faculty development grants in preparing the manuscript for publication. I am also grateful to the Jeremiah Kaplan Family Foundation and the Posen Foundation for the Study of Secular Jewish History and Culture for supporting Jewish studies at Hampshire and thus offering me an intellectual home.

And finally, I would like to thank my family, especially Dannah Rubinstein, an ideal travel companion and field researcher, and my parents, Boris and Halina Rubinstein, aunt Annette Rubinstein and uncle Alexis Arroyo, for information on our family history. Most important, I am indebted beyond words to Justin Cammy, my partner in all things, for our beautiful family and for unstinting love, advice, and guidance.

Introduction

What does it mean to be an American Jew today? What does it mean to be
a member of any tribe in the twenty-first century?
                                        —Tiffany Shlain and Ken Goldberg, *The Tribe*[1]

Nice Jewish Critics among the Indians

In 1991, in anticipation of the Columbus quincentenary, Chippewa/Anishinaabe
author Gerald Vizenor published *The Heirs of Columbus*, in which Christopher
Columbus is reimagined as a "crossblood," a Mayan Indian and a Marrano
Jew, whose descendants, led by Stone Columbus, the protagonist of the novel,
create a sovereign nation at Point Assinika in the Pacific Northwest. Columbus's
voyage is not one of discovery but is rather imagined by the novel as a return
to his homeland.[2] The Mayans, the novel argues, are related to Sephardic Jews,
being descendants of the lost tribes of Israel. Blood is a concrete and scientific
means of measuring kinship: Columbus's heirs share a "genetic signature" that is
a condition for membership in the new "natural nation" they have created (126).
In the novel, both Mayans and Sephardic Jews carry and write "their stories in
the blood," a phrase that, as Arnold Krupat has noted, occurs approximately
fifty-three times in the 189-page novel.[3] These stories in the blood, additionally,
have "power to heal."[4] The healing power of the novel seems to inhere in Vizenor's
trickster discourse, his rehabilitation of the story of Columbus to "defang the

monster who enslaved Indians, and opened the door to their slaughter and subjugation . . . in order to gain control over it for tribal people."[5] I begin with Vizenor's novel because, in the course of referencing nearly every political issue facing American Indians from blood quantum and tribal sovereignty to Western anthropology and contestations over cultural property, Vizenor also stages a dramatic encounter between the Jewish reader and the Native text.

In a crucial scene, the crossblood Felipa Flowers is in England to recover the stolen bones of Pocahontas. She meets Pelligrine Treves, an antiquarian book collector of American Indian and associated texts who is descended from Marrano Jews. The most unusual text in his collection, Treves says, is a first edition of Arnold Krupat's *The Voice in the Margin*, with marginal notes by a "notable novelist" pretending to be the Pulitzer Prize–winning Kiowa/Cherokee writer N. Scott Momaday:

> "Who wrote the notes?" asked Felipa.
> "That much is confidential," said Treves.
> "The margins, then," said Felipa.
> "Krupat wrote that Momaday offered an 'invariant poetic voice that everywhere commits itself to subsuming and translating all other voices,' and so on, to which the novelist made a marginal note, 'but not enough to subsume your arrogance and dialogic domination.'"
> "Sounds like an esoteric word war to me, but at the same time the sense of oral stories in the printed word is mythic, the remembered poet over the noted critic," said Felipa.
> "Indeed, but Krupat's discussion of 'racial memory' drew the sharpest marginal responses," said Treves. "The novelist noted, 'Krupat gives head to footnotes, how would he know about tribal memories?'"
> "Krupat would be the trickster in the margins," said Felipa.
> "The book is great, and the notes are cruel," said Treves.
> "The politics of tribal creation stories never ends," said Felipa. (111)

In his substantial discussion of *The Heirs of Columbus*, Chadwick Allen further elaborates upon Krupat, a well-known scholar of Native American literature, and his argument with Momaday. According to Allen, Momaday's notion of blood memory, reinforced through all of his work beginning with *House Made of Dawn* (1968), "achieves tropic power by blurring distinctions between racial memory and narrative."[6] Allen reads Momaday's invocations of racial, "genetic" tribal memories as a clear "appropriation and redeployment" of the U.S. government's attempts to control "authentic" American Indian identities through legislation concerning "degree of Indian blood," or blood quantum. But Krupat argues in *The Voice in the Margin* that the phrase "blood memory" is "absurdly racist" and objects to such "mystifications" of American Indian identity. In *The Turn to the Native,* Krupat continues: "I do not believe that there is any gene for narrative orientation or preference or that stories can be inherited 'naturally,' remembered, listened to, or heard 'in the blood'" (60). The use of such phrases is, in Krupat's words, "politically retrograde" (62).

Although on the one hand the contest between Krupat and Momaday could be read as the collision between the "disparate projects" of "indigenous recovery and Western inquiry," Allen also notes that Krupat's resistance to "blood" or genetic memory emerges out of "a post-Holocaust anxiety over the idea of fixed racial or 'blood' categories" and adds that "out of context Momaday's assertion distressingly echoes Nazi racialist beliefs."[7] However, I suggest that Momaday's troping of memory as racial in fact recalls Freud's arguments concerning Jewish identity, worked through both in his preface to the Hebrew edition of *Totem and Taboo* (1930), in which Freud invokes the "essential" nature of Jewishness, and in *Moses and Monotheism* (1939), which, despite the book's apparent heresy, can be read as an investigation and defense of Jewish "character" in defiance of Nazi culture.[8] Like Momaday, Freud argues that no doubt "there exists an inheritance of memory—traces of what our forefathers experienced, quite independently of direct communication and of the influence of education of education by example. When I speak of an old tradition still alive in a people, of the formation of a national character, it is such an inherited tradition, and not one carried on by word of mouth, that I have in mind."[9]

In his preface to the Hebrew edition of *Totem and Taboo*, Freud, like Momaday, blurs the boundary between a mystical understanding of Jewishness and science or rational inquiry. Freud considered himself an adherent of the rational and secular values of the Enlightenment but nevertheless wrote that he "never repudiated his people" and, what is more, believed he was "in his essential nature a Jew" and had "no desire to alter that nature." Freud's approach to the collective psychology of religion in both *Totem and Taboo* and *Moses and Monotheism* suggests further the affinities between the origins of psychoanalysis and modernist anthropology. Franz Boas too was a secular Jewish heir to the German Enlightenment who either transcended or evaded the notion of tribal Jewishness through "scientific" inquiry into "primitive" cultures elsewhere.[10]

In beginning this project about Jewish interpretations, projections, and appropriations of imagined Indians with Krupat's work, I am most interested in the ways in which *Jewishness* emerges as a mediating third term in this argument over indigenous texts and Western interpretive practices. Vizenor "upsets *all* sides" by praising Krupat as a "trickster in the margins" and by having a wounded Jew, Holocaust survivor Pir Cantrip, join the nation of the Heirs of Columbus as a genetic scientist.[11] In response to the margin's challenge to Krupat's Westernness ("Krupat gives head to footnotes, how would he know about tribal memories?"), Vizenor, in his linking of Sephardic Jews, Holocaust survivors, and Mayans through mystifications of blood and genetic science, rehabilitates Jews as *both* tribal and enlightened.[12]

Krupat himself stages a dialectic between tribal and Enlightenment ways of reading in his *The Turn to the Native* (1996), which addresses "questions of identity as they shape the criticism of contemporary Native American literature" (ix). Krupat was writing against, among other things, what he discerned to be a problematic emergent trend in Native American literary criticism, that is, a "tribally centered" or more nationalistic, ideological criticism, which Krupat reads as invested in protecting Native literary scholarship as the special province of Native critics. In her recent defense of tribal theory, Penelope Myrtle Kelsey describes the reticence of Native American literary scholars to use "Western-derived theory" as concern for "recolonizing Native texts."[13] She, like other Native scholars, argues a turn to indigenous knowledges as legitimate and organic theoretical and critical models for reading Native texts.

As a pioneering non-Native scholar working in the field, Krupat builds a defense of a critical position that attempts to understand Native American literature in relation to Euroamerican culture using poststructuralist critical theory yet is at the same time sensitive to the particular histories, epistemologies, and experiences out of which modern Native texts emerge: what Krupat has elsewhere described as "ethnocriticism." He therefore reads selected late-twentieth-century novels—by Native writers Momaday, Leslie Marmon Silko, and Vizenor, among others—as cosmopolitan, hybridized texts, against the grain of tribal theory. The last chapter of Krupat's academic study, however, is an autobiographical essay titled "A Nice Jewish Boy among the Indians." This is a piece that Krupat calls a "vocational autobiography": "I focus on what I think of as vocational identity, tracing my own personal history in order to suggest that who we *are* is an important function of what we *do*" (xi). In this way, Krupat's pseudo–travel narrative enacts the drama of Jewish-Indian encounter through the practice of reading and criticism:

> Who am I? I know who I'm not. I'm not—although the Lakota film-maker, Harriet Skye, at dinner one evening thought I might be—a Navajo. Nor am I a Lakota, Seneca, Cheyenne, or Paiute; I'm not a Native American, not

an Indian. Doing what I do, however, prompts questions about my "tribe" or "nation" more frequently these days than in the late 1970s, when I first began to publish on Native American literature. Now, as Linda Alcoff notes of one Canadian case, "white" critics are being asked by some Native peoples to "move over," to leave the field to those who are what they write about. I've already argued that, from an ethical and an epistemological point of view, it makes no sense to exclude any would-be participant from the critical conversations that make up the contemporary interpretation of Native American literatures. Nor does it make sense politically to reject the aid of allies just because they are not "us."

No, I'm not an Indian. I'm a Jew, the son of working-class Jewish immigrants. But I "do" Native American literature. (89)

One of Krupat's objectives in his vocational autobiography is to insist upon class as a significant and legitimizing category of difference: "It's only lately that I have begun to see class as having something to do with my attraction to contemporary Native American writers, many of whom, like me, came from below" (111). Krupat's memories of his working-class Jewish origins, however, are marked by a sense of alienation and cultural impoverishment. Unlike, for instance, Acoma poet Simon Ortiz, who writes of his first language, Aacqumeh, that the language he heard "from birth to six years of age in the Acoma family and community was the basis and source of all [he] would do later," Krupat does not associate the Yiddish of his childhood with a rich oral culture and vibrant cultural life.[14] He writes:

> My grandmother was not a storyteller. . . . I never heard a traditional Yiddish tale of dybbuks and inspired rebbes from my grandmother's mouth; I never knew there were such tales until I read them in books. . . . If there was anything left of an earlier and quite rich Yiddish cultural life on the Lower East Side, I was entirely unaware of it, growing up in the 1940s and 1950s. . . . I fled Yiddish for English as rapidly as I could, and in the family circle, as far back as I can remember, when spoken to in Yiddish I would answer only in English. Later, I would aspire to French, and once in Paris, in the rue des Rosiers, in the Jewish quarter, I would admit, in French, to an old man who spoke to me in Yiddish that, yes, it was true, I was an American Jew whose French was far better than my Yiddish. (90–91)

Yet Krupat does draw parallels between his family's recent history, Jewish history, and Native history: "My grandmother not only did not tell folk stories but also did not tell of personal, historical experience. Perhaps that would have been too painful, for some small part of her experience—the experience of violence and oppression, which I learned about late and sketchily from my mother—roughly parallel the historical experience of some Native Americans" (91). Krupat imagines his grandmother and mother, hiding from marauding Cossacks under hay in a neighbor's barn, as feeling the same fear as "Cheyenne and Lakota women had felt hiding with their children from raiding soldiers" (91).

Krupat's story, as he acknowledges, is not unique; like so many American Jews, he seeks to leave the tribe to become himself: "In the miserable public schools of the Lower East Side, I became a convert to the Enlightenment. And neither the ethnic, national, and religious appeals from the 'provinces' nor the postmodernist appeals from the metropolitan centers have yet managed to urge me to apostasy" (101). Krupat admits himself to be what "T. S. Eliot found detrimental to the cultural and political health of (Christian) nations . . . a 'free-thinking,' cosmopolitan Jew," like Franz Boas, who was, in Leonard Glick's terms, "an enlightened universalist who had transcended both ethnic provincialism and supernatural religion."[15] Krupat never had a sense, he writes, "of the way in which I might form my personal or vocational identities on the basis of Jewishness or class position" (102).

What, then, attracts a cosmopolitan "post-Jewish" child of the Enlightenment to another species of "tribal" creative expression? Krupat struggles between a sense that selfhood is enmeshed in cultural "particulars" and a romantic desire to forge a "real humanism" that transcends tribal or national consciousness. Indeed, Krupat's sense of struggle and negotiation is reflected stylistically in his decision to include an anonymous "voice," or rather voices, represented in italics, who counter, question, criticize, and offer alternative narratives throughout the autobiography.

Krupat's community is, he writes, is a "chosen, consensual, affiliative one—modern, rationalist, secular, diasporic, transnational, and cosmopolitan rather than a community of birth, blood, religion, nationality, and the like" (128); he is at home in the "culture of criticism." And yet, he writes, he paradoxically focuses his criticism on the cultural texts of Native Americans, which, with few exceptions, "insist on a geocentrism that borders on autochthony" (125). He resolves to feel at home, so to speak, with this contradiction, and decides that his story is really a variation on a classic twentieth-century narrative of Jewish Americanization, where reading American literature was, for the sons and daughters of Jewish immigrants, the way to "modern and Western culture generally" (128). As he notes:

But now it is possible—my own trajectory is an illustration of the possibility—for the sons and daughters of immigrant Jews to read American literature *first* as a means of expanding their horizons to modernity and the West, *then* of (not contracting but) *localizing* and focusing on the Native American and African American components of American history and culture without which the United States simply cannot be understood and, ultimately, of making whatever efforts they can to read the world. (129)

Second-generation Jewish immigrants, Krupat imagines, can become modern and Western through reading American literature; but it is through imaginative contact with Native American and African American texts that they can finally become *American*.

Krupat's negotiations between Jew and Indian, cosmopolite and native, modern and ancient, Enlightenment individualism and tribal collectivities thus introduce the terms of this study. *Members of the Tribe* offers a literary history of Jewish representations of American Indians. On a most basic level I suggest that Jewish representations of Indianness are distinct within a larger Euroamerican history of encounter and representation.[16] Freud's, Boas's, and Krupat's dynamic encounters with tribalism—these blood-longings—emerge from the conflicted historical relationship of Jews with Enlightenment liberalism and rationalism.

Implicit in a Jewish engagement with Native America is the legacy of Jewish anxiety and desire generated by what Cynthia Ozick has called the "Napoleonic bargain." Modern Europe extended to the Jews a promise of citizenship that was contingent upon the Jews' profound transformation: "The wish of His Majesty is, that you should be Frenchmen; it remains with you to accept the proffered title, without forgetting that, to prove unworthy of it, would be renouncing it altogether."[17] In order to prove worthy, Jews would have to be "made to fit, and for that they needed to be transformed, cleaned-up, and normalized, even as they were still marked as Jews."[18]

Jews were to be made over as individual modern citizens. "The Jews," declared one member of the French National Assembly in 1789, "should be *denied everything as a nation, but granted everything as individuals*. They must be citizens. . . . It is intolerable that the Jews should become a separate political formation or class in the country. Every one of them must individually become a citizen; if they do not want this, they must inform us and we shall then be compelled to expel them. The existence of a nation within a nation is unacceptable to our country."[19]

By some accounts, modernity perfectly suited the Jews. Yuri Slezkine argues that Jews had in fact suggested its very terms: "Modernization is about everyone becoming urban, mobile, literate, articulate, intellectually intricate, physically fastidious, and occupationally flexible. . . . Modernization, in other words, is about everyone becoming Jewish."[20] Jews were the "most successful of all modern tribes," Slezkine continues, but "they were also the most vulnerable."[21] Even as it promised enfranchisement, the language of European Enlightenment shifted the burden of citizenship onto the Jews, producing a "tacit regime of tolerance" where Jews were continually compelled to demonstrate their commitment to the nation-state.[22] Laura Levitt argues that "liberal assimilation produces a subject who is almost but not quite dominant. The harder this subject tries to fit in, ironically, the more s/he differs. Instead of sameness, these efforts produce an excess that always marks this subject as other."[23] In Europe, Slezkine writes, Jews combined "spectacular success with irredeemable tribal foreignness."[24]

Modernization and secularization affected eastern European Jews in particular ways. Eastern Europe became the site of secular, cultural Jewish nationalism as well as other forms of radical and secular Jewish political involvement, including, most crucially, socialism and communism. Jewish varieties of political and cultural nationalism both mimicked and rejected the nationalisms of the West. Jews revived and cultivated Yiddish and Hebrew, recovered and documented Jewish folk traditions, and fostered autonomously Jewish creative industries. Nationalism and communism, the twin legacies of Jewish eastern Europe, would come to serve as powerful mediating ideas between immigrant Jews and their imaginary Indians.

This brief conversation about modernity, Europe, and the Jews is really to introduce the migrations of those European Jews to the United States, which for Jewish immigrants offered unique opportunities for self-making. Alternatively allying themselves with or defining themselves against other groups considered unassimilable into the liberal experiment, Jews found that they could strenuously write themselves into the national project. Perhaps as a result, Stephen Whitfield notes, America "has most fully tested the category of the Jew."[25] This book thus constitutes a contribution to ongoing discussions about the ways in which Jews negotiated their Americanness in relation to other cultural groups in the United States. I am indebted to Werner Sollors's characterization of the immigrant drama as the ongoing negotiation between "descent" culture and "consent" culture, as well as his arguments about ethnicity as not a "thing" but a "process."[26] Cultures—especially a particularly syncretic Jewish culture, as David Biale argues—continually refine, revise, and reinvent themselves in response to, and in interaction with, other cultures.[27] Identities—especially Jewish identities in a modern, open, and continually self-inventing U.S. culture—are likewise not fixed and essential but rather constructed, in flux, and performed, often over and against identities constructed as sometimes other and sometimes kin.[28] "Ethnographically," Jeffrey Feldman writes, "Jewishness is a cultural process whose very terms are in flux."[29] Jewish representations of Indianness thus often imitated wider Euroamerican cultural fantasies, but as frequently they functioned as challenges to or interventions into them. Crucially, it was not only "American" identity that was at stake when Jews "played Indian" but *modern* identity as well. As the two travel narratives I discuss in the following section suggest, imaginative engagements with Indians pointed the way not always or only forward to an ever-elusive Americanness but also frequently "back" to an equally dynamic Jewishness.

Found Tribes

> Then must you speak
> Of one that lov'd not wisely but too well;
> Of one not easily jealous, but being wrought,
> Perplexed in the extreme; of one whose hand
> Like the base *Indian* threw a pearl away
> Richer than all his tribe . . .
>> —William Shakespeare, *Othello*, V.ii.343–48, First Quarto (1622)

> . . . of one whose hand
> Like the base *Iudean* threw a pearl away
> Richer than all his tribe . . .
>> —First Folio (1623)

The confusion between Othello, the Indian, and the "Iudean" (Jew), in the folio and quarto copies of *Othello*, refers not only to a racial confusion in *Othello* but also to a religious and national one: Othello is a convert to Christianity, and his obscure religious origins are as threatening as his "blackness." *Othello* has been read as a rewriting of *The Merchant of Venice*: both take place, at least in part, in Venice; both feature outsiders; and in both an interloper steals a girl away from her father.[30] The variations between versions of *Othello* suggest an overlapping of the categories of Moorishness or blackness, Jewishness, and Indianness (all, not coincidentally, victims of Catholic Spain) in the uncertainty of Othello's position vis-à-vis Old and New World, East and West.[31]

A typographical slippage between "Indian" and "Iudean" is evident as early as but is not limited to the *Othello* folio and quarto; it was in fact rather common. Judith Laikin Elkin notes that confusion between Jew and Indian is apparent in documents of the Spanish colonial period: "In manuscript, and even in print, *iudio* easily becomes *indio* and vice versa."[32] These orthographic slips mirrored, Elkin argues, actual confusion in European minds between Indians and Jews. Both Christians and Jews in the tumultuous seventeenth century were caught up in the throes of millenarianism, which was to a significant degree invested in the thesis that the Indians of the New World were in actuality the descendants of the ten lost tribes of Israel, dispersed and disappeared in the aftermath of the Assyrian conquest of ancient Israel in the eighth century B.C.E.[33]

Participation in this argument, however, had somewhat different political implications for Jews, Protestants, and Catholics. Ten-tribist theories would come to have a particular appeal to English Puritanism in the process of imagining its own unique relationship with the American continent, one that identified or interpreted the New World as part of a sacred arc of biblical exodus and return. For missionaries intent upon the conversion of the native populations of the Americas, the confusion of Indian and Jew allowed for an historical reinforcement of the theological conviction that both were ripe for conversion, and that converting both would hasten the end of days.[34] In Spanish-held territory, however, this confusion also resulted in the persecution of both Indians and the settlers of the New World who happened to be *conversos*, or New Christians (Jews converted to Christianity).[35]

Menassah ben Israel, a rabbi who as a child had escaped the Portuguese Inquisition to Amsterdam, became a publicist of the idea that the lost tribes were to be found in the New World and that they were preparing for the end of days.[36] Ben Israel published *Esperanca de Israel* in 1650, and in that same year dedicated its English translation, *The Hope of Israel,* to Oliver Cromwell and his Parliament, in his appeal to allow the resettlement of Jews in England. Because he published his treatise in several European and Jewish languages, *Esperanca de Israel* serves as an unusual early modern Jewish text that crossed boundaries not only between the Sephardic and Ashkenazi Jewish communities but also among Jewish, Protestant, and Catholic readers in northern and southern Europe and across the Atlantic. Even before the publication of these treatises, ben Israel's theories had apparently already been widely circulated in England and in the New World.[37]

The source for the myth of the Jewish origins of the New World, an idea that American writers of varying faiths and ethnicities invoked again and again over the centuries, was a fantastic adventure tale, narrated to ben Israel and circulated by word-of-mouth and written correspondence all over Europe and the New World even before ben Israel made it the opening chapter of his treatise, as he noted in his dedication in the 1650 Spanish edition: "The famous narrative of Aaron Levi, also known by the name of Montezinos, has been widely circulated in the last few years."[38] Ben Israel published the *Hope of Israel*, the first chapter of which consisted of Montezinos's *relacion*, in Spanish and Latin simultaneously, and it was quickly translated into English, Dutch, and after some decades Hebrew and Yiddish.[39]

Aaron Levi, or Antonio de Montezinos, was a New Christian, descended from Jews converted in 1497. He was born around 1604 in Villaflor, Portugal, a well-known center of Marranism.[40] Like many other conversos, he went to the West Indies, where he lived until 1644. He then traveled to Amsterdam, where he remained only six months and where ben Israel interviewed him, before setting sail again to Recife, Brazil, which he reached in about 1645. Recife was the first Jewish community in the New World, flourishing in the period of Dutch Brazilian rule. Montezinos died there two years later. In the words of Henry Mechoulan and Gerard Nahon, "he was relatively young when he died, having spent the best years of his life in a Marrano's state of dissimulation and anxiety."[41]

Through the tropes of disguise, passing, performance, and discovery, Montezinos's tale negotiates between the interlocked conventions of conquest and captivity narratives. The narrative begins when Montezinos, or Aaron Levi (the Hebrew name he seems to have adopted while in Amsterdam), while traveling in the company of several Indians whom he has engaged to carry his goods from the port of Honda, in present-day Colombia, over the Cordillera mountains into the province of Quito, is struck with his companions by a "great tempest": "Every one began to count his losses; yet confessing that all that and more grievous punishments were but just, in regard for their many sins . . . the notorious cruelty used by the Spaniards toward them was sent of God, because they had so ill treated his holy people, who were of all others the most innocent" (105). Montezinos is a Jew passing as an Iberian Christian, apparently sympathizing with his assumed identity to the extent of rebuking his Indian companions for their criticisms of Spanish rule. Francisco, one of the Indians, answers him that the "miseries and calamities" inflicted upon the Indians by a "cruel and inhumane people" would not go unrevenged.

After this encounter, Montezinos continues to Cartagena, where he is imprisoned by the Inquisition, presumably for suspected Judaizing. His mask begins to slip: while in prison he prays, in a variation of the traditional Hebrew morning prayer: "Blessed be the name of the Lord, that has not made me an idolater, a barbarian, a blackamoor, or an Indian." But as Montezinos utters the word "Indian," he corrects himself: "the Hebrews are Indians" (106). Montezinos is miraculously released, and convinced that a divine power has spoken the truth through him, he seeks out Francisco in Honda. One of the dramatic centerpieces of the narrative is Montezinos's confession of his

Jewishness to a fellow victim of the Spanish, the Indian Francisco, who takes him on an arduous journey to a hidden tribe who claims to be descended from the tribes of Reuben and Joseph—that is, two of the ten lost tribes.[42] It is not just that Montezinos's journey to his secret brethren is made possible by his revelation of his "true" identity; rather, his journey in fact dramatizes his return to his true identity and his rejection of his Spanish-Portuguese mask. Francisco's quest has as its aim the spiritual cleansing of Montezinos: he is permitted to eat nothing but "parched maize"; he must throw away his European trappings, what he has in his knapsack, and his cloak and his sword; and he must put on shoes made of "linen packthread" and follow Francisco, biblically, with his staff (107).

The found tribes tell Montezinos in Hebrew and "through signs" that the time is imminent when they are at last to issue forth into the world, but in the meantime they could not allow visitors to discover them. Francisco then confesses to Montezinos that other tribes had persecuted these "special" people but that tribal magicians had issued a warning to desist, declaring that "the God of these children of Israel is the true God; that all which is engraven upon their stones is true; that about the end of the world they shall be lords of the world; that some shall come who shall bring you much good, and after that they have enriched the earth with all good things, those Children of Israel going forth out of their country, shall subdue the whole world to them, as it was subject to them formerly" (110). Montezinos's tale then ends with multiple declarations of brotherhood and kinship: the secreted tribe embraces Montezinos and assures him that "we are all your brethren," and then Francisco bids farewell to Montezinos "as a brother" (111). Montezinos thus moves from disguise back to his Jewish origins, which are also Indian. This brotherhood forged in a rejection of Spanish conquest, however, mirrors the very language of conquest: once Spain is defeated during the end of days, "the Children of Israel . . . shall subdue the whole world to them" (110).[43]

For Jews and Puritans alike it was the eschatological implications of Montezinos's adventure tale that became its salient features. If the first half of *The Hope of Israel* is devoted to an exhaustive analysis of all possible evidences that Hebrews were in fact to be found among the Indians, its second half is entirely concerned with how these were signs pointed to the end of days and the messianic age. Throughout my discussions, in fact, messianism will continue to work as an animating force in the imaginative linking of American Indians and Jews. Millenarian excitement surrounding the English and French revolutions, for instance, saw a revival of the Jewish Indian theory, spurred by the publication in 1775 of James Adair's *History of the American Indian*, in which Adair argued at length the Hebrew origins of Indians, along with the reissue of ben Israel's *Hope of Israel*. Mordecai Noah, discussed in the following chapter, quoted liberally from Adair in his 1837 *Discourse on the Evidences of the American Indians Being the Descendants of the Ten Lost Tribes of Israel*. The Jewish Indian theory suggested to Christians an essential role for indigenous Americans in developing God's climax to human history, and saw America as central in the drama. Non-Jewish belief in the theory in turn served to historically hallow a Jewish engagement and identification with Indians. For nineteenth-century Indian rights activists like Pequod William Apess, as we shall see, invoking Indians as Jews served to legitimate pleas for tribal cultural autonomy.

In beginning with Montezinos and New Spain, I do not mean to elide the profound differences between Spanish and Anglo histories of conquest and colonization, nor their very different imperial policies concerning both Jews and indigenous peoples.[44] Nevertheless, I would like to suggest that the narrative's tropes of adventure, masquerade, passing, discovery, mediation, and kinship are significant early expressions of the dynamics of encounter and theatricalization that superintend later Jewish narratives "among the Indians." Montezinos's *relacion* of his adventures among the Indians, before whom he performs as both colonizer and colonized, Spaniard and Jew, alien and brother, resonates in later tales.

More than two and a half centuries after the publication of Montezinos's narrative, another Jewish traveler from Europe would offer a strangely parallel narrative of travel among the Indians, albeit produced in a dramatically different milieu. From the first official arrival of a handful of Portuguese Jewish refugees in North America in 1654, Jews comprised a minute population in the United States. The first wave of Sephardic immigrants who arrived by way of Amsterdam, London, and the West Indies were soon overtaken by German Ashkenazi immigrants in the mid-nineteenth century. Many of these Jews were merchants, traders, and peddlers; indeed, for several hundred years, any actual encounters between Jewish immigrants and Native Americans usually occurred in the context of trade.[45] Political upheavals and economic hardship in eastern Europe, however, produced about two and a half million Yiddish-speaking immigrants who flooded the United States between the 1870s and 1924.

Beginning at the turn of the century and peaking in the 1930s, the Yiddish press in eastern Europe and the United States featured a number of articles on Native American themes. A popular Yiddish children's journal published in Vilna featured a number of Native legends and histories.[46] Several Yiddish newspapers ran ethnographic or historical features on Native ceremonial dances and Indians in Mexico. Many features were more explicitly political.[47]

One of these was written by poet and journalist A. Almi in 1919 for *Der Moment*, published in Warsaw. Almi had emigrated from Warsaw to the United States in 1912, at the age of nineteen, during the height of eastern European immigration. His essay "Tsvishn indianer" ("Among Indians") was part of a series of articles that grew out of his travels across North America; the piece's subtitle is "Impressions of an American Journey." He begins his dispatch by addressing his readers' expectations, predicting their surprise at what would be considered his unusual subject matter: "Strange!—you will think—why all of a sudden Indians?"[48]

But in the course of his travels across the United States and Canada, Almi writes, he has often found himself among the "unhappy children of the red race," descendants of those who "for a few buttons" were stripped of their country. Almi, in a tone of heavy irony, briefly sketches a history, from Spanish conquest onward, of conversion and "Americanization": Indians, "having absorbed civilization from the 'palefaces'—drinking schnapps, suffering from swindlers and prostitution—in short, [are now] civilized men!" (5). Almi describes spending a night on a train where the majority of the passengers were Indians, "men and women, young and old." "The unhappy songs that they sang all night" in their melancholy remind Almi of "our own Jewish *nigunim* (melodies)." He writes: "I saw a people in *golus* (exile) in their own land" (5). He is thus uniquely positioned to "understand" the Indians:

> The handful of French and English passengers who found themselves in the car looked at them with contempt, scorn, and pride, like men of property look upon strangers . . . the only stranger who understood the Indians, who sympathized and felt for them, was a young Jew from Poland—me. (5)

But he yearns to see Indians in their "real" home, far away from "civilization," those Indians who have inspired the "sentimental romances" of American poetry, "dancing" around their "fires" with their "bows and arrows" (5). He wants to see them in "their own homes," living according to the traditions of their ancestors, without "strangers" around them, and speaking "their own language." In other words, Almi articulates a fantasy about cultural purity and autonomy that increasingly, as the piece continues, acquires resonances of Jewish nationalism.

Eventually, Almi visits Kahnawake, a Mohawk community near Montreal, where his fantasies about Indianness are both confirmed and challenged. He happens to arrive during a celebration and describes streets filled with throngs of celebrants, wearing both "national" costumes "hung with feathers" as well as "European" clothes. Almi feels himself to be strange, visible, a white man, albeit, he says, one with a "split tongue"—that is, idiomatically in Yiddish, the gift of eloquence, but here perhaps suggesting his sense of dual identity, both "white man" and Jew. In the air he can hear Indian melodies, but unlike those he heard in the train, these melodies are "joyful, victorious, filled with hope and faith" (5). Almi befriends a young man of about thirty, who introduces himself as a doctor and who, Almi discovers, studied at McGill University in Montreal. He has returned to his village, having decided that he cannot live among the "palefaces" and must be "among his own." Almi is impressed, if surprised, with his new friend's worldliness, which includes skepticism about the recent "peace" in Germany. Almi recounts his companion's remarks:

> "As long as the whites," he said to me, "have not remedied the history of oppression they have wrought against the red race, there can be no true peace. No peace will reign as long as injustice reigns against one nation or even group of people." In his opinion, the "peace conference" should create an Indian republic. "We have never lost hope," he exclaimed, "that our liberator will come."
>
> I listened to this Indian doctor and looked into his eyes, to see if this wasn't a Jew speaking. Nearly the same sorrow and bitterness vibrated in his voice, and the same consoling messianic yearning—*our* messianic yearning. A Red Messiah!
>
> A certain legend, unbidden, sprang to mind—that the Indians were of the ten lost tribes, discovered by some rabbis from the time of Columbus. Who knows—I thought to myself—but that a wonder occurred, that there was, hundreds of years before Columbus, intercourse between Asia and America. . . .
>
> About Jews, my Indian did not know a great deal. But when I told him, he was moved to proclaim: "It is nearly like that with us!" . . . And pressing my hand, he offered: "Don't lose courage, justice must, in the end, prevail!" . . .
>
> Thus spoke a "wild Indian," and his comrades, who had surrounded us, nodded their heads. Running muddled through my head the entire time was: "Red Jews . . . Red Messiah . . . Red Messiah . . . Red Jews . . ." (5–6)

Almi's travel narrative sees a Jewish-Indian kinship around oppression and yearning for sovereignty and self-determination. Almi prompts his readers to overlay, as he does, the devastation of European Jewry during World War I onto the position of Native Americans in North America. He sees a people both "in exile in their own land" and also a people with nationalist aspirations, articulated in messianic terms. This is a sense of identification that emerges out of a modern experience of war, displacement, and migration. But at the same time Almi invokes the lost ten tribes, Jewish mythology's "red Jews," revealed in Montezinos's adventure tale to be New World natives.[49]

Imaginary Jews, Imaginary Indians

Jewish fantasies of Indianness were themselves responses to a white Christian culture that occasionally sharpened its sense of "Indianness" over and against its ideas about Jews. If, in the early nineteenth century, Jews and Indians were racially, historically, and religiously linked in the Protestant imagination, in the early twentieth century, American moderns came to demonstrate their commitment to a national artistic culture through a constructed sense of Indianness that they persistently cast against Jewishness. Just as European modernists turned to so-called primitive art for inspiration, American moderns turned to Indians, who came to be read as both authentically "American" and naturally modernist. This turn to the native was conditioned by anxieties caused by the massive influx of immigrants from eastern and southern Europe at the turn of the century.[50] American modernism, in its search for a native form of expression, came increasingly to rely on troubling racial and cultural typologies: if the Indian was natural, artistic, and "American," then the Jew was commercial, intellectual, and alien. Ideologies and attitudes that seemed otherwise to be at odds deployed these opposed typologies. Fascism, nativism, Marxism, and modernism were all, as we shall see in the chapters that follow, invested to some degree in this dialectic of Indianness versus Jewishness. *Members of the Tribe* is thus not just about how Jews in the United States have imagined Indians in relation to themselves, and themselves in relation to Indians, but how Jews have imagined both in relation to white Gentile culture's ambivalent representations.

I am in conversation with the substantial body of scholarship concerning Jewish-black relations, particularly that part of it that responds to Michael Rogin's famous arguments about Jewish ethnic and racial masquerade.[51] As Rogin writes, "Jews were middlemen not only in their economic and cultural positions but also in their racial and sexual identification: they were positioned between white and black and between men and women."[52] Laying claim to black culture and identities through blackface and other performance strategies, to summarize Rogin's significantly more complex and nuanced argument, helped ambiguously raced and sexed Jews "become white." But at the same time, such racial masquerade helped Jews foreground their own Jewishness as performed and negotiated, and what is more, thus identified Jewishness with an American tradition of self-making and unmaking. Jews, observes Ted Merwin, did not just perform as ethnic others in early-twentieth-century visual culture; they also performed as themselves.[53] Karen Brodkin argues further that Jews succeeded in "becoming white folks" most spectacularly in the postwar period, as they were afforded the class mobility denied other racially stigmatized groups.[54] Many discussions of the period assume a willed Jewish "invisibility" in a postwar culture of changing ethnic identities and affiliations. But, as Josh Kun has argued in another context, even in the era of upward mobility and strenuous assimilation, Jews continued to insist upon a kind of difference, however ambiguously defined.[55] In this contemporary multicultural moment, when asserting racial otherness—particularly in an academic context—can involve a certain privilege, Jews have thus become, in David Biale's words, "doubly marginal": marginal to mainstream white Christian culture but also marginal to other minorities.[56]

The chapters that follow, through a series of literary readings, thus trace a shifting and unstable dynamic, where Jewish-Indian kinship can easily give way to opposition and, especially in the contemporary moment, competition. "Playing Indian, Becoming American" describes analogous Jewish topoi of response to Indians over the long nineteenth century, one directed by the dynamics of encounter, the other by theatricalization. "Jewish redface" performances in vaudeville and on Broadway in fact have at their root Mordecai Manuel Noah's and Solomon Nunes de Carvalho's nineteenth-century performances of Indianness, Americanness, and Jewishness, which themselves must be read against the role of Indians in other nineteenth-century literary nation-building projects. In "Going Native, Becoming Modern" I elaborate upon literary modernism's fascination with the Indian-poet and examine a series of Yiddish translations of Indian chants that appeared in the modernist journal *Shriftn* in the 1920s. "Red Jews," about Jewish writers from the Left, moves from Tillie Olsen's and Michael Gold's earnest invocations of Indians to Nathanael West's projections of Indians and Jews into his satire of fascism, nativism, and ethnic performance to John Sanford's and Howard Fast's identifications of Indians with communism, Zionism, and the antifascist struggle. "Henry Roth, Native Son" focuses on Henry Roth's complicated appeals to Indianness, read against his relationship with Eda Lou Walton, the rediscovery of *Call It Sleep* in a countercultural moment marked by romantic Indian appropriations as well as rising ethnic nationalisms, and Roth's own conversion to Zionism. And finally, "First Nations" addresses contemporary contestations between Jews and Indians over cultural and territorial sovereignty, in literary and political discourse as well as in museum spaces. I move from Bernard Malamud's final, unfinished novel,

The People, which I read as anticipating the struggles over Holocaust memory and ethnic power that mark contemporary identity politics in the United States, to recent texts by Sherman Alexie and Michael Chabon, among others, who resituate an increasingly strained Jewish-Indian encounter as mediated through memorial objects, museum spaces, and alternative histories.

Constantly interrogating and examining their own indigenousness and their own sense of being "at home," Jews found in the figure of the Indian a mirror for their simultaneous and interacting desires for, and anxieties about, tribal and national belonging. In identifying sympathetically with Indians, many Jews could register a covert resistance to an American political culture that historically policed the kinds of difference it could tolerate.[57] At the same time, beginning in the nineteenth century Jews in fact helped to *create* the ways in which Indians have been imagined and consumed by the larger American public, through their increasing prominence in commerce, anthropology, literary criticism, entertainment, and mass and popular culture. Jews—primarily but not only as anthropologists, filmmakers, translators, or critics—in many cases set themselves up as mediators between Native and Euroamerican cultures, even if they did not necessarily see themselves engaged in these maneuvers as Jews. To a certain extent, then, Indians in the modern Western imagination may be read as complex and ambivalent *Jewish* projections.

Perhaps, from an indigenous perspective, literary/critical and scientific/anthropological establishments and the Western modes of analysis they employ have come to be associated, for better or for worse, with Jews and Jewishness.[58] It might seem odd in this context to yoke Indian activist Ward Churchill and postmodern theorist of Jewish diaspora Jonathan Boyarin, but both link the stereotyping of Indians in the Americas with Jews in Europe to in fact privilege a Native history of imperialist conquest and genocide, mediated through Israel and Palestine, thus effecting a transformation of a Jew-as-Indian topos into one that identifies the Palestinian as Indian.[59] These contestations have less to do with Israel itself than with perceptions, resentments, and assertions of ethnic power in American public culture. Jews and Indians, that is to say, can be both agents and instruments in an unstable rhetoric of Jewish-Indian identification and disidentification.

Ultimately, I do not presume to argue historical or cultural analogies or parallels between Jews and Indians (or between Palestinians and Indians) but rather explore how and why individuals and groups deploy a *rhetoric* of similarity and kinship, as well as displacement and supersession, around competing narratives of homeland, nationhood, exile, and genocide. These multiple and polyvalent Jewish identifications with and projections of Indians are driven, more than by a desire to fix a marginal racial identity as "white" and therefore "American," by what I consider to be a historically unresolved Jewish dialectic between liberalism and tribalism, staged in a distinct American political and cultural arena that permits Jews to be *both* individuals and members of a tribe.[60]

(1)

Playing Indian, Becoming American

Two Doomed Peoples

Ben Katchor's 1998 graphic novel *The Jew of New York: A Historical Romance* begins in 1830, five years after the sovereign Jewish nation of Ararat envisioned by diplomat, journalist, and playwright Major Mordecai Noah in upstate New York failed. The New York City in Katchor's graphic novel, like his contemporary renderings of New York in such strips as *Julius Knipl, Real Estate Photographer*, is peopled by Jewish dreamers, visionaries, and entrepreneurs. Katchor's urban Jewish businessmen include Isaac Azarael, "a middleman in the oriental button trade"; Yosl Feinbroyt, who sells kabalistic designs to a handkerchief embroidering company; Abel Marah, "importer of religious articles"; Enoch Letushim, a Jew from Palestine peddling soil from the Holy Land; and the "impresario" Hershel Goulblat, who exhibits Elim-Min-Nopee, a Hebrew-speaking Indian. The actual historical figure of Mordecai Noah reigns over the novel as its model of Jewish entrepreneurial utopian dreaming. I begin here with Katchor's postmodern narrative because it serves to introduce interlocked themes of Jewish-Indian masquerade and theatricality, travel, and encounter that drive the nineteenth- and early-twentieth-century texts that are the subjects of this chapter.

I begin with a brief discussion of James Fenimore Cooper, Henry Wadsworth Longfellow, and Herman Melville, in addition to Katchor, to introduce the ways in which Jews and Indians could be yoked together in the service of literary nation-building. I then discuss Mordecai Manuel Noah and Solomon

Nunes de Carvalho, two nineteenth-century Jews who both adopted and challenged the rhetoric of their contemporaries. I continue with a discussion of turn-of-the-century Jewish representations of Indians both on the stage, with vaudeville entertainment in both Yiddish and English, and in the popular press, concentrating on the frequently reprinted story of Nahum Blanberg, the Jewish Indian chief. Katchor's novel, like the texts I discuss in this chapter, meditates on wandering and rootedness, performance and identity, and the dream of a New World homeland for the Jews.

The Jew of New York begins with a play, also called The Jew of New York and planned by the New World Theater Company, which is a "thinly veiled burlesque" of Major Noah's life written by a notorious anti-Semite. At the same time, Nathan Kishon, a refugee from Noah's failed nation, disembarks in Manhattan after having spent the last five years wandering in the wilderness of upstate New York. Kishon has in fact "gone native": wearing only a bedsheet and sleeping outside on a patch of grass, he is mistaken for an Indian by the residents of the city. The novel constantly references and plays with ten-tribist theories, quoting both Noah himself as well as other nineteenth-century texts, real and imagined. A character called only "the Man in an India Rubber Suit" walks through the city, reading aloud from a ten-tribist tract that catalogs the similarities between Indians and Jews. Hiram's Museum on Broadway features Elim-Min-Nopee, the Hebrew-speaking Indian: "A RARE, LIVING MEMBER OF ONE OF THE 10 LOST TRIBES OF ISRAEL! RESCUED FROM THE WILDS OF UPPER NEW YORK STATE."[1] As one character observes of this Indian masquerading as a lost Jew, "The idea of a New Jerusalem discovered in the wilds of New York State is irresistible to the casual Sunday school student of the Old Testament. . . . By comparison, we, the Jews of the old world, appear to have been thoroughly corrupted by European culture and are Jews in name only" (59). However, Noah's proclamation that Indians, descendants of the lost tribes, should join his new Jewish nation is resisted by Indians in the novel. A band of Indians invited by Noah to participate in his dedication ceremony declare that they "cannot be subsumed by Major Noah's tribe of Jews. . . . What proof has been offered of their descent from a common mother? They, understandably, suspect trickery and deceit" (15).

Impersonation and masquerade are thus central preoccupations of this graphic novel. The character of Moishe Ketzelbourd, called "Maurice Cougar" by the Indians, is a crypto-Jewish fur trader who has adopted "Indian" ways in his travels upstate. When he learns that the beavers whose pelts he trades are becoming extinct, he begins an elaborate mourning process that mimics beaver behavior. Here, Katchor offers a parody of nineteenth-century discourse concerning the vanishing Indian: "His days were spent in a ceaseless frenzy of memorial oration. He dwelt at length upon the tragic inevitability of the Beaver's extinction, never mentioning the part he played in it" (24). Ketzelbourd eventually "becomes" a wild animal himself, and by the end of the novel he has been stuffed and mounted in Hiram's museum as a specimen of a rare South American beast, "the Bowery Behemah."

Jennifer Glaser, in her discussion of the novel, notes that Katchor's preoc-cupation with the interchangeable bodies and "imagined physical difference" of Indians and Jews points not just to nineteenth-century racial discourse but to a postmodern politics of ethnic difference, and thus comments on contemporary anxieties about the "waning content of Jewish ethnic difference."[2] Katchor also juxtaposes Noah's failed homeland in the New York wilderness with what became in the twentieth century a new Jewish promised land—New York City.[3] In what Glaser calls a "uniquely contemporary project," Katchor thus portrays "the Jews of New York in their New World search for an American homeland situated between assimilation and separatism."[4]

Katchor's very contemporary project is also very much aware of its nineteenth-century sources, which include Israel Zangwill's 1899 short story "Noah's Ark."[5] Nathan Kishon seems to be modeled on Zangwill's protagonist Peloni, a German-Jewish poet, who, alone in heeding Noah's call to populate Ararat, is guided to the island by a "half-naked red Indian," his "long-lost brother" (106–7). He waits alone on the island for months, makes friends with the Indians, and picks up some of their language. Having gone native, he finally receives word that Noah has abandoned his project and now believes in a Jewish restoration in Palestine. Peloni then encounters the "famous chief of the Iroquois" Red Jacket, and the two characters, "the puny stooping scholar from the German Ghetto, and the stalwart, kingly savage," talk about the city that is now "dead before birth" (120–21). In that moment Peloni realizes that they "were indeed brothers: the Jew who stood for the world that could not be born again, and the Red Indian who stood for the world that must pass away. Yes, they were both doomed."[6]

Zangwill's story suggests the ways in which *both* Jews and Indians, in much nineteenth-century discourse, were always-vanishing or even already-vanished. Indians "disappeared" to make way for territorial expansion and settlement; Jews disappeared to be reborn as individual American citizens. Cooper and Longfellow offered the most popular literary articulations of a vanishing race. In the final lines of Cooper's *The Last of the Mohicans* (1826), "the sage of the Delaware" mourns: "The pale-faces are masters of the earth, and the time of the red-men has not yet come again."[7] In the last lines of Longfellow's epic *Hiawatha* (1855), having encountered the true religion of the "Black-Robes," Hiawatha sails "west" into the "Hereafter." Longfellow eulogized a vanished Jewish nation in rather identical terms in "The Jewish Cemetery at Newport" in 1852:

> But ah! What once has been shall be no more!
> The groaning earth in travail and in pain
> Brings forth its races, but does not restore,
> And the dead nations never rise again.[8]

Throughout the Revolutionary period and the early republic, the small Jewish community had fielded criticisms of "clannishness" and insufficient republican feeling.[9] If a living Jewish and Native presence threatened the unity and stability of a young nation, then imagining as "natural" their disappearance as nations underscored the triumph of the American experiment.

Herman Melville's *Pierre, or the Ambiguities* (1852) belongs in this discussion insofar as it describes nineteenth-century American identity as negotiating a shifting landscape of Indianness and Jewishness. Pierre's family is identified with the nation; he is descended from Revolutionary War heroes and his estate, Saddle-Meadows, "bore the cyphers of three Indian kings, the aboriginal and only conveyancers of those noble woods and plains."[10] Moreover, Pierre has discovered, near his ancestral seat in an unspecified countryside, a stone that serves as evidence of the ancient presence of Jews in America:

> Pierre happened to brush aside several successive layers of old, gray-haired, close cropped, nappy moss, and beneath, to his no small amazement, he saw rudely hammered in the rock some half-obliterate initials—"S. yᵉ W." . . . But who,—who in Methusaleh's name,—who might have been this "S. yᵉ W.?" Pierre pondered long, but could not possibly imagine; for the initials, in their antiqueness, seemed to point to some period before the era of Columbus' discovery of the hemisphere. Happening in the end to mention the strange matter of these initials to a white-haired old gentleman, his city kinsman . . . this not-at-all-to-be-hurried white-haired old kinsman, had laid his tremulous hand upon Pierre's firm young shoulder, and slowly whispered—"Boy; 'tis Solomon the Wise." (133)

Pierre's family's territorial claims are legitimized through the imprimatur of vanished Indians and ancient Hebrew kings. Pierre's national identity may be founded on his affiliation with vanished Indians and Jews, but it is Indianness and Jewishness that, through a shifting series of associations, threaten that very identity. The mystery of Pierre's half-sister Isabel's parentage, vaguely and inconclusively described as "French," is ethnically and racially charged. Isabel's defining physical quality is not merely her beauty but her darkness: she is "the olive girl" (51) with the "dark, olive cheek" (46) and the "jettiest hair" (118). Isabel's darkness is left unexplained: she is a generalized ethnic whose "unknown, foreign feminineness" (112) reveals the instability of the national family. When Pierre flees with Isabel to the city, it is as if "a frontier man be seized by wild Indians, and carried far and deep into the wilderness, and there held a captive, with no slightest probability of eventual deliverance" (307). Manhattan, the wilderness in which Pierre eventually meets his end, was by the 1830s already known to be inhabited by "the Tribe of Judah," mostly new immigrants from central Europe. In 1853, Cornelius Matthews compared the Jews of Chatham Street (in what would become the Lower East Side) to the ancient Native inhabitants of Manhattan, quipping: "The old Redmen scalped their enemies; the Chatham clothes-men skinned theirs."[11]

Cooper's contemporary Mordecai Manuel Noah, impresario and entrepreneur of Jewish-American-Native identity, and Longfellow's and Melville's contemporary Solomon Nunes de Carvalho, a traveler disguised among the Indians, offer complex performances of Americanness, Indianness, and Jewishness that, in their determination to be at home in America, challenge their non-Jewish contemporaries' nineteenth-century visions of Jews and Indians as vanished or, if present, irredeemably alien. I depart from many other accounts in situating the roots of Jewish travel and performance "among the Indians" in the nineteenth century, and even earlier. In making Noah and Carvalho continuous with early-twentieth-century performances of Jewish-Indian encounter on the stage and in the popular press, I suggest that each generation of immigrants in the United States provoked anew national and racial literary anxieties produced by a polyglot, polyethnic America.

Staging a Nation: Mordecai Manuel Noah

Mordecai Noah wrote in the preface to his most successful play, *She Would Be a Soldier, or the Plains of Chippewa* (1819): "National plays should be encouraged. They have done everything for the British nation, and can do much for us; they keep alive the recollection of important events, by representing them in a manner at once natural and alluring. We have a fine scope, and abundant materials to work with, and a noble country to justify the attempt."[12] Noah expressed his nationalist fervor primarily through a privileging of the native that incorporated Jews, Indians, and Protestant Americans.[13] Noah was also, paradoxically, a Jewish nationalist. The *American Hebrew*, in 1908, in a retrospective piece on Noah, wondered: "The tenacity with which Noah held to his Jewish nationalistic ideals is all the more remarkable in view of the fact that he was so thoroughly American."[14] Nearly a century before the official birth of Zionism, Noah advocated the return of Jews to Palestine and the creation of a "temporary" and autonomous Jewish "nation" in America.[15] Among the decrees for the new Jewish-American nation was the assertion that "Indians, being in all probability the descendants of the ten lost tribes of Israel, must be made sensible of their condition and reunited with their brethren."[16]

Throughout Noah's life, he developed a reputation as spokesperson for the Jews, cultivating correspondences not only with Jewish community leaders all over the world but also with Presidents John Adams, Thomas Jefferson, and James Madison. The crux of Noah's nationalist project was the defining of the American character, in which he sought to combine, often problematically, a peculiar breed of nativism with a program of ethnic tolerance. Noah would attempt to address early-nineteenth-century Jewish anxieties about citizenship and difference in the early republic largely through a dynamic of theatricalization: in print, on stage, and in civic life.[17]

Noah's columns for the *New York National Advocate* appeared between 1818 and 1820 and helped to make the *Advocate* one of the best-selling papers in New York. Their primary subject was domestic economy.[18] Noah reaffirmed Franklinian notions of austerity, thrift, and industry, a bias toward homegrown and homemade products, a belief in middle-class gentility, and a program of ethnic tolerance. Noah echoes J. Hector St. John de Crèvecoeur's narrator in *Letters from an American Farmer* (1782) in an 1819 column on immigrants:

> The consequences of this rapid emigration of industrious and moral Europeans will be wonderful in a few years. We have territory for millions of people, giving to each a farm. In a short time we shall hear the pipe of the Swiss goatherd playing in our valleys; we shall see the vine bent to the earth with clusters of ripe grape, and whitewashed cottages, flourishing villages, and manufacturing towns, springing up in the wilderness as if by magic; and this association of foreigners, this blending of habits, manners and language, will temper the genius and national disposition of the people, and give a softness, harmony, and judicious character to the American community.[19]

But just as Crèvecoeur's narrator's utopian vision collapses under the fractious weight of the Revolution, Noah's insistence on a harmonious ethnic "blending" in this column belies his awareness of the anxieties concerning ethnic and religious diversity that drove early-nineteenth-century discourse. His play *She Would Be a Soldier* makes these fractures explicit.[20]

Set during the War of 1812, on the fluctuating American-Canadian border, *She Would Be a Soldier* remained popular for fifty years, with almost half of its performances held on the Fourth of July, Evacuation Day (November 24, the day set aside to celebrate British troops' evacuation of New York City in 1783, thus marking the end of the Revolutionary War), or Washington's birthday.[21] The *New York Mirror* for September 24, 1836, in fact, listed Noah as one of the outstanding writers of the time, along with James Fenimore Cooper and Washington Irving.[22] *She Would Be a Soldier* features not a single Jewish character but rather a variety of sexual and ethnic cross-dressers, a pig farmer, British, French, and American soldiers, and, by some accounts, the earliest sympathetic Native American character to be seen on the stage.[23] The tensions inherent in the emerging polyvocality of America, the competing claims of immigrant citizens and American Indians, and the attempt to articulate a national identity constitute Noah's subject.[24]

The focus of Noah's play concerns a farmer, Jasper, a French immigrant and Revolutionary War hero who has promised his daughter Christine to Jerry Mayflower, a neighboring pig farmer. Christine, in love with Lieutenant Lenox, a wounded soldier she has nursed back to health, decides to escape her engagement, donning boy's clothes and crossing the American-Canadian border in search of Lenox. Once Christine reaches the American encampment, however, she spies Lenox flirting with Adela, the general's daughter. Feeling betrayed and deceived, Christine decides to enlist as a soldier, to meet with a quick death. Alternating with the camp scenes, in which we see Christine in military training, are sketches of Mayflower and Jasper searching for her, as well as the first appearances of America's enemies, represented by British Captain Pendragon and his French aide, LaRole, both stationed at York. During the climax of the play, the battle of Chippewa, the Americans defeat the British army and take Pendragon and LaRole, both disguised as Indians, prisoner, along with the Indian chief who had been fighting alongside them. Christine and Lenox are reconciled, as are Pendragon, the Indian chief, and the American general. The last lines of the play echo the Declaration of Independence, thus making explicit what Noah saw as a theatrical nation-building project: "Enemies in war—in peace, friends!"

The play's plot is a pastiche of popular set pieces and types of the day, most famously the "woman in breeches" popularized by John Daly Burk's *Female Patriotism, or the Death of Joan of Arc*, and Leveaux's opera *Leonore*, which had been the basis for Noah's earlier play *The Fortress of Sorrento*. Jerry Mayflower, a version of the stage Yankee, draws upon the bumbling, doltish, and simple Brother Jonathan character of such plays as Royall Tyler's *The Contrast*.[25] In Noah's permutation, however, the most recognizably "authentic" American stage character (as evinced by the "Mayflower" in Jerry's name) is also its most cowardly. As Mayflower notes with pride, in the battle of Queenstown, when the rest of his comrades cross a river to enter into the fray, he does not: "I was afear'd that in such a crowd, nobody would see how I fought, so I didn't cross at all. Besides, some one said, it were contrary to law and constitution, to go into enemy's country, but if they com'd into our country, it were perfectly legal to flog 'em."[26]

The cowardly antipatriot was a particularly surprising incarnation for Brother Jonathan, traditionally a "symbolic projection of American patriotism."[27] Instead, the play's most "authentic" expressions of nationalist, democratic, and revolutionary feeling are put in the mouth of the character of the Indian chief, a part said to have inspired John Augustus Stone to write *Metamora*, in which Edwin Forrest famously performed the stage role of Metacom, or King Philip.[28] During the scenes with Pendragon and LaRole, the Indian chief enters their inn and delivers what Craig Kleinman terms "a radical statement about borders, power, and whiteness" as he declares himself the equal of the king of England in his fight for "freedom":[29]

INDIAN: Who and what are you?

PENDRAGON: Who am I? Why, sir, I am the honourable captain Pendragon, of his majesty's guards, formerly of the buffs.

INDIAN: [Aside] The officer who is to be under my command. Well, sir, you have lately arrived from across the great waters: How did you leave my father, the King of England?

PENDRAGON: How! call my most gracious sovereign your father? Why, sir, you are the most familiar—impertinent—s'death! I shall choke—What the devil do you mean?

INDIAN: [Coolly] What should I mean, young man, but to inquire after the health of my father, who commands my respect, who has honoured me with his favours, and in whose cause I am now fighting.

PENDRAGON: Well, sir, if you have the honour to hold a commission from his majesty, I desire that you will speak of him with proper awe, and not call him your father, but your gracious master.

INDIAN: Young man, the Indian warrior knows no master but the Great Spirit, whose voice is heard in thunder, and whose eye is seen in the lightning's flash; free as air, we bow the knee to no man; our forests are our home, our defence is our arms, our sustenance the deer and the elk, which we run down. White men encroach upon our borders, and drive us into war; we raise the tomahawk against your enemies, because your king has promised us protection and supplies. We fight for freedom, and in that cause, the great king and the poor Indian start on equal terms. (45)

The Indian chief then orders Pendragon and LaRole to dress as Indian warriors, in which guise all three are eventually captured and brought to trial by American troops (Pendragon and LaRole still comically clutching opera glasses and a snuff box, respectively). At this moment Noah uses the chief to critique the young nation's imperialistic policies, and the following commentary can, Kleinman asserts, be read as a comment on the Jewish diasporic condition as well:

Your friend? Call back the times which we passed in liberty and happiness, when in the tranquil enjoyment of unrestrained freedom we roved through our forests, and only knew the bears as our enemy; call back our council fires, our fathers and pious priests; call back our brothers, wives, and children, which cruel white men have destroyed.—Your friend? You came with the silver smile of peace, and we received you into our cabins; we hunted for you; our wives and daughters cherished and protected you; but when your numbers increased, you rose like wolves upon us, fired our dwellings, drove off our cattle, sent us in tribes to the wilderness, to seek for shelter; and now you ask me, while naked and prisoner, to be your friend! (58)

The Indian chief functions as one of the directors of identity play when he orchestrates the passing of Pendragon and LaRole, and as one of the directors of political reorganization at the play's conclusion when he abruptly makes a peace pact with the American army. The Indian chief, in much the same way the Brother Jonathan figure had in other plays, functions first as a critique and then as an affirmation of American nationhood.[30] But the quote from the Declaration of Independence meant to evoke narrative and rhetorical consensus at the conclusion of the play—"Enemies in war—in peace, friends!"—still leaves unresolved the profound friction and irreconcilability between immigrant and Native American desires.[31]

Noah's concluding affirmation ends up only exposing the seams of the political and cultural fragmentation brought into being by the play—Democrat versus Federalist, immigrant versus native, Indian versus colonizer. Jews, in this national ferment, are rendered invisible in and by the play. If Noah meant to celebrate a polyethnic America, he also revealed a certain anxiety about its effects. If post-Revolutionary America was polyglot, multinational, multiethnic, and politically contentious, much popular cultural production articulated a desire for a nation consolidated, monovocal, and whole. Noah's play seems to participate in this project of political and cultural unification but ends up rather exposing its seams.

In 1832, Noah, writing to playwright William Dunlap, summed up his life in what he suggested was the theater of politics:

> You desire me to furnish you a list of my dramatic productions; it will, my dear sir, constitute a sorry link in the chain of American writers—my plays have all been *ad captandum*: a kind of *amateur* performance. . . . [M]y "line," as you well know, has been in the more rugged paths of politics, a line in which there is more fact than poetry, more feeling than fiction; in which, to be sure, there are "exits and entrances"—where the "prompter's whistle" is constantly heard in the voice of the people; but which, in our popular government, almost disqualifies us for the more soft and agreeable translation to the lofty conception of tragedy, the pure dictation of genteel comedy, or the wit, gaiety, and humour of broad farce.[32]

As we shall see, Noah's performance of multiple ethnic and political identities in his most radical piece of theater—a founding ceremony for a Jewish American sovereign nation—does the same sort of cultural work as his play, dramatically demonstrating the way in which American nationalist rhetoric could be adapted in the service of a project that called into question the very possibility of a unitary nation.

There existed several efforts to establish autonomous communities or polities within the early United States, and many, like the Cherokee Nation in its 1827 constitution, used the rhetoric of American nationalism to justify their efforts. In the early nineteenth century, in keeping with the newly legitimized ethnic and social polyphony of postrepublic America, Catholics, Irish, Germans, and other "Utopians" planned colonies for themselves in North America. At the same time, the American Colonization Society began to advocate the repatriation of African Americans to Africa. A number of proposals for Jewish colonies emerged in the years following the War of 1812: Moses E. Levy tried to induce Jews to migrate to Florida; Samuel Myers envisioned a Jewish colony in the frontier west of the Mississippi. As early as 1750, a Scottish nobleman named Alexander Cuming had proposed settling three hundred thousand Jewish families in, interestingly enough, "the Cherokee Mountains."[33]

Noah's scheme for a Jewish-American nation was unique in its elaborate theorization and in the way in which he consciously exploited both the American rhetoric of liberty and refuge as well as other minority groups' bids for cultural autonomy, especially in his invitation that Indians join their "brethren" in Ararat. Noah succeeded in simultaneously involving the Jewishness of the American Indian and the Americanness of the Jew in both his politics and his literature. Years later, Noah speculated in his 1837 treatise *Discourse on the Evidences of the American Indians Being the Descendants of the Ten Lost Tribes of Israel*: "Weren't the Indians organized into tribal units with the land belonging to the tribe, rather than to the individual as in ancient Israel? Also, like the ancient Israelites, each tribe recognized a Chief as their head. True, many Indian tribes no longer practice circumcision, yet hadn't the Jews in their forty years of journeying into the desert set aside the rite because of dangers from the elements?"[34] Noah's reading of the Jewishness of the American Indian in his *Discourse* is based on tribal territorial allocation: land has replaced circumcision as the marker of Jewish identity. This emphasis on the Jewishness of Native American communal land ownership practices—perhaps informed by the Cherokee Nation's constitution, which emphasized Cherokee communal property ownership—is in keeping with Noah's famous "grand effort," an attempt to establish a Jewish state on Grand Island in the Niagara River in 1820, which purported, in the words of his biographer Jonathan Sarna, "to save the world, promote America, develop New York State, improve the Jewish condition, and aggrandize himself—at one and the same time."[35]

As the *American Hebrew* noted, "Grand Island, upon which Noah dreamed of establishing the Jewish city of 'Ararat,' is a little larger than the island of Manhattan. There was not a single Jew on Grand Island then, and it is questionable whether Noah himself ever set foot upon it. He imagined that the Jewish city must be founded in some primitive region far away, and he chose a spot that was at that time in the distant West."[36] Noah presented his petition to be allowed to buy the property for the purpose of turning it into a Jewish colony before the New York legislature in 1820, where he was met with resistance on the grounds that preference for one sect would open the way for "Dutch, Swiss, French &c. [who] might wish similar assistance."[37] The land in question had been purchased by the state of New York from its Indian inhabitants; Britain, meanwhile, claimed ownership of the island. Noah was not able to purchase the island until 1824, when, through his journalistic connections, he began to publicize his dedication ceremony, which he had scheduled to coincide both with the Jewish New Year and with the celebration marking the completion of the Erie Canal.

Noah mined both the mass appetite for public pageantry and his own theatrical sensibilities. The dedication ceremony was staged in a Buffalo church; Red Jacket, the elderly Seneca chief, attended, and Noah, dressed in a Richard III costume lent by the Park Theatre, led a procession from the Masonic lodge to the church. The Ararat cornerstone lay on the communion table, crowned with silver cups of wine, corn, and oil and inscribed with the Hebrew *Sh'ma* ("Hear O Israel the Lord our God the Lord is One") and with "ARARAT: The Hebrews' Refuge, founded by MORDECAI MANUEL NOAH; In the month of Tisri, 5586, corresponding with September, 1825, and in the 50th year of American Independence." The band played "Judas Maccabeus," the organist played "Jubilate," and the congregation sang "Before Jehovah's Awful Throne." A rector conducted an ecumenical service, after which Noah, as "Judge of Israel," addressed the congregation. He announced the foundation of a city of refuge, a haven for European and Middle Eastern Jews suffering from persecution, to be called Ararat (the name of the biblical mountain upon which Noah's ark had landed), and proclaimed the reestablishment of a "sovereign independent" Jewish nation, "under the auspices and protection of the constitution and laws of the United States of America."[38]

These ceremonies were greeted with a great deal of criticism, from non-Jews as well as Jews. Jews criticized Noah for organizing evangelical Christian support for his scheme. His promise that Ararat would speed the collection and "improvement" of the Jews appropriated the Christian belief that Jewish restoration would presage the millennium. Indeed, one of Noah's letters of support came from Erasmus H. Simon, an agent of the American Society for Meliorating the Condition of the Jews, which had set up a Jewish colony in New Paltz for conversionist purposes. The Jewish-Christian service at St. Paul's Church had offended many. Noah's political opponents jeered at his theatrics, called the scheme a "land-jobbing business," and suggested that the whole endeavor was a plot to swindle wealthy European and American Jews out of their money.

Noah interpreted Jewish criticism as anxiety over the impending immigration of European Jews to Ararat, "from the fear that the conduct of Jewish emigrants might possibly bring them into disrepute."[39] Noah had envisioned Ararat as a way of modernizing world Jewry, a haven "where our people may so familiarize themselves, with the science of government, and the lights of learning and civilation [*sic*], as may qualify them for that great and final restoration to their ancient heritage, which the times so powerfully indicate."[40] Neither Indians nor European Jews ever flocked to Ararat; in 1833, the island was sold for timberland.[41]

If the Cherokee constitution of 1827 used the language of the U.S. Constitution in order to distinguish the Cherokee Nation and its communal notions of property ownership from the United States, then Noah's proclamation attempted, problematically, to use the U.S. Constitution as absolute justification for his separatist scheme, which he attempted to represent as an inevitable development in the trajectory of the nation. Just as "a few pilgrims, driven to our continent by European persecution, have laid the foundation of a splendid empire . . . [so] a few Jews in this happy land admonished by the past, and animated by anticipations of the future, may increase rapidly and prosperously."[42]

Noah termed his proclamation another "Declaration of Independence," a strategy that was especially common among groups who believed themselves excluded from the original document.[43] Like the contradictions of Noah's position on immigration and naturalization, the paradoxes inherent in Ararat resulted in an unreconciled tension between integration and separation, between his gestures toward the U.S. and the New York constitutions and the declaration of his and the Jews' independence from them.

The problematic politics of Noah's Ararat, however, were overlooked by his critics, who preferred to satirize his spectacular theatrics. Noah had transformed a public pageant into a choreographed performance of American multiculturalism in which he fashioned himself into, at once, a Christian, a Jew, an American, an Israelite, and a British monarch. Indeed, Noah offers a concentrated reenactment of the characters from his most popular play: he plays Christine (a Christian); Mayflower (an American); Pendragon (a British monarch); and the Indian chief (a Jew and Israelite, descended from the ten lost tribes).

Some years later, during the 1830s, when Irish Catholic immigration became a central political concern in New York, Noah supported measures aimed at restricting the political activity of aliens. Noah's political stance was accompanied by a change in nationalist rhetoric: he bemoaned the "changes which may be produced in the character and habits of native born citizens by the influx of foreigners" and insisted that "Native Americans must control the country."[44] Many of Noah's contemporaries wondered aloud how a Jew could justify a nativist stance; one commentator found it "very funny" that any member of "a tribe who have been aliens and renegades throughout the world" should even "talk of aliens."[45] However, Noah's nationalism, his interest in Indians' Jewish origins, and his nativism were all attempts to claim for the Jewish-American citizen the title of "Native American," and to disaffiliate Jews from the question of immigration and naturalization.

In his *Discourse on the Evidences of the American Indians Being the Descendants of the Ten Lost Tribes of Israel*, Noah writes, after detailing the discovery of a "Phoenician city" on the Palenque River in South America, that this proves "beyond a shadow of a doubt, that we, who imagined ourselves to be natives of a new world, but recently discovered, inhabit a continent which rivalled the splendor of Egypt and Syria, and was peopled by a powerful and highly cultivated nation from the old world" (22). Noah's "we" inverts the categories of native and immigrant: "we" are natives of a new world; those who were native before "us" were, in reality, immigrants from the old world. American Indians and Jews, in Noah's argument, were to be included in Protestant America's narrative of nativeness and citizenship—or rather, an American nativeness that transcended citizenship—whereas African Americans and Irish immigrants, though they could be naturalized, nevertheless stood distinctly outside Noah's "we," his imagined axis of autochthonous Americanness.

Solomon Nunes de Carvalho:
A Marrano among the Mormons

Nineteenth-century Native activists too could deploy the rhetoric of Jewish-Indian kinship, if in very different ways, to assert autonomy and legitimacy. In 1829, Pequod activist William Apess drew upon ten-tribist theories in arguing that "I humbly conceive that the natives of this country are the only people under heaven who have a just title to the name, inasmuch as we are the only people who retain the original complexion of our father Adam."[46] In his 1833 essay "An Indian's Looking Glass for the White Man," Apess continues to draw upon Jewish-Indian kinship, asserting that "Indians are counted Jews," in developing his antiracist critique: "Did you ever hear or read of Christ teaching his disciples that they ought to despise one because his skin was different from theirs? Jesus Christ being a Jew, and those of his Apostles certainly were not whites. . . . Now if the Lord Jesus Christ, who is counted by all to the a Jew, and it is well known that the Jews are a colored people, especially those living in the East, where Christ was born—and if he should appear amongst us, would he not be shut out of doors by many, very quickly? And by those, too, who profess religion?"[47] Apess draws upon a nineteenth-century racial discourse that Noah had managed to sidestep: he argues that both Indians and Jews are "colored" peoples, just like Jesus himself, thus pointing to the racially unfixed positioning of Jews in the early-nineteenth-century United States.

Solomon Nunes de Carvalho, an American-born Sephardic Jew with roots in the West Indies, and possibly the first Jewish photographer in America, repeatedly calls himself a "white man" in his *Incidents of Travel and Adventure in the Far West* (1856). His 1850 daguerreotype self-portrait, however, reveals an individual whose features could be read much more ambiguously. Carvalho's travel narrative is both autobiographical and ethnographic, confessional and evasive, creating an effect of a self both revealed and masked. Read alongside his racially ambiguous self-portrait and the portraits he created of the Indians he encountered, Carvalho's narrative is a complex exploration narrative that works in addition as an exercise in self-fashioning and masquerade.

Carvalho had become an authority in the young field of photography and daguerreotype; he had invented a method of varnishing prints so that they would be protected without having to put them under glass.[48] John Fremont, in his fifth expedition through the West, determined to find a northern railroad route, had fastened upon the original idea of documenting the expedition through photographs to be published alongside the report of the expedition. In was in this capacity that Carvalho was asked to join Fremont's expedition in 1853. He is generally only discussed now as the creator of the "lost photographs" of Fremont's fifth expedition.[49] They were believed to have been destroyed in a fire in 1881, but one plate has since surfaced: an illustration of a Plains Indian village.[50] Fremont never published his own account of the expedition, having been distracted by his fledgling political career. Carvalho, however, kept a diligent journal and regularly sent letters back to his family. He edited these documents into a published narrative in 1856.[51] This narrative, along with the ghosts of the disappeared daguerreotypes, remains the only detailed record of Fremont's difficult wintertime expedition across the Rockies.

Because Carvalho edited his narrative for publication knowing that it would serve to help Fremont in his presidential campaign, it is entirely possible that any references to his Jewishness were excised from the narrative with an eye toward what would be a national and overwhelmingly Christian audience—all the more reason, then, to read the narrative as a collection of evasive procedures designed to both suggest and deflect. The result is a travel narrative that in many ways circumvents the triumphalist conventions of the Euroamerican narrative of discovery, adventure, and conquest—whether of nature or natives. Carvalho crafts an unusual literary voice for a western adventurer in the heyday of imperialist expansion and acquisition: curious, absorptive, willing to suspend judgment, self-mocking, and self-effacing.

Carvalho was known to be a pious, observant Jew.[52] Though he frequently quotes Scripture in his narrative, he withholds details about how he negotiated personal religious observance during the expedition. Indeed, Carvalho does not explicitly admit his Jewishness, and his Jewishness is only covertly alluded to in rare, significant moments in the narrative. Like Montezinos, Carvalho

performs various identities, but where Montezinos ends his journey of rediscovery among a tribe of Indians he interprets to be lost Israelites, the climax of
Carvalho's journey occurs in Salt Lake City, where he finds himself recuperating
among the Mormons, whose strange, exotic customs in many ways substitute
ethnographically for the Indians who would normally occupy this narrative
and representational space.

Instead, the Indians of Carvalho's narrative are assimilated, however uneas-
ily, into the community of the expedition: "The party consisted of twenty-two
persons; among them were ten Delaware chiefs; and two Mexicans. The officers
were: Mr. Egloffstien, topographical engineer; M. Strobel, assistant; Mr. Oliver
Fuller, assistant engineer; Mr. S. N. Carvalho, artist and daguerreotypist; Mr.
W. H. Palmer, passenger" (18–19).[53] The Delaware "chiefs" meet up with the
party in Kansas: "27th—today we met our Delawares, who were awaiting our
arrival. A more noble set of Indians I never saw, the most of them six feet high,
all mounted and armed *cap-a-pie*, under the command of Captain Wolff, a 'Big
Indian' as he called himself, and all understood it. 'Washington,' 'Welluchuas,'
'Solomon,' 'Moses,' were the names of some of the principal chiefs" (31). The
catalog of the names of the Delaware principal chiefs includes archetypically
American, Native, and Jewish names: one character even shares Carvalho's own
name, Solomon. As the party begins its preparations for the journey, Carvalho
documents his feelings of "persecution," not for his Jewishness, which at this
moment is concealed from the reader, but for the fact that his photography
equipment is heavy and the muleteers do not want to carry it: "The packing
of the apparatus was attended with considerable trouble to the muleteers, and
also to the officer whose duty it was to superintend the loading and unloading
of the mules; and they all wanted to be rid of the labor. Hence the persecution
to which I was subjected on this account" (33).

Throughout the early chapters of the narrative, letters from Carvalho to his
family written during the journey alternate with personal journal entries and
reminiscences written later and stitched into the account. Thus, the different
"voices" of Carvalho's narrative offer multiple views and interpretations of
the expedition. The letters are mostly descriptive and ethnographic, focused
primarily on the party of Delawares. These letters represent a Carvalho who
initially imagined that this expedition would be a "journey among the Indians,"
and he had outfitted himself for this purpose with trinkets designed for trade
with the "natives." Here he places himself in an easily recognizable genre of
Euroamerican encounter narrative dating to Columbus. But increasingly, a
more self-conscious and "persecuted" voice of Carvalho's journal vies with and

eventually overtakes the more recognizably ethnographic and authoritative—we could even say, "hegemonic"—voice of the letters.

Carvalho increasingly fashions himself into a kind of accidental explorer, whose cleverness and willingness to deprecate himself must compensate for his inexperience and lack of physical prowess. For instance, Carvalho as healer frequently "cures" his Delaware companions, whom he repeatedly calls his friends, of various ills, using the supply of remedies he has, with foresight, packed in his luggage. When visiting a Cheyenne village, after making pictures of various inhabitants and their dwellings, Carvalho as bearer of advanced technology delights the village by turning their brass ornaments into silver by coating them with the "quicksilver" he carries with him for his photography. Later in the narrative, Carvalho also acts as interpreter: "Col. Fremont requested me to see from what it [voices of women in 'bitter bewailment'] proceeded. . . . Understanding the Spanish language, I gleaned . . . that the horse our Delawares had killed the evening before, some twenty miles away, belonged to one of the squaws then present, who valued it very highly and demanded payment" (91). Much later, Carvalho includes a dictionary of phrases and numbers from the "Piede dialect" (224–25).

In an extended and rather comical sequence in which he describes his first buffalo hunt, Carvalho the "city slicker" recounts mistaking an "old bull" for a cow and getting lost, and when he eventually makes his way back to camp—where no one has noticed his absence—and tells his Delaware companions about his kill, "the whole party laughed at me." Finally, Captain Wolff tells Carvalho, "When Captain Wolff kill buffalo, he cut out the tongue. Indian shoot buffalo, bring home tongue. Carvalho no bring buffalo tongue, he no kill buffalo." Carvalho decides that he can't argue with this "powerful" and "perfectly logical" argument (55) and says no more.

The narrative takes a more serious turn as the party makes its way across the desolate Rockies in the snowy depths of winter. Carvalho describes killing their horses and mules for food as their supplies dwindle. It is at this point that his earlier squeamishness in the face of raw meat is explained: these are religiously forbidden foods, which he must eventually force himself to eat in order to survive: "When it became necessary to slaughter our animals for food, I refrained from eating it in the vain hope of killing game, until exhausted nature demanded recuperation. I then partook of the strange and forbidden food with much hesitation, and only in small quantities" (113). This is the only direct reference to Carvalho's Jewishness in the entire narrative, a subtle revelation that inevitably recasts his behavior up until that point.[54]

As the situation of Fremont's party grows increasingly desperate, Carvalho's allusions to Scripture change. That is to say, the part of his narrative that recalls Euroamerican narratives of discovery and conquest and the part that confesses personal vulnerability and fear at a certain moment converge to become a narrative of desperation in the wilderness and eventual spiritual redemption—that is, a variation of a captivity narrative. Here, however, Indians are not captors but companions in hardship, and even saviors, as the first succor to reach the desperate party is a band of Utah Indians who conduct them to their camp. The party had lived for fifty days on horsemeat, and one member of the expedition, Oliver Fuller, died just as the party set out for Parowan, a Mormon settlement in the Little Salt Lake Valley.

At this moment in the narrative, Carvalho confesses a nearly total dissolution of self:

> I felt myself gradually breaking up. The nearer I approached the settlement, the less energy I had at my command; and I felt so totally incapable of continuing, that I told Col. Fremont, half an hour before we reached Parowan, that he would have to leave me there; when I was actually in the town, and surrounded with white men, women, and children, paroxysms of tears followed each other, and I fell down on the snow perfectly overcome.
>
> I was conducted by a Mr. Heap to his dwelling, where I was treated hospitably. I was mistaken for an Indian by the people of Parowan. My hair was long, and had not known a comb for a month, my face was unwashed, and grounded in with the collected dirt of a similar period. Emaciated to a degree, my eyes sunken, and clothes all torn into tatters from hunting our animals through the brush. (135–36)

Like Montezinos, Carvalho has been stripped of previously identifying characteristics that would have marked him as white, urban, urbane, middle class, educated, Jewish. Here, finally, he "becomes" an Indian. For Montezinos, this crisis of self and journey of reclamation ends climactically with Montezinos embracing his Jewish-Indian, countercolonial identity. Carvalho remains among the Mormons as Fremont continues on his way to California and slowly regains his strength and, with it, his accustomed cosmopolitanism. Eventually, Carvalho himself goes west from Salt Lake City, where there was no Jewish population, to Los Angeles, where there were perhaps thirty Jews, and though he does not mention this, historians know that he helped to organize the small Jewish population there into the first Jewish society in Southern California, the Hebrew Benevolent Society of Los Angeles.[55] Carvalho does not describe his stay among the Jews of Los Angeles, however; in fact, he no longer alludes to his Jewishness at all, with perhaps one exception. He resumes his ecumenical mask. But it is in his extended and conflicted account of the Mormons of Salt Lake City that I read a covert, secretive, and evasive narrative about religious and national difference, where Mormons, rather than Jews, are religious and national "others."

Carvalho reacts to Mormon polygamy initially with disapproval: "Mr. Heap had married three sisters, and there were living children from them all. I thought of that command in the bible,—'Thou shalt not take a wife's sister, to vex her.' But it was no business of mine to discuss theology or morality with them—they thought it right" (137). Eventually, impressed by the orderliness and cleanliness of Salt Lake City, remarking on the absence of vice (drunkenness, gambling, prostitution) among the Mormons he encounters, Carvalho offers this ambivalent defense: "Their religious teachers of Mormonism, preach to them, as they call it, 'Christianity in its purity.' With their perfect right to imbibe new religious ideas, I have no wish to interfere, nor has any one. *All religions are tolerated, or ought to be, in the United States*" (145, italics added).

He observes, "These Mormons are certainly the most earnest religionists I have ever been among. It seems to be a constant self-sacrifice with them, which makes me believe the masses of people honest and sincere" (185–86). Carvalho develops a friendship with Brigham Young, the governor of Utah, and paints a number of portraits of local Mormons. He also accompanies Young during his negotiations with several local tribes of Indians, a chapter worth discussing in some detail.

Carvalho begins his account of Young's negotiations with the Indians with a description of a Mormon meeting, during which, he notes, "Apostle Benson also preached a sermon on the restoration of Israel to Jerusalem, which would have done honor to a speaker of the Hebrew persuasion; they call themselves Ancient Israelites of the order of the Melchizedek priesthood" (185). If Montezinos's narrative proposes a Jewish-Indian ancient brotherhood confirmed in the present through rejection of Spanish rule, then Carvalho suggests, if somewhat ambivalently, a certain Jewish-Mormon ancient kinship, here consolidated through a species of proto-Zionism. This kinship, however, is somewhat tempered by Carvalho's account of the infamous Gunnison massacre, which had prompted these negotiations.

A group of Mormon emigrants on their way to Salt Lake City had killed an elderly Parvain man, part of a group of Indians who had entered their camp asking for food. In response, a group of Parvains attacked Captain Gunnison's exploration party, who were, like Fremont, attempting to chart a railroad route across the Rockies. The Parvains had then allied themselves with the

Utahs, Pahutes, and Payedes and "were determined," Carvalho observes, "to continue in open hostility." Carvalho then offers a somewhat radical statement of sympathy: "The various tribes of Indians, who had, at different times, been wantonly and cruelly shot down, like so many wild beasts, by the American emigrants to California, were now incited to revenge" (187).

An Indian agent had convinced the chiefs of the tribes to enter into peace negotiations with Young, to be held in the camp of Wakara, the Utah chief. As an observer of these proceedings, Carvalho fashions himself into a mediating figure, sympathetically imagining the positions of both Mormon and Indian participants. What is more, he convinces all the chiefs to sit for their portraits, of which only that of Utah chief Wakara has survived. Carvalho's detailed account of the slaying of the Parvain chief by Captain Hildreth and his party of emigrants, and the events leading up to the attack on Gunnison's camp, is actually narrated by Kanoshe, the "celebrated chieftain" of the Parvains who is persuaded by Carvalho to relate the "facts" of the case while sitting for his portrait (197).

Carvalho's increasing willingness to entertain equally the perspectives and narratives of Mormons and Indians—both marginalized, vilified, and exoticized populations in the nineteenth century—is an impressive imaginative feat. But their narratives emerge at the expense of his: that is to say, at the moment that Carvalho "breaks up" and then puts himself back together, his ethnographic impulse displaces his autobiographical one. The resumption of his portrait painting reflects his preferred location as observer. But in his portraits as well as in his narrative, it seems, Indians again served to mediate Carvalho's unstable relationship with "whiteness." Carvalho does not exoticize his subject; Wakara's hair and dress are decidedly western. Wakara's features, around the nose, eyes and eyebrows, and lower lip, recall those of Carvalho's in his self-portrait; they wear similar solemn expressions and similarly knotted neckties. In Wakara, his only surviving portrait from his adventures in the far West, it is possible to read something of Carvalho himself.

Traveling Narratives, or "vi azoi a yid iz gevorn a hoyptman fun vilde indianer"

One of the remarkable features of Montezinos's narrative is the way in which it, like its protagonist, "traveled" among and between Jews and then between Jews and their non-Jewish neighbors. The narrative of Montezinos, told and retold by different authors in different languages, articulates the anxieties and dangers of a certain Jewish historical moment, discernible in its ending with its

Portrait by Solomon Nunes Carvalho, half-plate daguerreotype, ca. 1850. Courtesy Prints and Photographs Division, Library of Congress.

fantasies of Jewish reclamation and assertions of power. The early years of the twentieth century, a time of increasing desperation for Jews in eastern Europe, saw the height of eastern European Jewish immigration into the United States as well as the beginnings of an energetic anti-immigration movement. Turn-of-the-century Jewish performances of Indianness likewise refract the particular preoccupations of their moment, most crucially Jewish immigrants' anxieties as new Americans and their desire for a starring role in the drama of American westward expansion.

Solomon Nunes Carvalho, *The Later Chiefs of the Utahs*, portrait of Wakara.
Reproduced with permission by the Gilcrease Museum.

If for Noah western New York State constituted the "frontier," by 1893 the frontier had been pushed to its western limit, and the "West," as Richard Slotkin notes, "became a landscape known through, and completely identified with, the fictions created about it."[56] These "fictions," dependent on the highly sophisticated visual modes of circulation produced by mass culture, were often characterized by performance as much as, or more than, text. The World Columbian Exposition in Chicago in 1893, for instance, has become strongly identified with both Frederick Jackson Turner's famous address to a meeting of American historians, "The Significance of the Frontier in American History," in which he argued that the "closing" of the frontier constituted the end of the formative first "epoch" in American history, as well as with Buffalo Bill Cody's representation of that frontier—his expanded and spectacular Wild West show, which was not, in fact, an official part of the exposition.[57]

For more than thirty years (1883–1916), "Buffalo Bill's Wild West" was one of the largest, most successful, and most popular stage entertainments in the world, as it toured both North America and Europe, not coincidentally, during the height of eastern European Jewish immigration to the United States. Buffalo Bill Cody, the impresario and main attraction of his own spectacle, had fastened upon a winning formula: that of historical "authenticity." "Buffalo Bill's stroke of genius," as Arthur Kopit would remark nearly a century later upon the debut of his play featuring Buffalo Bill, "was to get real people from Western history into his show. Of course, he would alter the facts . . . Buffalo Bill became involved in the dilution of history because he made what happened into a fiction; and he used real people to fictionalize themselves."[58]

Sitting Bull, Chief Joseph, Geronimo, and scores of Indians who had fought against the U.S. government only a few years previously reenacted "famous battles" and "historical scenes" in the arena and were joined by "real cowboys," by former scouts Buffalo Bill and Wild Bill Hickok (who had already been made famous by their appearances in numerous dime novels), and by accomplished western performers like Annie "Little Sure Shot" Oakley. Buffalo Bill, in imitation of the Declaration of Independence and Noah's closing lines of *She Would Be a Soldier*, introduced his slogan: "An Enemy in '76, a Friend in '85."[59] More than functioning as the condition for performance, "friendship" between Indians and whites was consolidated in the very act of performance, thus naturalizing and rendering inevitable the Indians' defeat, performed over and over again in the arena.

The presence of Indians performing as themselves confirmed the illusion of historical fidelity and authenticity that was so essential to the success of the "Wild West." In contrast, across the country, a very different kind of western spectacle presented itself to an urban, immigrant, Yiddish-speaking audience.[60] In 1895 a musical playlet called "Tsvishn Indianer," by Khanan-Yakov Minikes, was performed at New York's Windsor Theater as part of a larger bill that included a more standard Yiddish melodrama.[61] In "Tsvishn Indianer," Harry and Willie, two Jewish "New York peddlers" meet in "a small place in Kansas" as each tries to sell his wares to the local Indian tribe, headed by Chief Kalomfulo. This piece is the antithesis—and also an exposé—of Buffalo Bill's Wild West, in that its wildly inauthentic Yiddish-speaking "Indians" enact not a "scene from history" but rather what is revealed at the playlet's end to be only an extended advertisement for a wholesale clothing business:

KALOMFULO: (angry) Keep your clothes for your wild kinfolk back East! Us westerners want good stock and know what good is!
WILLIE: (sighs, aside) When there's no luck, you can't make a broom shoot!
KALOMFULO: So, Harry, let's see your suits.
HARRY: (hands over his whole pack) Here, brown majesty.
KALOMFULO: How many suits in your pack?
HARRY: 25.
KALOMFULO: And the price?
HARRY: $30 a suit.
KALOMFULO: Good, here's money. (He gives him money.)
WILLIE: (aside) Now that's what I call luck! He gets it coming and going. He'll be a second Jay Gould!
KALOMFULO: Next time bring more clothes. Goodbye! (He and his followers exit.)
WILLIE: No Harry! I can't stand it any more! Either you know black magic or I'm not Willie! (25)

Eventually, Harry reveals his "secret":

HARRY: (takes a book out of his breast pocket and holds it up high) 1-2-3!
WILLIE: (opens his eyes, is amazed) What's this? A book?
HARRY: This is the catalogue of Louis Minsky of 55, 57, and 59 Canal Street in New York. Get a catalogue like this, do you hear? Rrrr! . . . Do you see? There are no tricks, you just have to be a good businessman, you have to know where to buy. Only fools believe in success; the smart ones believe in themselves. Start buying from L. Minsky, the largest, most up-to-date and cheapest whole-sale dry goods store and manufacturer of clothing, at 55, 57, and 59 Canal Street, New York. Then you'll see that in a couple of years you too can be a little Jay Gould. (26)

Mark Slobin, in his introduction to his translation of "Tsvishn Indianer," warns the contemporary reader about the "brash language, racial stereotyping, and crass commercialism" of the piece: "This is not," Slobin notes, "what we have been taught about the Yiddish stage" (18). But it is also not, he argues, an anomaly, and not only does the playlet characterize "low" Yiddish entertainment of the period but also "leads to the films of Mel Brooks and others" (18).[62] The playlet, though it certainly dips into the worst racist stereotyping concerning

Indians, is also highly aware of its own fakery. It is explicit about its "crass commercialism," unlike Buffalo Bill's Wild West spectacles, which pretended to "educate" their audiences. And yet, it is possible to detect a trace of historically literate irony in the playlet's Indians, who this time refuse to be sold, so to speak, another fake bill of goods.

Other vaudeville artifacts also took on Buffalo Bill's Wild West as the point of departure for their own brand of urban, ethnic humor. "I'm a Yiddisher Cowboy" might well have been inspired by an actual cowboy who toured with Buffalo Bill, William Levi "Buck" Taylor, billed in the program as the "King of Cowboys":[63]

> Way out West in the wild and woolly prairie land,
> Lived a cowboy by the name of Levi.
> He loved a blue blood Indian maiden,
> And came to serenade her like a "tough guy."
> Big Chief "Cruller Legs" was the maiden's father,
> And he tried to keep Levi away,
> But Levi didn't care, for ev'ry ev'ning
> With his Broncho Buster, Giddyap! Giddyap!
> He'd come around and say:
>
> *Chorus:*
> Tough guy Levi, that's my name, I'm a yiddish cowboy.
> I don't care for Tomahawks or Cheyenne Indians, oi, oi,
> I'm a real live "Diamond Dick" that shoots 'em till they die,
> I'll marry squaw or start a war, for I'm a fighting guy.
>
> Levi said that he'd make the maiden marry him
> And that he was sending for a Rabbi,
> The maiden went and told her father,
> He must not fight because she liked the "tough guy,"
> "Cruller Legs" gave the "Pipe of Peace" to Levi,
> But Levi said I guess that you forget,
> For I'm the kid that smokes Turkish Tobacco,
> Get the Broncho Buster, Giddyap! Giddyap!
> Go buy cigarettes.[64]

The marriage of Tough Guy Levi with his Indian maiden represents a union of warring opposites: cowboy with Indian, mongrel immigrant with "blue blood"

"I'm A Yiddish Cowboy (Tough Guy Levi)." Frances G. Spencer Collection of American Popular Music, Crouch Fine Arts Library, Baylor University, Waco, Texas.

native, the newest American with the oldest. In his discussion of the song, Harley Erdman asserts that it performs positive possibilities for America's melting pot, "as if in the meeting and mating of these two grotesque extreme anomalies lay all the myriad possibilities of the nation."[65]

In Tin Pan Alley, Jews could be both Yiddish cowboys and Yiddish Indians: in 1909 a musical challenge to "Tough Guy Levi" appeared in the form of "Big Chief Dynamite," an urban Jewish pawnbroker turned violent Indian revolutionary, intent upon enacting revenge on the "Yiddish cowboy," penned by the same composer, Al Piantadosi:

BIG CHIEF DYNAMITE
Cohen got tired from the simple life
And turned his pawnshop over to his wife.
Says he "I'll go and show your cowboy Jew,
Right away a thing or two
I'll go out west and join an Indian band
We'll wipe those cowboys from the prairie land
With grip sack full of bombshells
I'll start a reg'lar fight
For the Indians call me 'Big Chief Dynamite.'"
(spoken) oo-whoopska, oo-whoopska

Chorus:
Big Chief Dynamite, oi, oi
I'm a tough Jew Indian boy
Who's afraid from the western life,
What I care for the cow-boy's knife?
Tough Guy Levi and his bunch
I will eat them for my lunch.
Come on, cowboys
I don't care a Whoop for all that's on the prairie
Dynamite's a tough guy too, you see.

Tough Guy Levi heard about the threat
Said he I'll make it hot for Cohen you bet
And right away he sent for brother Sylvest
To drive back Cohen from the west,
"Come one," said Cohen, you and your brother too.
You'll look like thirty cents when I get through
Sylvest and Levi started
To fight with all their might,
"It's a shame," said Cohen, then threw the dynamite.
(spoken) oo-whoopska, oo-whoopska[66]

"Big Chief Dynamite" seems to refer to a popular pseudohistorical tale of a Jewish Indian chief, circulated in both American Jewish and Yiddish newspapers

"Big Chief Dynamite." Lester S. Levy Collection of Sheet Music, Special Collections, Sheridan Libraries, Johns Hopkins University Library.

between 1909 and 1910. The story began as a feature in the *American Hebrew* in 1909, written by J. Fuchs, who regularly contributed entertaining, semifictional sketches to the paper. These sketches blurred the line between fact and invention, often claiming a basis in historical fact while also acknowledging some liberties with the crafting of narrative voice. In this case, Fuchs provided a note to "Nahum Blanberg, Indian Chief," which read: "This story is based in part upon certain extremely curious facts, for which I have the authority of Mr. Ossian Lang,

"They Turned at Last to Me for Counsel." Illustration in "Nahum Blanberg, Indian Chief," *American Hebrew*, May 28, 1909.

editor-in-chief of the 'School Journal' and staff contributor to the 'Forum.'"[67] The tale is narrated by "Nahum Blanberg" himself, in quotation marks, giving the sense of a true tale "as told to" J. Fuchs. The style is purposefully archaic, biblical, and formal, and neither satiric nor comical:

In the year 5636 after the Creation of the World, Alexander the Second, Emperor of Russia, declared war against the Turk. He drew the sword as

Haman, his brother, had done before him, but the Lord bore with him for five years ere he destroyed him, as it is written: "The Lord's soul hateth him that loveth violence," Psalms XI. 5. At the outbreak of the war I had three years of military service behind me. I was a lusty youth then, strong as an ox and free from all fear, save the fear of the Holy One, blessed be He. But in my innermost heart I loathed the thought of fighting the enemies of the house of the son of Agag. And therefore, when our regiment got marching orders, I deserted the colors at the death of night and hastened home, with the *Malachha-moves* in pursuit behind me. (82)

The first paragraph exhibits several flourishes that become characteristic of the whole piece: first, the story is told in "Jewish time," that is to say, according to a Jewish calendar, taking place in 5636 rather than 1876. Second, the story, while recognizably set in recent history, frames itself biblically: Alexander the Second is the brother of Haman and is described as a son of Agag and later on as Pharaoh. And finally, Hebrew and Yiddish words are frequently inserted into the narrative with no gloss so that an effect is created of a text that presumes a multilingual, or at least heteroglossic, reader and of a reader who consumes the tale as though it were a translation.

Nahum Blanberg and his mother decide to flee Russia, through Poland, into Germany. From Hamburg, they eventually make their way to New York, "two strangers in a city of strangers." This was an archetypal journey, a popular trajectory for emigrating Russian Jews, and the same journey described by Mary Antin (save that Antin and her family ended up in Boston) in her bestselling autobiography *The Promised Land*, published only two years after "Nahum Blanberg, Indian Chief." But here Blanberg's travels diverge from Antin's. An immigration official at Castle Garden, "marveling" at Nahum's "great strength and size," recommends that he try his luck out West as a trader: "He told me of far-off parts whither I had better go to grow up with the country. . . . [H]e counseled me truly telling me to try my luck in borderlands, where honest, hardworking traders are needed" (82). Leaving his mother in the care of "good Jews" in New York, Blanberg "traveled night and day, by rail and by stagecoach, till I reached what is known now as the town of Laguna, in the country of Valencia, New Mexico, with a hundred dollars in my pocket and goods worth several hundred more. Behold now how it came to pass, that I attained to wealth and honors in this Indian village of Laguna where I am sitting in the seat of a judge now and where you, my heirs and sons, shall sit in judgment after me, in the fear of the Lord and in obedience to His Holy Law" (83).

This narrative, it thus appears here, is addressed to Blanberg's "sons and heirs," who, like priests or kings in ancient Israel, will inherit their father's position of leadership. Blanberg continues with his story of material success in the West, noting proudly that he is the only white man "that went around unarmed" and never drank "ardent spirits." Thus, Blanberg notes, "I lived like the Indians to whom the whites denied strong drink they wouldn't do without themselves. As for fire-arms, I had left war and murder behind me where I fled from, and stood in no need of them, meaning harm to no one" (83).

As for the Indians among whom Blanberg lives, "They were heathen in those days, before God turned toward me their hearts and minds, and as helpless as babes at the breast. They could neither read nor write, nor could they figure correctly or measure values in common trade—they were sheep without a shepherd and I soon found out what wolves were preying upon them and in what way" (83). Evidently, this is not a narrative about a crypto-Jew's return to his faith but rather a neo-Puritan conversion narrative in which Blanberg's pacifism and purity turn "savage" innocents toward the "true" faith. The villains of the story are the corrupt Indian agent and the dissolute Indian chief, who are in league together to reap illegal profits off the sale of the tribe's pottery. Meanwhile, Blanberg becomes fluent in both English and "the Red Man's tongue" and earns the trust of the tribe with his honest business dealings and his piety. The tribe decides ultimately to depose their chief and to appeal to Blanberg, who assumes responsibility for the tribe's financial affairs. At this, the Indian agent "storms" at the Indians and "told them I was a Jew and that they had better distrust me, as one of the misbelievers. Thereupon they told him that the Great Spirit with *him* was in his mouth, but with *me* in my hands, and if I was a Jew, they were all willing henceforth to learn the ways of the Jews and to abide by their law" (84). Blanberg teaches his new tribe "the Torah and the Sayings of our Sages—their memory for a blessing!" (84). Blanberg concludes:

> Know this: I had found a people poor, and I was a poor man myself, just escaped from oppression. God made me lift from them the yoke of oppression and made us rich, both me and my people. . . . I knew that the Holy Law of my fathers had completed its circuit from the land of the rising sun to that of the setting. I have been found worthy to spread it. (84)

Although in many ways this narrative echoes European narratives of conquest and religious conversion (particularly in the description of indigenous peoples "eager" to convert), this tale also frames itself in a continuous tradition, from biblical narrative through modernity, of Jewish persecution and redemption. What is more, the narrative also adopts the familiar archetype of the clever and honest immigrant's material success, and even suggests a parable about labor exploitation: Blanberg saves the Indians—honest and talented, if ignorant, workers—from the exploitation of a corrupt boss and government. Blanberg is a curious amalgam of conquistador, Moses, Horatio Alger hero, and labor union organizer. The story is thus unable to reconcile its colonial and countercolonial impulses: Blanberg helps the tribe assert itself against the agent of the U.S. government and exploitative bosses, but he assumes their paternalistic roles. He asserts the "natural" goodness of the "red men" but discusses how they do not stop "drinking, gambling, and beating their wives" until he has taught them the principles of Jewishness. The story imagines, at its end, the spread from east to west not of Christianity, civilization, capitalism, or democracy but rather of Judaism—which is implied to be completely compatible with all of the above. This curious narrative, I suggest, is deeply responsive to particular anxieties associated with the precarious place of Jews in the turn-of-the-century Russian empire and in Europe generally, as well as the evolving place of Jews as immigrants and their participation as "Americans" in a rapidly expanding United States.

Blanberg's story, it seems, was widely assumed to be true. On June 11, 1909, Philip Cowen, another writer, contributed a response to Fuchs's story in the *American Hebrew*:

> In THE AMERICAN HEBREW of May 28, there was published under the above title, a story by J. Fuchs that merits a few words in the behalf of historic truth, lest an interesting incident in American Jewish history be altogether forgotten. . . . [I]t is an actual fact that a Jew was an Indian chief, who exercised all the powers that a chief could exercise after the white man drove his tribe into a corner. It is also true that this Indian chief was a man of sterling character, who ruled his people wisely, and brought them to understand the ways of the white man so far as they were commendable. Here, however, excepting perhaps as to the locality, the real facts end so far as the writer of "Nahum Blanberg" is concerned, for fiction reigns thereafter.[68]

The real Blanberg, according to Cowen, was not from Russia but from Germany and from a relatively well-to-do family. He did not marry a Jewish woman from New Orleans, as Fuchs's Blanberg does, but rather "took to wife an Indian maiden, none other than the chief of the tribe, and thus it was that he became an Indian chief." Here, Cowen's version of the tale becomes less one of a democratic, bloodless workers' revolution and rather a tale of adoption and kinship:

> The chief loved Nahum because he had been so faithful a friend and counselor unto the remnant of the tribe, and he had been adopted into the Indian fold in the customary fashion of the red man. And when the old chief was about to join his fathers, he yielded his scepter to his son-in-law as his heir, and passed it over to him in accordance with the traditions of his tribe, and the choice of the dying chief was welcomed by the remnant of his people. (143)

Nahum raises his children as Jews, and decides ultimately to move to an unnamed large city where his children would have Jewish associations. Here the narrative becomes a drama of racial disguise and passing: "He hoped that the dark eyes and the olive complexions of his beautiful daughters would be taken simply as indication of Castilian heritage, but dreaded that the fact of Indian blood in their veins would become known to the people among whom her dwelt, and blight the lives of his loved ones. He, therefore, put the seal of silence on the lips of those of his family in the East who knew the full story of his life" (143). For this reason, Cowen keeps the secret of Blanberg's true identity, but hopes to someday "deposit" the account with the American Jewish Historical Society.

The actual historical figure upon whom Nahum Blanberg was based was most likely Solomon Bibo, whose biography can indeed be found on the American Jewish Historical Society's website (http://ajhs.org).[69] Bibo was a Jewish immigrant from Prussia who, with his brothers, had established a mercantile business throughout New Mexico and opened a store in the Acoma Pueblo. He married an Acoma woman, and the Acomas elected him as governor of the Acoma Pueblo in 1885. He served as governor for about four years. It seems that Bibo's tenure among the Acomas was rather contentious and divisive; he advocated a policy of assimilation and modernization for the Acomas, which pitted him against other tribal factions that argued for the preservation of traditional religious and cultural life. By 1909, when his fictionalized story was published and discussed in the *American Hebrew*, Bibo had left the Acoma Pueblo—perhaps because of the cultural battles in which he was embroiled—and was living in San Francisco with his family, where he operated a large grocery store and where at least one son celebrated his bar mitzvah.

Nahum Blanberg, evidently, exerted a more romantic appeal than Solomon

Bibo on a turn-of-the-century readership. "Nahum Blanberg, Indian Chief" was reprinted in the *American Israelite* (published in Cincinnati) in 1910, where it took up most of the front page, retitled "Nahum Blanberg: How a Jew Became an Indian Chief."[70] From there, the story migrated to the Yiddish press and was translated and published in 1910 in *Undzer Lebn* (Our Life), a Yiddish weekly published out of Warsaw. The translated title was "Vi azoy a yid iz gevorn a hoyptman fun vilde indianer" ("How a Jew became a chief of wild Indians") and an accompanying note read, "A mayse gegirndet oyf emese fakten dertseylt fun hoyptman aleyn, Nahum Blanberg" ("A story founded upon true facts narrated by the chief himself, Nahum Blanberg").[71]

Nahum Blanberg, not J. Fuchs, is the author of this Yiddish piece: its status as true tale, and Nahum Blanberg as a living person, is now undisputed. Moreover, the translator, attributed here only through initials, A.Z.C., has taken some liberties with Fuchs's ornate and formal style, as the first few lines in Yiddish demonstrate: "I had served three years in the Russian army, when Alexander II declared war upon Turkey" ("Ikh hob shoyn gehat gedint dos drite yor in rusishen militer, als Aleksander der tsveyter hot erklert terkay a krig" [2]). But not only does this translator dispense with Fuchs's biblical flourishes, A.Z.C. also engaged in some rewriting: "I had since childhood been educated in *kheyders* and *yeshivas* [traditional religious Jewish schools] and feared, by nature, wars and bloodshed" ("Ikh bin gevorn fun kindvays ertsoynen in di kheyderim un yeshives un hob b'teyve faynt gehat milkhomes un blut-fergisung" [2]). Blanberg's pacifism and gentleness are here heightened even further than in the original. Blanberg runs away from the army, in the English original, "with the help of friends and neighbors who may still be alive and within reach of Pharaoh's yad [hand]." In the Yiddish, Blanberg runs away from his barracks, donning civilian clothes given to him "by a friend, with whom I often took my *Shabbes* meals" ("bay a fraynt, vu ikh fleg esn shabbes" [2]). That is to say, this Yiddish translator adds several touches to the story's Russian beginning that reframe Blanberg's origins as familiar, intimate, and recognizable rather than epic and biblical. In the hands of this Yiddish translator, America becomes a mythic land, and in these sections the translator adds certain stereotypical language and images. For example, when Blanberg arrives in New Mexico, this translator adds that the country is peopled with "wild Indians" ("iz geven demalt bezetst fun vilde indianer" [2]). Later, where the English version has the Indians talk about the Great Spirit, in the Yiddish version this Great Spirit is named Manitou, a name popularized perhaps primarily by Longfellow's *Hiawatha*, and in any case not linked with the peoples of New Mexico.

Moreover, the Yiddish translator/adaptor, having evidently decided that the original was not exotic enough in describing Native customs, even adds a scene in which the tribe of Indians holds a dance in Blanberg's honor:

> In my honor the Indians made a great revelry, during which they danced the "great oxen dance." Eight men, for four days, several times a day, danced this folk dance for all assembled, in which they artfully imitated the movements of various animals, and especially the movements of the wild ox (bison). The dancers were thus clad in the skins of wild oxen, with horns and tails and painted faces in different colors. They presented me with a valuable riding horse and a bow with arrows. (3)

The writer here is presumably describing a "Buffalo dance," in this case accurately linked to the tribes of the Southwest. Possibly derived from an ethnographic account, this description reflects typical Euroamerican fantasies about Indianness, not least in the translator's decision to insert it gratuitously into the narrative. Finally, it is Blanberg's return to Jewishness that is foregrounded in the Yiddish version. Here, he does not "convert" the tribe among whom he lives, but rather because he begins to yearn for his familiar texts—his Bible, his Talmud, and so on—he begins to tell them stories and legends. The Yiddish version of the tale ends when Blanberg finds a Jewish wife.

Blanberg's advocacy of exploited indigenous workers certainly appealed to a secular, intellectual, radicalized eastern European Yiddish-speaking audience. Blanberg as the immigrant who, even among "wild Indians," cannot forget his own indigenous traditions, also certainly appealed to a readership ambivalent about the promises of the New World. Like the narrative of Montezinos, the tale of Nahum Blanberg/Solomon Bibo exerted a romantic appeal on both sides of the Atlantic not necessarily for what it had to say about Indians but rather for what it had to say about Jews and their roles as immigrants and new citizens in the United States.

Trickster Jews and the Wild West

I associated with all kinds of races and creeds and it don't bother me at all. In fact, I was in a bill with a colored act fellow named Shelton Brooks. He wrote "Darktown Strutters Ball" and "Some of These Days." I used to go rowin' on the lake with him. And I remember we were sittin' in the park,

Shelton and I, and there wuz a coupla goils sittin' on another bench and they probably just saw the show. So Shelton says, "Nat the goils are floitin' with you." "Shelton," I said, "what am I gonna do with you?" "Oh, tell them that Ah'ma Indian."

This one you'll like. In Chicago while I wuz wo'kin' with my wife, when we weren't married we had separate dressin' rooms and naturally I'd give her the best room. So one night the manager comes up to me and says, "Nat, you're dressin' with those Indians on the bill." "I don't want to dress with no Indians. Put me in the boiler." That was a new kind of thing for me, dressin' with Indians. But he says, "That's all we got." So I said allright. So I walked into that dressin' room and just as I'm comin' in, I hear four of five of those Indians convoicin'[?] in Jewish. The act was called an Indian act but it had one Mexican, one Indian and the rest wuz was Jewish. And that was the foist time I ever felt at home with a buncha Indians.

—Nat Reynard, *American Life Histories: Manuscripts from the Federal Writer's Project, 1936–40*

This former vaudevillian's anecdote repeats an old joke that "Indians" on the vaudeville stage (and later, in Hollywood films) were usually performed by Jews but also suggests that the early-twentieth-century vaudeville theater served as a literal staging ground upon which Jews, Indians, as well as various other "others" met and mingled—and perhaps, in the words of Nat Reynard, felt "at home."[72] If Jewish immigrants usually encountered "real Indians" through trade and through ethnographic fieldwork, it seems another possible site of encounter was the vaudeville circuit. However, it was likely more often the case that Jewish performers donned redface, a phenomenon that has increasingly attracted attention by scholars, including Michael Rogin, Andrea Most, and Peter Antelyes. The comical encounter between an urban ethnic, usually a New York Jew, and the Wild West as invented by William Cody performed in "Tsvishn Indianer"; burlesque songs such as "Yonkl the Cowboy Jew," "I'm a Yiddish Cowboy," "Moshe from Nova Scotia" (about a Jewish Eskimo), and "Big Chief Dynamite"; and Fanny Brice's Ziegfeld Follies song "I'm an Indian" would continue to play out on the stage in such productions as Donaldson and Kahn's Ziegfeld production *Whoopee!* (1929; filmed in 1930) and George and Ira Gershwin's *Girl Crazy* (1930).[73] Noah's own New York, whose Lower East Side was at the turn of the twentieth century home to the densest Jewish immigrant population in the country, would eventually produce the urge from the margins to comically undermine the mytho-history in which Noah was so deeply invested. As Rogin writes, "When the Jew goes west as vaudeville Jew—as Eddie Cantor—he at once facilitates and subverts the melting pot."[74]

In *Whoopee!* Eddie Cantor plays Henry Williams, who, Gentile name notwithstanding, is a neurotic New York Jew who has moved "out West" for his health. He is conscripted by Sally Morgan—who is supposed to marry the local sheriff but is in love with an Indian "half-breed" named Wanenis—to help her run away. Henry and Sally are pursued by Sheriff Bob, which then provides the opportunity for Henry Williams/Eddie Cantor to disguise himself as a Greek cook, as a minstrel in blackface, and finally, when Sally and Henry reach Wanenis's reservation, as an Indian. In this disguise, Henry sells Indian trinkets to an unsuspecting wealthy tourist. Rogin explains, "The message is that Jews would have a gotten a better price for their land."[75] In a comical inversion of "Tsvishn Indianer"'s Jewish peddlers and Indian customers, he delivers a sales pitch in a rapid Yiddish, and sings and dances an "Indian melody" that "sounds more like a Hasidic *niggun*."[76] The tourist, a New England blueblood, is totally fooled. Further, as Most notes, "When Henry is invited to smoke a peace pipe with Chief Black Eagle, he sings (to the tune of 'Old Man River') 'Old Black Eagle and old man Siegal.'"[77] Later, when the chief offers to make him an Indian, Henry exclaims, "Big Chief Izzy Horowitz!"[78] Redface does not "disguise but rather calls attention to the Jew under the costume."[79]

Girl Crazy also features a New York Jew who ends up an accidental westerner; the character Gieber Goldfarb (played by Jewish vaudevillian Willie Howard) is a New York taxi driver who has driven playboy Danny Churchill out West to his father's cattle farm, which Danny promptly turns into a "dude ranch for city folks." Like Henry Williams, Gieber Goldfarb appears in various guises, including an Indian, a sheriff, and a woman, and impersonates a variety of famous performers, including Al Jolson in blackface and Eddie Cantor. Most writes: "The disguises [Henry Williams and Gieber Goldfarb] choose to hide behind render them invisible to the members of the stage community while they remain distinctly visible to the audience. Gieber and Henry do not follow the expected path of assimilation by trying to blend into the powerful white majority of cowboys and ranchers. Rather, ironically and brilliantly, Gieber and Henry escape their pursuers by becoming women, blacks and Indians—members of the disempowered groups inhabiting the Western landscape."[80] In both musicals, Most argues, the movement between Jews and Indians is "direct and self-conscious. . . . Indians become Jews and Jews become Indians."[81] When Gieber is in Indian costume, he meets Eaglerock, described by the playwrights as a "real Indian," who is simply dressed, speaks perfect English, and is just back from college. Gieber tries to communicate with Eaglerock in a made up

"Indian" language, Eaglerock responds in Chinese and German, but the two do not understand one another. It is only when Gieber switches to Yiddish that Eaglerock responds in kind, and the two "exit speaking animatedly."[82]

In these vaudeville and vaudeville-inspired productions, Jews do not perform as "actual" Indians as much as "*perform the role* of the Indian stereotype in order to reap the benefits of the mythic associations without suffering the stigma faced by real Indians on reservations."[83] In Most's argument, these Jewish characters subvert both racial and gendered identities by turning the "entire (non-Jewish) Wild West into a theatrical world in which performance determines identity."[84] By the 1930s, however, the "Wild West" already was a "theatrical world"; it was Buffalo Bill Cody who most famously turned the West into the "Wild West," where, indeed, performance determined identity, in that all of his "actors" essentially performed as themselves. Rather, these performances marked a series of moments in which Jews and other urban ethnics decided to enter and star in Buffalo Bill's self-consciously theatricalized America, a mythos from which they had historically been excluded. These productions, Rogin argues, dwell on "the relationship between the excluded rather than substituting one group for the other . . . [making] humor from the outsider status of Indians and Jews."[85] But even so, Rogin continues, Jewish-Indian burlesque "participates in the tradition it ridicules."[86]

A 1949 newsreel, for instance, described Sophie Tucker being "inducted" into an "Indian tribe" in Canada: "The last of the red hot mamas" is crowned "sister of flowers," tries a few steps of a "tribal dance," gives the "Six Nations an eyeful," and generally "whoops it up." In our final glimpse of her she is, as the announcer describes, "mugging in Mohawk."[87] Such scenes of urban and urbane Jews in theatricalized encounters with a mythical American West and its mythologized inhabitants, clearly culminate in Mel Brooks's late-twentieth-century turn as a Yiddish-speaking Indian chief in *Blazing Saddles*, in Gene Wilder's Polish immigrant rabbi crossing the continent in *The Frisco Kid*, and in Rob Morrow's New York Jewish doctor trapped in a tiny Alaskan village in the 1990s television series *Northern Exposure*.

Performance and impersonation, encounter and mediation were, through the nineteenth and early twentieth centuries, related and analogous endeavors. The texts discussed in this chapter, laced together over the long nineteenth century through tropes of Jewish-Indian encounter, kinship, and resemblance, give a sense of the ways in which Jewish writers and performers could use travels "among Indians" to theatricalize, disguise, and Americanize themselves all at once. Now I turn to aesthetic modernism, left radicalism, and Zionism as powerful twentieth-century matrices for Jewish-Indian engagement.

⟨2⟩

Going Native, Becoming Modern

To bump into a wooden Indian was to bump into good luck, a hundred times a week.

—Mary Antin, *The Promised Land*

The palefaces dominated literature throughout the nineteenth century, but in the twentieth they were overthrown by the redskins.

—Philip Rahv, "Paleface and Redskin"

The imaginary Indian offered a convenient and infinitely flexible figure upon which to work out questions of American identity, from the seventeenth century up through the fledgling twenty-first. In the twentieth century in particular, Indians, as well as other so-called primitive peoples, would additionally come to serve as a site through which Americans could define what it meant to be modern.[1] The kind of modernness embodied by Indians, as we shall see, served specific nationalist incentives. These moments of imaginative encounter, representation, and masquerade, as we have come to see, had particular resonance for Jewish writers in America, for many of whom the memory of immigration was fresh and the process of acculturation unfinished.

Mary Antin, in her 1912 autobiography *The Promised Land*, articulated the feeling, often echoed, that the eastern European Jewish immigrant experienced in the passage to America not only a journey in space but a journey in time. "I began life in the Middle Ages," Antin wrote in her introduction, "and here am I still, your contemporary in the twentieth century, thrilling with your latest thought."[2] After all, it was not only the unassimilable foreignness of Jewish immigrants that caused widespread popular anxiety; it was also their perceived primitiveness.[3] Antin both participates in and assuages this anxiety, as she describes her "medieval" origins and at the same time assures her readers of her speedy and thorough modernization. To come to America was to enter the modern age; to Americanize was to become and to remain essentially modern. "To be alive in America," wrote Antin, "I found out long ago, is to ride on the central current of the river of modern life" (278). Calling herself the "youngest of America's children" (286), this self-designated universal immigrant and American claims not only the nation's "shining future" but its "whole majestic past" (286).

When, in *The Promised Land*, the young Antin bumps into her wooden Indian (250) and drops her medicine, the accident's immediate effect is the solidification of Antin's friendship with the pharmacist, Mr. Pastor, whose symbolic name communicates his status as another idealized "native" American. The wooden Indian represents a moment of encounter between immigrant and native, during which conflict resolves into friendship ("Of course we were great friends after that, and this is the way my troubles often ended on Dover Street" [250]); each friendship brings Antin closer to triumphant Americanization.

Susan Hegeman has argued that both modern anthropologists (led by German-Jewish immigrants Franz Boas and Edward Sapir) and modern literary intellectuals (such as Van Wyck Brooks and Waldo Frank, another German Jew) were engaged in the project of redefining modern American "culture," a term that has come to absorb both the social-scientific and the aesthetic. For those engaged in the defining and refining of an American "culture," the Indian would serve both as the subject of ethnological study, affirming Boas's program of "cultural relativism," and as the model for an indigenous art. As Hegeman has said, the context of both projects was "complexly modernist."[4] A focus on primitive societies, through their difference, could serve to reinforce American modernity. On the other hand, in the work of many moderns, such as Mary Austin, Georgia O'Keeffe, Jean Toomer, and William Faulkner, Indians, the Southwest, and the rural South loomed large and served not as foils for modern experience and expression but as vehicles for modern experience and expression. Indians, that is to say, were, in the words of writer, ethnographer, and activist Oliver La Farge, *both* "primitive" and "modern."[5] Indian chants, art, and rituals thus served a multitude of useful purposes for a creative culture both influenced by and anxious to distance itself from recent artistic trends in Europe, which itself was beginning to turn to "primitive" cultures for modernist inspiration.

Although it is more accurate, in light of the recent scholarship expanding our notions of aesthetic modernism, to speak of multiple and diverse modernisms in a variety of geographical centers, I would venture to say that American modernism in its most ascendant form was particularly committed to the idea of nationhood, as opposed to the internationalism or cosmopolitanism generally attributed to Anglo-European modernism, perceived to have arisen out of the rootlessness of modern life.[6] Persistent historical debates about a national language, racial and ethnic identity, and the relationship between American citizenship (a naturalized status) and Americanness (a natural, or native, status) were reenergized and recontextualized in the early twentieth century.[7] As Alan Trachtenberg writes, "The fundamental shift in the representation of Indians, from 'savage' foe to 'first American' and ancestor to the nation, was conditioned by the perceived crisis in national identity triggered by the 'new immigrants' of the late nineteenth and early twentieth centuries."[8]

The year 1924 saw the passage of both the Reed-Johnson Act, which established restrictive quotas on immigration, and the Indian Citizenship Act, which declared "all non-citizen Indians born within the territorial limits of the United States . . . to be citizens of the United States." Walter Benn Michaels argues that both acts participated in a recasting of American citizenship, changing it from a status that could be achieved through one's actions (immigrating and becoming "civilized" or naturalized) to a status that could be better understood as inherited.[9] Naturalized immigrants were perhaps American citizens, but they were not American; the Indian's Americanness antedated his citizenship—he had been an American long before becoming an American citizen.

Michaels thus pinpoints the 1920s as the moment in which "culture" replaced "race" as a way of thinking about national identity. He too focuses on the Indian as the contested site of culture, specifically modernity, aesthetic modernism, and American identity: "the emergence of nativist modernism involved . . . the transformation of the opposition between black and white into an opposition between Indian and Jew."[10] Jewish responses to this opposition, however, are not discussed by Michaels and are precisely what I seek to recover in this discussion.

Indianness thus functions in this context as a category, used to focus and legitimize literary and aesthetic tastes and trends. When Philip Rahv wrote his 1939 essay about the "split personality" of American literature, he chose to describe the two poles not as patrician and plebeian but as "paleface" and "redskin."[11] This is the cult of Henry James, Rahv writes, versus the cult of Walt Whitman: theory versus experience, sensibility versus energy, refinement versus "gross, riotous naturalism." That criticism is "chronically forced to choose between them" has resulted in "truncated works of art": what is at stake for Rahv is nothing less than the possibility of a fully realized national literature. The mode of twentieth-century literature, Rahv writes, belongs to the redskin, who is a "purely indigenous phenomenon," a "juvenile," on the one hand a "crass materialist, a greedy consumer of experience" and on the other a "sentimentalist, a half-baked mystic listening to inward voices and watching for signs and portents." Rahv considers writers Dreiser, Lewis, Anderson, Wolfe, Sandburg, Caldwell, Steinbeck, Farrell, and Saroyan all redskins; the Jewish writer is, he insinuates, a paleface: "As for the paleface, in compensation for backward cultural conditions and a lost religious ethic, he has developed a supreme talent for refinement, just as the Jew, in compensation for adverse social conditions and a lost national independence, has developed a supreme talent for cleverness."[12] Rahv, that is to say, participates in an early-twentieth-century critical discourse about a national literature that casts the Jew against the Indian. That Rahv seems to prefer the paleface to the redskin ("at present the redskins are in command of the situation, and the literary life in America has seldom been so deficient in intellectual power") is beside the point.[13] Rather, Rahv's arguments indicate the terms with which, or against which, the writers in this study wrestled.

I concentrate in this chapter upon modernist poetry, and upon Yiddish literary modernism's engagement with American modernism and modernist intertexts, performed not on the vaudeville stage but in the rarefied pages of a literary journal. Identification with Native Americans made it possible for the Yiddish writer to imaginatively inhabit the bodies both of Indians and aspirers to Indianness, natives and aliens, primitives and moderns, and in the process to both imitate and critique the racism and elitism of Anglo-American modernist literary practices. Through the binding together, against the grain, of Indian and Jew, the Yiddish writers I discuss here participated in a conversation that resolutely excluded them, a conversation about the possibilities for a modern, national literature.

The Primitive, the Modern, and the Jews

Bay dem breg fun Gitchee-Gumee,
Bay dem yam-vaser dem heln,
Dort geshtanen iz Nokomis,
Mit ihr finger kegn mahriv,

Ibern vaser kegn mahriv
Tsu di purpur abend-volken.

—Henry Wadsworth Longfellow, *The Song of Hiawatha,*
Yiddish translation by Yehoash

But from the dust and sand, if you stop anywhere,
The breath of the Indian follows you there.

—Mani Leyb, "The Bit of Land," translated by Jehiel and Sarah Cooperman

Yehoash's (Solomon Bloomgarten's) translation of Longfellow's 1855 poem
Hiawatha in 1910 asserted the rich capacities of the Yiddish language as well
as the Yiddish poet's cosmopolitanism. So argued critic Khaym Zhitlovski,
who wrote an introduction to the Yiddish translation of the epic poem. "In
our opinion," he writes, "we are the most cosmopolitan people in the world."
Translation helps the Jewish cosmopolite to "understand the soul of the non-
Jew," Zhitlovski writes, and in the case of Yehoash and Longfellow, to cultivate
sympathy with a people who live in harmony with nature.[14]

When Zhitlovski wrote his introductory essay, he could hardly have antici-
pated Ezra Pound's mandate, published three years later, to translate foreign
texts so as to "train" oneself as a modernist poet. Zhitlovski's introduction
not only rehearses Pound's feeling that "translation is good training" but also
anticipates American modernism's linking of cosmopolitanism and a romantic,
pseudoethnographic American primitivism. Longfellow, in *Hiawatha,* had
adapted both the meter of the Finnish *Kalevala* and the substance of Henry
Rowe Schoolcraft's research in Indian legend. Zhitlovski, however, for all his
sympathetic participation in Longfellow's project, momentarily indulges in a
bit of irreverence. How is it that Yehoash fastened upon this particular poem
to translate? asks Zhitlovski rhetorically. Surely, he answers himself, the poet is
not obligated to answer that question. Rather, "it's Longfellow's good luck!" to
be translated into Yiddish. This moment, a cheerful pronouncement of Yiddish's
status as a major language, read against Yiddish poet Mani Leyb's portrait of
an American landscape haunted by a vanished Indian, together represent the
competing tensions of early American-Yiddish modernist writing as it fashioned
itself against and around the early-twentieth-century American literary scene.[15]

By the first decade of the twentieth century, the handfuls of artists, intellectuals, poets, and writers who had arrived along with the millions of eastern
European Jewish immigrants had managed to create a flourishing literary
and artistic marketplace in New York.[16] American influence on immigrant

literary production expressed itself at first through energetic and voluminous translation: Harriet Beecher Stowe, Jack London, and Walt Whitman were all translated into Yiddish. *Hiawatha* was translated not only into Yiddish but into Hebrew as well, by Shaul Tshernikhovski in 1913. Most relevant to my discussion here, the years 1920 and 1925–26 saw renderings of Native American chants into Yiddish in the journal *Shriftn*, the first preeminent venue for Yiddish modernist writers, primarily members of the group Di Yunge (the young ones), the first self-proclaimed Yiddish aestheticist and modernist group to emerge in New York.

Di Yunge included poets like Y. Y. Shvarts, whose 1925 epic *Kentucky* was hailed by his colleagues as establishing the right of Yiddish to be regarded as a part of American literature. Prose fiction writer Isaac Raboy became well known for writing novels about farming (*Herr Goldenbarg*, 1913) and the American prairie (*Der Yidisher Cowboy*, 1942). In contrast with their politicized, activist predecessors at the turn of the century, the labor or "sweatshop" poets, the Yunge emphasized their disengagement from political didacticism, their concern with beauty and transcendence, their ability to assimilate and represent a range of poetic personae, and their intimacy with the geographic reaches of America. The Yunge's insistence upon their "Americanness" has been read both as evidence of their anxious and incomplete acculturation and as a gesture to an urban immigrant as well as an overseas eastern European Yiddish readership hungry for the exotic and unfamiliar.[17] I want to suggest in addition that their turn to typically "American" subject matter was crafted in great part by the emergent discourse in U.S. literary circles about the possibilities for a modern, national literature.[18]

The Yunge's assertion of both modernness and Americanness via Indianness emerged through its imaginary dialogue with a nascent American modernist movement that was itself involved in an ongoing and unresolved negotiation concerning native identity, language, and literature. Although the members of the Yunge published several other journals, I focus here on the group's journal *Shriftn* (Writings, 1912–26), which, I argue, self-consciously engaged, through translation, imitation, and subtle critique, with *Poetry: A Magazine of Verse*, begun by Harriet Monroe in Chicago in the same year. Monroe and Ezra Pound, her "foreign correspondent," struggled to define the borders and languages of American modernism. Imagism and free verse, and Walt Whitman and American Indians as the American antecedents of both, were promoted in the pages of *Poetry* alongside Pound's cosmopolitan, international offerings. Neither Monroe's Americanism nor Pound's globalism would include the Yiddish poet. *Shriftn*'s modernism, as a result, gestured in specific ways toward this anti-Semitic, Anglo-American modernist movement and at the same time attempted to suggest its own difference.

Monroe's proposed journal was the first of its kind—devoted exclusively to poetry and to publishing the poets whose experimental verse was rejected by established publications. The groundbreaking work of *Poetry* was later eclipsed by later comers—the *Little Review, Seven Arts, Others*, and the new *Dial*. And Monroe's successes as an editor were later passed over in favor of tales of her mistakes—her distaste for T. S. Eliot, James Joyce, and E. E. Cummings, for example. In 1912, however, the state of poetry in America was by all accounts lamentable; within several years of *Poetry*'s initiation the nation was in the grip of a "poetry renaissance," attributable in great part to the efforts of *Poetry*.[19]

Modernist interest in the Indian, both as subject and as new artist/poet, was consolidated in part by the magazine, as well as by Ezra Pound's launching, in its pages, of the imagist movement in 1912 when he named Richard Aldington's and H.D.'s poetry *imagiste*. Monroe had hired Ezra Pound, then a young poet and critic with a developing reputation in England, as her foreign correspondent. *Poetry* became the outlet, briefly, for his imagist movement, publishing, in 1913, his essay "A Few Don't by an Imagist," and Monroe continued to support experiments in *vers libre*. Pound's discovery of Rhabindranath Tagore and his encounter with Ernest Fenollosa's interpretations of Chinese poetry enabled an analogous American turn to Native American song, reconstituting the Indian, in the process, as imagist poet.[20] Pound himself was not specifically interested in the Indian question, but he paved the way by encouraging translation, particularly translation from poetry that lacked stanzaic form and therefore was identified, often mistakenly, as *vers libre*.[21]

Pound, however ambivalently, also saw explicit connections between Whitman, imagism, and modernism: Whitman's "crudeness" could be understood to be reaching into the same primitivist strain that Pound sought, for instance, in Chinese poetry. Pound's poem "A Pact," which appeared in *Poetry* in 1913, addresses Whitman in true Whitmanesque fashion: "We have one sap and one root / Let there be commerce between us."[22] Just as *Shriftn* announced its first issue in 1912 with a translation of Whitman's internationalist poem "Salut au Monde," *Poetry* featured in *its* first issue an essay by Alice Corbin Henderson titled "A Perfect Return," which chronicled Whitman influence first on French poets, then on English poets, and foresaw the return of Whitman to America, by way of this international circle of interest, because of the new emphasis on *vers libre*.[23] Indeed, Whitman, as a continual presence in and justification for the magazine, was featured prominently in every issue of *Poetry*, which featured on every title page an epigram by Whitman: "To have great poets there must be great audiences, too." This, Monroe's motto, stood in direct contrast to Margaret Anderson's intention (and Pound's) in the *Little Review* to make "no compromise with the public taste."[24]

Monroe was particularly interested in furthering the cause of American poetry, intending to pass over William Butler Yeats, for instance, in favor of Vachel Lindsay as the recipient of a two-hundred-and-fifty-dollar Guarantor's Prize for the most distinguished publication of *Poetry*'s first year. The prize went to Yeats at Pound's furious insistence, when he wrote: "Either it must be respectfully offered to Mr. Yeats, or the americans [*sic*] must admit that they are afraid of foreign competition. . . . You CAN not divide the arts by a political line. . . . You ought either to have specified the award as local, or you ought not to have accepted [Yeats's] stuff."[25] Monroe acceded to Pound, and a one-hundred-dollar second prize, limited to American contributors, was hastily raised for Lindsay. Her reply to Pound's infuriated harangue read, in part:

> In a more general way I would say, however, that it is easy for you, living in what one of our papers calls "the world's metropolis" to charge with imbecility us "in the provinces." If we are provincial, we shall always be so until we cease to take our art and art opinions ready-made from abroad, and begin to respect ourselves. This magazine is an effort to encourage the art, to work up a public for it *in America*.[26]

This spat provoked the first of Pound's several resignations from the magazine, until he fully and explicitly transferred his allegiance to the *Little Review* in 1919 or so.[27]

Throughout his association with Monroe's magazine, the tension between Pound's cosmopolitan project and her nativist one engendered an ambivalent journal, the product of two competing modernist agendas. Monroe's intense interest in creating an indigenous brand of modernism, at odds with Pound's determination to "print one French poem a month" continually provoked Pound's disgust, as when, writing to William Carlos Williams in 1920, he sniffed: "Amy Lowell's perfumed—would be putrid even if it had been done by a pueblo Indian, or written on the highest pinnacle of Harriet's buggerin rocky mts."[28]

Alice Corbin Henderson, Monroe's associate editor, agreed with Monroe in determining the cultural orientation of the magazine. Henderson introduced the verse of Sherwood Anderson to the magazine in 1917 and advocated the publication of cowboy ballads; Monroe, as it happens, did not share either enthusiasm.[29] Henderson's June 1914 editorial, "Too Far from Paris," argued that the American poet must realize himself in "direct relation" to the American "experience" and held up Lindsay as an ideal. She wrote:

> It may be that the spirit of Whitman is still, in any large sense, to capture. It will be captured and transmuted into expressions varying widely in outward form if the American poets realize their birthright and heritage of individual genius. . . . We cannot forecast Mr. Lindsay's future. He is already, as Mr. Yeats said, assured for the anthologies. But his example is valuable. He is realizing himself in relation to direct experience, and he is not adapting to his work a twilight tone which is quite foreign to him, as it is, generally, to the nation.[30]

Poetry continued to foster the experimental verse of such American writers as Lindsay, Edgar Lee Masters, Wallace Stevens, and Carl Sandburg. A special Indian issue of *Poetry* appeared in February 1917. It included a number of "interpretations" of Indian song and dance, a list of anthropological texts in which readers would find more poems and myths (which indeed served as the basis of later collections, most prominently George Cronyn's *Path on the Rainbow*), a plea by Monroe calling for further exploration and preservation of this literature, and a protest against the government policy of suppressing Indian culture: "the danger is that the tribes, in the process of so-called civilization will lose all trace of . . . their beautiful primitive poetry."[31]

In her apparent hunger for "primitive" material, Monroe, it seems, wrote to the editors of the Yiddish modernist journal *In zikh* (1919–40), inquiring: "Unfortunately we cannot read your journal. We would like to know what language it is printed. Is it Chinese?" The Inzikhistn, the generation of Yiddish modernists who followed the Yunge and "rebelled" against their aestheticism, indignantly wrote in their 1923 issue:

> *Poetry* is published in Chicago. Several Yiddish daily newspapers are printed in Chicago. Yiddish periodicals, collections, books are published there. There are certainly also Chinese laundries in Chicago, and the lady-editors of *Poetry* have probably seen a ticket from a Chinese laundry in their lifetime. And, after all that—not to mention that an intelligent person may know the difference between the way Chinese and Yiddish look—to ask whether a Yiddish journal is Chinese does not reflect very positively on the intelligence of the *Poetry* people. . . . How long will Yiddish literature be unknown among the Gentiles? How long will they think of us—in literature—as Hotentots?[32]

Implying a feminized and privileged modernist establishment (the "lady-editors of Poetry" have "probably seen a ticket from a Chinese laundry"), the *In zikh* editors lash out at the indiscriminate romanticism of the primitivist modernism celebrated by *Poetry*. The Inzikhistn reject the perceived label of primitive. Not only is Yiddish *not* Chinese, Yiddish poets are also *not* "Hotentots" (that is, Africans). Monroe, however, was not entirely uninterested in the untapped potential market signaled by *In zikh*; the two journals had a brief but unfruitful correspondence. Monroe writes in the notes to *Poetry*'s February 1924 issue:

> The exchange editor's curiosity was aroused by *In Sich* [*sic*], a magazine of modern Yiddish verse. This information concerning its contents was acquired only through correspondence, in English, with the magazine's editor, A. Leyeless. In Gentilian ignorance we rashly offered to find a Jewish poet who would read the magazine and briefly evaluate it for readers of POETRY, and we were promptly honored with what seems to be a complete file. But we have not yet happened upon any one sufficiently versed in both Yiddish and poetry to have an appreciative comprehension of the magazine. (287)

A translator was never found, and the *In zikh* file still languishes, presumably, in the *Poetry* archives. Indeed, this aborted exchange is symptomatic of *Poetry*'s relationship with Jewish writers in general. *Poetry* published the work of Edward Sapir, Maxwell Bodenheim, and Louis Untermeyer, whose 1922 poem about Heine, "Monologue from a Mattress," most likely featured in its final lines the only Hebrew words to appear in *Poetry* during its first ten years: "Wait . . . I still can sing—*Sh'ma Yisroel Adonai Elohenu,/Adonai Echod . . . /* Mouche—Mathilde . . ."[33] But the journal rarely addressed, in its reviews or its editorials, the issue of the Jewish, or immigrant, writer. One exception, however, occurs in a July 1923 editorial by Florence Kiper Frank (herself, evidently, a writer on Jewish subjects), titled "The Jew as Jewish Artist," the primary argument of which is that the Jew will not produce great works of American literature until he ceases to be a Jew. Frank writes:

> The Jew in modern American poetry has nothing to say as a Jew. This assertion in spite of my friends Mr. Louis Untermeyer and Mr. Maxwell Bodenheim, who have both written recently on the subject!—and of certain ingenious attempts in these pages to classify the lengthy rhythms of Mr. James Oppenheim and of others of his group as Hebraic. The lengthy rhythms of Mr. James Oppenheim are the rhythms of Whitman, who of course derived from the flow and parallelism of the lyric and dramatic passages of the Old

Testament. But certainly the Whitmans of modern poetry are not pre-eminently Jews ... the Jew has not, with perhaps the exception of Heine, produced an outstanding genius in modern literature. ...

I cannot become convinced that what the Jew has to say in the modern world he will say as a Jew. ... And here it seems to me he becomes significant as symbol. For if genius can only grow out of the deep ground, then perhaps genius—in the sense of the great, outstanding figure—will be no more. ... This de-nationalized Jew, this de-religionized expatriate of spiritual solidity—looking back perhaps with nostalgia, perhaps feeling about into this new world with a curious, rising excitement, is—it seems to me—the modern intellectual.[34]

Contemporary accounts of literary modernism tend to emphasize and valorize its connection with the exiled or dislocated artist, exemplified by Pound, Eliot, Joyce, and later, the Lost Generation, and in this way implicitly celebrate the Jew as modernist subject or "symbol" (for instance, Leopold Bloom). The earliest American accounts, however, of "modern poetry," as in Frank's editorial, or, for instance, Mary Austin's introductory essay to *The American Rhythm* (1923), sought to define it as growing organically out of the poet's experience of the environment, emphasizing its connection to place. In this valorization of indigenousness and autochthony, the "denationalized" Jew had nothing to say in modern art "as a Jew," nor as an American.

If Di Yunge, the first Yiddish American modernists, were intently following the first manifestations of an indigenous American modernism in the pages of *Poetry*, as I argue they were, Frank's editorial would have deflated the very heart of their project. Even more stingingly, by 1923, when her editorial was published, the number of Yiddish modernist journals was at an unprecedented high; just as *Poetry* had paved the way for the *Little Review*, *Others*, *Seven Arts*, and the new *Dial*, so had *Shriftn* ushered in *Der inzl*, *In zikh*, and a revised *Tsukunft*. All were implicitly invested in the legitimacy of the modernist, and American, Jewish artist.

Shriftn, Modernism, and America

There were, clearly, differences between *Poetry* and *Shriftn* in terms of content and appearance. *Shriftn* published prose fiction as well as poetry, and the volumes came out annually as thick collections as opposed to monthly; this was due to the exigencies of the market for elite Yiddish literature, in which both money and readers were scarce. Despite its differences, however, *Shriftn* can be fruitfully compared in many ways to *Poetry* in the duality of its project and in its importance as a forum for emerging poets and writers, mostly members of the Yunge. Conceived of and published by David Ignatov, *Shriftn* was a cosmopolitan and internationalist publication but at the same time was self-consciously "American," though the only native American poetry translated and transformed in the pages of *Shriftn* were Whitman and Indian chants. In this way, Whitman, Philip Rahv's archetypal "redskin," centrally links *Poetry* and *Shriftn*. *Poetry* displayed Whitman's epigram in every issue, and, in its early years, mentioned Whitman in some capacity in nearly every issue. Whitman and Indians served as early indigenous examples of *vers librists* and imagists and in this way made an argument for the natural affinity of America and American artists for modern poetry. Yiddish poets in America had very early on engaged with Whitman; the turn-of-the-century "sweatshop poets" celebrated Whitman as a protosocialist.[35] For *Shriftn*, however, as for *Poetry*, Whitman was both a native American and a cosmopolitan modern.[36] *Shriftn* thus announced its first issue, also published in 1912, with a Yiddish translation of Whitman's global poem "Salut Au Monde."

The negotiation in this poem between the local and the global was continually reflected in *Shriftn*. A typical issue in 1914 featured Mani Leyb's poem "Shtiler, shtiler" ("Hush, hush"), which quickly assumed the importance of a manifesto as the representative piece of the Yunge's apolitical aestheticist program; David Ignatov's novella "Phoebe," in which the protagonist accepts a position on a Vermont farm and finds himself embroiled in a pathological and dangerous affair with an American girl who is the product of an intermarriage between Jew and Gentile; and Isaac Raboy's *Herr Goldenbarg*, in which a Jewish immigrant stakes a land claim in the "vayter vest" (distant west). The 1914 issue, in its translation section, featured excerpts from the *Iliad*, Friedrich Nietzsche, Hermann Hesse, and Robert Louis Stevenson—although this last was not as odd a choice when one considers that his circle, for a time, had included a young Harriet Monroe. The journal regularly showcased art, reviews, and essays in addition to poetry and translation. Aware of the trends at work in English journals, it published translations of Whitman and the Zohar, the *Rubayyat*, Aesop's *Fables*, and Tagore, inspired in great part by Pound and *Poetry*. At the same time, the Yunge's programmatic statement, published in their first, short-lived journal, *Di yugend* (1907–8), aimed to "create for Yiddish literature in America its own, independent home":

> Yiddish literature here in America has been boarding out with the Yiddish
> press that treats it as a stranger, a stepchild. The purpose of the press is either

to turn a profit or to spread certain social or nationalistic ideals. It has never had any pure or authentic interests in literature. . . . As professionals, the young Yiddish writers in America are in love with literature, and it hurts us to see Yiddish *belles-lettres* in exile here, being treated with cynical abandon. We have united . . . to create for Yiddish literature its own, independent home to free it from its bruising, battering exile.[37]

Ignatov claimed authorship of this unsigned editorial.[38] In 1912, when Ignatov published the first issue of *Shriftn*, Reuben Eisland would write in its pages, in the first definitive essay on the Yunge, that the group, different as each of its members were, constituted a real, legitimate movement that had brought Yiddish literature out of its provincial, "almost primitive" state into a national artistic flowering.[39] Ignatov, described by Wisse as the leader and most fervent promoter of the group, was a writer of symbolist prose fiction but perhaps was more effective, like Harriet Monroe, as an editor. Ignatov also wrote in English and submitted his English-language stories and novellas to American publishing houses and to the *Dial*, although none were accepted.[40] He also, apparently, was in brief correspondence with John Gould Fletcher, whose imagist verse Pound had introduced to *Poetry* in 1913. The illegible, damaged 1919 letter that remains among Ignatov's papers seems to suggest that he had intended to translate Fletcher, possibly for appearance in *Shriftn*: "I look forward with pleasure to seeing my own work in translation, also [this section is illegible] . . . some of your work." Ignatov, Eisland, Mani Leyb, and Zishe Landau constituted the core of the group, and others associated with it included Y. Y. Shvarts, Joseph Rolnik, Moyshe-Leyb Halpern, M. J. Haimovitch, Isaac Raboy, and Joseph Opatoshu.[41]

Eisland's private papers reveal an explicit and sophisticated engagement with the American literary modernist scene, particularly as it was crafted in the pages of *Poetry*. Featured among his letters and manuscripts are poems, copied out by hand, by Pound in English ("The Altar," "The Flame"); a Pound poem translated into Yiddish ("Dance Figure"); an undated photograph of a young Pound; lists of poets' names—apparently reading suggestions—that include Bodenheim, Padraic Colum, John Gould Fletcher, and Conrad Aiken; Chinese poems by Po-Chui, Wu-Li, Lu Yun, all translated into Yiddish, and, finally, elaborate copies of what are labeled "Indian" symbols, with handwritten notes in Yiddish at the bottom noting the similarities between the Indian and Hebrew terms for God.

The connections with *Poetry* are profound. Pound's "Dance Figure" was one of the group of poems "Contemporaria" that marked his debut in the

pages of *Poetry* (the other two were published in *Personae* in 1926). The poets
Eisland had jotted down all had made prominent appearances in *Poetry*, many
for the first time. *Poetry* continually featured translations of Chinese poems,
albeit not the ones in Eisland's papers, and *Poetry*'s consistent preoccupation
with the Indian, and with the similarity of Indian verse with modern imagism,
underscores Iceland's musings on the similarities between Indian and Hebrew
religions in antiquity.

Eisland, the theorist of the group, in his essay "Di Yunge" in *Shriftn*'s first
issue, profiles Rolnik, Mani Leyb, Landau, and Shvarts and, in conclusion, marvels
at the aesthetic accomplishments of the Yunge given the "grey, monotonous life
in the American Jewish streets where all the members of the Yunge live; where
all is harsh, coarse, and materialistic, where there is no vestige of tradition and
where the exaggerated yellow press deadens the flavor of all that it publishes,
which is of the most banal sort."[42] In this way Eisland establishes a rather
different relationship between the American poet and his environment than
that forwarded by Austin, Henderson, and Frank: one in which nativeness and
modernity could be achieved as a matter of will.

Translating America

Valt Vitman bin ikh, a kosmos, der zun fun mekhtigen manhaten,
Shturemdik, gufik, zindik, un ikh es, un trink un frukhper zikh,
Kin sentimentaler,
Kin muster iber man un froy, kin muster bazunder fun zey,
Azoy fil basheydn vi umbasheydn.

—Walt Whitman, *Song of Myself*

Hi-ihiya naiho-o! Lomir zikh nemen zingen.
Lomir zikh nemen freyen. Hitciya yahina-a.
Lomir zikh nemen zingen, lomir zikh nemen freyen.
Dos gezang fun der groyser kokuruze. Hitciya yahina-a.
Dos gezang fun der kleyner kokuruze. Hitciya yahina-a.

—Indian Rain Song

Yiddish interest in the Indian and in Whitman would become an act of interpretation and transformation designed to assert the simultaneous modernism
and Americanness of the Yiddish immigrant poet. These intersected in *Shriftn*
in great part through acts of translation, thus reconstituting the Indian and

Walt Whitman as, paradoxically, quintessentially American and alien: that is, as both Americans and Jews. Engagement with the Indian and with Whitman could serve as a gesture of, at once, a desire to participate in a rapidly developing culture of modernism and a resistance to the subsuming power of that culture. By concentrating here on the question of translation in the pages of *Shriftn*, I hope to situate Whitman and the Indian in a particular matrix of Yiddish-American modernism, one that sought to fuse the cosmopolitan and the local, the international and the American, the cultural and countercultural, thus both echoing and reconfiguring *Poetry*'s brand of primitivist, "nativist modernism."

Andre Lefevere asserts that translations, or rewritings, are always produced under either ideological or poetological motivations or constraints, depending on whether the rewriters "find themselves in agreement with the dominant ideology of their time."[43] Tejaswini Niranjana adds: "Translation thus produces strategies of containment. By employing certain modes of representing the other—which it thereby also brings into being—translation reinforces hegemonic versions of the colonized, helping them acquire the status of what Edward Said calls representations, or objects without history."[44] Many theorists of translation assume that the direction of translation is always either between major cultures or from the minor to the major culture and not vice versa. In the case of Yiddish literature, we must adjust the power differential inherent in the project of translation and consider the reverberations of a possibly subversive translator from a minor language and culture, translating a major literature's "re-expression" (to use Mary Austin's phrase) of yet another minor language and culture.

Pound, notes Lawrence Venuti, saw translation as a means of "cultivating modernist poetic values like linguistic precision."[45] In 1918 Pound wrote that "Translation is good training, if you find that your original matter 'wobbles' when you try to rewrite it. The meaning of the poem to be translated can not 'wobble.'"[46] Venuti argues that Pound's self-fashioning as modernist poet-translator, confronting and competing against Victorian translators whose poems he chose to revisit, is an example of the ways in which translation practices could be instrumental in the fashioning of an authorial identity and that this construction "is at once discursive and psychological, worked out in writing practices open to psychoanalytic interpretation" (76). If the translator fashions an authorial identity through the selective translation of certain texts, then cultural, collective identities are likewise crafted through translation of the foreign:

> Translation forms domestic subjects by enabling a process of "mirroring" or self-recognition: the foreign text becomes intelligible when the reader recognizes himself or herself in the translation by identifying the domestic

values that motivated the selection of that particular foreign text, and that are inscribed in it through a particular discursive strategy. . . . Sometimes, however, the values may be currently marginal yet ascendant, mobilized in a challenge to the dominant. (77)

This particular dynamic accurately describes the modernist immigrant Yiddish translator: through an effective transformation of Whitman and of American Indians into "Yiddish" poets, the translators I discuss in this section, in modernist fashion, meant to "modernize" the Indian and Whitman, and at the same time to "naturalize"—in the sense of both make *natural* and make *American*—the Yiddish poet.

Y. Y. Shvarts, author of the 1925 epic poem *Kentucky,* cited Whitman as a direct inspiration and translated "Salut Au Monde" for the first edition of *Shriftn* in 1912. Whitman meant this particular poem to express a "world vision" that would "temper and balance his nationalism."[47] The poem is a breathtaking geographical and cultural catalog, which includes glances at the Jew: "You Chinaman and Chinawoman of China! you Tartar of Tartary! / You women of the earth subordinated at your tasks! / You Jew journeying in your old age through every risk, to stand once again on Syrian ground! / You other Jews, waiting in all lands for your Messiah." Whitman, a famous tinkerer, revised the poem definitively in 1881, removing a number of lines that were descriptive of the United States, thus "limiting his point of view outward from America to other lands."[48] Shvarts, however, uses an older version of the poem, retaining all of the American references. The title of the poem is preserved in French in its roman letters in the Yiddish journal, thus crafting an even more emphatically multilingual poem than Whitman himself would have been capable of. Whitman revised the poem so that it would be even more cosmopolitan, as evidenced by the excising of the "American" lines. That Shvarts would leave those lines in seems to reflect the cultural binaries that *Shriftn* announced itself as negotiating from its very inception.

L. Miller's translations of sections 6 and 24 of *Song of Myself,* "A Woman Waits for Me," and "O Captain! My Captain!" appeared in 1919. Section 6 of *Song of Myself* is a discourse on the nature of grass; section 24 begins famously: "Walt Whitman, a kosmos, of Manhattan the son, / Turbulent, fleshy, sensual, eating, drinking, breeding." Miller inserts "A Woman Waits for Me" between these sections, then concludes with "O Captain! My Captain!" Whitman's most "widely known and least characteristic poem" with its regular metrical scheme, and a poem that Whitman later confessed he felt uncomfortable with.[49] Miller, in "anthologizing" Whitman, means to translate him in all his incarnations:

transcendental, crude, sensual, and finally, nation-making, political poet. However, he also engages in quite a bit of editing and subtle rewriting. The entire second half of section 24 is cut. Miller also uses a pre-1881 edition, as evidenced by his preservation of the line "Valt Vitman bin ikh, a kosmos, der zun fun mekhtiken manhaten" ("Walt Whitman am I, a kosmos, of mighty Manhattan the son"), rather than Whitman's final version: "Walt Whitman, a kosmos, of Manhattan the son."

Indeed, it is this line that encapsulates the dual possibilities that both Whitman and the Indian as poet could represent for the Yiddish immigrant poet: both a "kosmos," cosmopolitan, international, and a son of Manhattan—native, local, American. Consider, in addition, the difference between "Walt Whitman, a kosmos," and "Walt Whitman *am I*—*Valt Vitman bin ikh.*" The Yiddish poet becomes Whitman, through a kind of translatorly ventriloquism, at the same time that Whitman, through this emphatic utterance, becomes a Yiddish poet.

Ignatov used George Cronyn's 1918 anthology *Path on the Rainbow* as his unattributed source for his translations of Native American chants in the 1920 issue of *Shriftn*, which itself was inspired, Cronyn writes, by *Poetry's* 1917 Indian issue.[50] Cronyn's dedication reads, in part: "None [of the songs and chants herein translated] exhibit the slightest traces of European influence; they are genuine American Classics." By dispensing with all of the prefatory framing material of Cronyn's collection, Ignatov engages in his own form of rewriting, one that removes American Indian lyric from the ethnographic context of Cronyn's collection and reconstitutes the Indian poetry as Yiddish in both spirit and context. At the same time Ignatov claims for the Yiddish journal its own status as "American classic."

The connection between these reconstituted Indian songs and modern imagism is explicitly and consistently outlined both by Harriet Monroe and by Mary Austin. Austin wrote in her introduction to Cronyn's volume:

> That there is such a relationship any one at all familiar with current verse of the past three of four years must immediately conclude on turning over a few pages. He will be struck at once with the extraordinary likeness between much of this native product and the recent work of the imagists, *vers librists,* and other literary fashionables. He may, indeed, congratulate himself on the confirmation of his secret suspicion that imagism is a very primitive form; he may, if he happens to be of the Imagist's party, suffer a check in the discovery that the first free movement of poetic originality in America finds us just about where the last Medicine Man left off. But what else could he have expected?[51]

Ignatov, author of "Phoebe," itself an ambivalent morality tale about the seductions of America, mined Cronyn for his Native American sources, but in the process he took poems out of order, chopped them up, and spliced some together, without regard for the careful ethnography that determined their order. Thus, a Zuni corn-grinding song is merged with a Pima rain dance; a section that in Cronyn was a prologue appears at the end of a sequence, instead of at its beginning. Information about individual tribal ritual and region that frames each contribution in the English anthology is simply omitted in Ignatov's version. Ignatov produces both a tribute to America's indigenous poetry and at the same time an impish affront pitched against the white ethnological and literary institutions that oversaw its production and consumption.

Shriftn's 1925–26 issue, its last, featured in its translation section a mini-"anthology" of international, non-Western verse: Japanese haiku, Chinese and Egyptian poetry, and more Indian chants. Ignatov was a collaborator, but Meyer Shtiker was the actual translator of the Indian verse. His unacknowledged source was Mary Austin's *The American Rhythm*, published in 1923; in her introduction to *Path on the Rainbow* she had sketched out the ideas that were to form the principle argument of the essay that opens her 1923 collection of "re-expressions" of Indian poetry: that "American poetry must inevitably take, at some period of its history, the mold of Amerind verse, which is the mold of the American experience shaped by the American environment."[52] Once again, Whitman and Indians are yoked: Austin "confesses" that her interest in Whitman "swelled perceptibly in the discovery of how like the Indian's his method is."[53] Yet, despite this radical declaration that spiritual, poetic, and national value was to be found embedded in long-neglected native forms, Austin's privileging of the Indian involves some troubling characterizations of other groups. "In any group of jazz performers," she writes, for example, "you can see the arm jerk, recalling the tortoise rattle, the whole torso quiver with the remembered rolling clash of shells."[54] In a 1920 article for the *Nation* titled "New York: Dictator of American Criticism," she wrote:

> Recently in a London journal one of these critics had fun with the general movement of non-New York American writers to absorb into their work the aboriginal, top layer of literary humus through which characteristically national literature, if we are ever to have it, must take root. He succeeded in making it appear that it appeared to him ridiculous. . . . One wonders what part is played in this schism between literature and the process of nationalization by the preponderance of Jews among our critical writers. There is nothing un-American in being a Jew; it is part of our dearest

tradition that no derivation from any race or religion inhibits a contribution to our national whole. We could not without serious loss subtract the Jewish contribution from our science or our economics, or dispense with the services of the younger Jewish publishers. It is only when the Jew attempts the role of interpreter of our American expression that the validity of racial bias comes into question. Can the Jew, with his profound complex of election, his need of sensuous satisfaction qualifying his every expression of personal life, and his short pendulum-swing between mystical orthodoxy and a sterile ethical culture—can he become the arbiter, of American art and American thinking?[55]

Indian and Jew are sketched by Austin as precise cultural opposites: natural versus overcultivated, native versus naturalized American, spiritual versus ethical, instinctual versus hyperrefined, connected versus disconnected with American landscape and environment. One irony of Shtiker's *Shriftn* translations is that they do not attempt to refute Austin's reading of the Jew as incapable of translating or interpreting American culture, or in this case American Indian culture. Notations as to which tribe each poem originated with are done away with, as is any sort of identifying terminology: for instance, Austin's "Sioux Song of Parting" is, in the Yiddish, simply a "Gezang baym tsesheydn zikh" (a "song of parting"). Like Ignatov, Shtiker engages in some editing of his source, cutting out pieces, for instance, of Austin's "Glyphs," and translating rather than transliterating the title, a term of her own invention, literally into *karbn* (a Yiddish word that means "score" or "notch").

Austin herself defined her methodology as not translation but "re-expression": "My method has been, by preference, to saturate myself in the poem, in the life that produced it and the environment that cradled that life, so that when the point of crystallization is reached, I myself give forth a poem which bears, I hope, a genetic resemblance to the Amerind song that was my point of contact."[56] Indeed, Austin increasingly came under attack for what many ethnologists considered her sloppy methodology. She knew no Native languages or dialects, was dependent upon bilingual translators, and the authenticity of her translations was frequently attacked.[57] As she wrote in her introduction to *The American Rhythm*: "I have naturally a mimetic temperament that draws me toward the understanding of life by living it. . . . So that when I say I am not, have never been, or offered myself, as an authority in things Amerindian, I do not wish to have it understood that I may not, at times, have succeeded in *being* an Indian."[58]

Shtiker adopts Austin's own translational strategies to a somewhat lesser degree, and the effect is both mimetic and subversive; by approximating Austin's own freewheeling methodology as cultural interpreter, by highlighting the compatibility of Yiddish and Native American lyric, and by decontextualizing Indian chants so that they are almost unidentifiable as such (if it were not for the header "Indianer gezangen"), Shtiker makes a plea for the "naturalness" of Yiddish and of the Jewish artist, in defiance of what he probably knew were Austin's cultural biases.

Translation and Transnationalism

Both *Path on the Rainbow* and *The American Rhythm* received mixed critical responses; most notably, Louis Untermeyer wrote a review of *Path on the Rainbow* in the *Dial* that prompted a months-long debate in the letters section. Untermeyer attacked the lack of critical apparatus in the volume ("many of these songs cry aloud for nothing so much as footnotes") and the "pretentious typography" that dictates the "arbitrary arrangement" of poems in a way that is "foreign to our native—though it may be native to Ezra Pound, 'H. D.,' and Richard Adington [*sic*]."[59]

Mary Austin responded in an elaborate defense of the volume in a letter to the *Dial* in which, in a rehearsal of her *Nation* editorial published a year later, she wrote: "That all these things seem to have been missed by the reviewer raises again the question as to whether we can ever have anything which is American literature, *sui generis,* until literary judgement begins to be American and leaves off being thoroughly New Yorkish."[60] The equation that Austin draws later in the *Nation* between New York criticism and Jewish critics, and the inability of either to appreciate authentic American poetic product, was, evidently, first suggested by Untermeyer's review of *Path on the Rainbow.*

Alice Corbin Henderson, unsurprisingly, gave *Path on the Rainbow* an enthusiastic review in *Poetry*, noting with pride the role the magazine had played in the volume's genesis. She also wrote:

> The appreciative interpretation of the poetry of another race is largely, one must believe, a gift. The whole art character of the Indian is of course more Oriental than European. Perhaps that is why we have so long failed to appreciate it. It is possible that Indian poetry may be more closely allied to Chinese poetry than to that of any other race; it has the same realism, the same concrete simplicity, and acceptance of the commonplace experience, as well as the exceptional, as the material of poetry. There are also many

points of similarity with Japanese verse, in spirit no less than in the brevity of many songs.⁶¹

By thus setting up the continuum between Chinese and Japanese verse, Indian verse, and American modernism, *Poetry* and the works it promoted in its pages set up the parameters of modern American poetry. As Monroe wrote in the introduction to the magazine's Southern issue, "Ever since *Poetry* began, it has believed in, and tried to encourage, a strongly localized indigenous art."⁶² This indigenous art, however, took as its inspiration Indian—and by extension "Oriental"—song, as translated by modernist poets who saw their own imagist project reflected therein. Even *Poetry*'s indigenous art had an undeniably cosmopolitan undercurrent, one that, despite its frequent use of the term "Oriental," also resolutely excluded the Yiddish poet.

Shriftn's American cosmopolitanism—cosmopolitanism that frequently took its cues from the international poetry fashionable in American literary circles—expressed itself, for instance, through translations of Tagore's 1914 play *Chitra* (in *Shriftn* 7 [1921]), the *Rubayyat* (*Shriftn* 4 [1919]), Aesop's *Fables* (*Shriftn* 6 [1920]), and more conventional German and Russian verse, in addition to the *Kalevala*, and Arabic and Egyptian poetry. The 1914 *Shriftn* featured an anthology of international verse, both "classical" and "modern."

The tension in *Shriftn* between American and transnational authorial identity manifested itself, however, not only through the journal's translation practices but also in its original verse, prose, and artwork. The first two issues recapitulated in extremely condensed form the history of the Jews up to the immigrant's passage to the United States: *Shriftn* 1 (1912) featured Ignatov's fictional retelling of the biblical story of Jepthah's daughter ("Der gibor"), the translation of Whitman's "Salut Au Monde," Eisland's essay introducing the Yunge, Zishe Landau's "Maiden-songs" ("Maidelshe-lider"), and Mani Leyb's "Evening and Night" ("Ovnt un Nacht") and concluded with Joseph Opatoshu's "Romance of a Horse Thief" ("Roman fun a ferd-ganef"), a novella that detailed the dark underworld of a Jewish horse thief in eastern Europe.

Shriftn 2 (1913) featured Moyshe-Leyb Halpern's "In a Strange Land" ("In der fremd"), a poem about the ship passage to America; Raboy's "The Lighthouse" ("Der licht-turem"), in which a Jewish immigrant farmer remembers his passage to America; Opatoshu's "Morris and His Son Philip" ("Moris un zayn zun Philip"), about the miseries of the New York ghetto; a photograph of Walt Whitman; and a poem by Peretz Hirshbein titled "Song of the Fool" ("Dos lid fun dem nar"). This last, following the photograph of Whitman, could be read as a parody of Whitman's all-absorptive ego, in which the Whitmanesque singer is at once menacing and absurd.[63] *Shriftn*'s first two issues reenacted the move from Europe to America, Old World to New, antiquity to modernity. If the immigrant's journey seemed to dominate, as a narrative, *Shriftn*'s debut issue, then by its sophomore effort its poets had sufficiently engaged with America to be able to evoke and parody America's premier poet.

Shriftn 4 (1919), the first issue to emerge after the war, featured a picture, once again, of Walt Whitman on its frontispiece, cityscapes of New York by the modernist artist Abraham Walkowitz, imagistic poems by Al. Gurieh, an essay by H. Leyvik on the Yunge, Lamed Shapiro's story "White Hallah" ("Vayse Chale") about an eastern European pogrom, and, in the translation section, Miller's Whitman translations and the *Rubayyat*. If the tone of the writers had become more elegiac, Whitman's guardianship over the journal, and the American cosmopolitanism he signified, remained unchanged. Moreover, *Poetry*'s preoccupation with an "American rhythm" finds its counterpart in Leyvik's essay that appeared in this issue. Leyvik writes: "No one in all of Yiddish literature has in the Yiddish word has heard so many sounds, so many rhythms, seen so many colors and visions, as the Yunge. They have discovered within the Yiddish word a thrill, a new love, a flashing beauty, concealed and hidden from all ears."[64] In rhetoric this echoes Austin's introduction to Cronyn's anthology, in which she writes of Indian verse-makers: "The poetic faculty is, of all man's modes, the most responsive to natural environment, the most sensitive and the truest record of his reactions to its skyey influences, its floods, forests, morning colors . . . it is only by establishing some continuity with the earliest instances of such reaction that we can be at all sure that American poetic genius has struck its native note" (xvi–xvii).

The experiments in imagism and free verse featured in *Poetry*'s early years, and their acknowledged sources of inspiration—Native American and Eastern poetry—were echoed in *Shriftn* first through translation and references to Whitman and later found expression in the original work published in the journal. Y. Tofel's essay "Modernism" appeared in *Shriftn* 5, in the fall of 1919. In it, he writes of the revolt of the young modern artist against "form that lies on the canvas like a tomb burying the soul:"

> He goes and searches . . . and sometimes he finds in the archives forgotten, neglected works of art. Sometimes he glimpses on old walls the pictures that he wishes to create. And what he learns was in him all along, before he began his search. The time has just revealed its own strength: just as the oak grows from the nut but the oak is present in the nut from the beginning.

The root of the tree is revolt. Revolt is also food from the earth: the atmosphere of modernism. (4)

The only thing "modern" about modern art, Tofel concludes, is its atmosphere of revolt—for its themes, even its forms, it reaches back into the distant (and not so distant) past and to different cultures, which offered the modern artist the Psalms, Chinese portraits, and French landscapes.

By this 1919 issue, the poetry featured included substantial contributions that experimented with free verse and Eastern imagery, some from poets who, like Tselia Dropkin, had begun to be associated with the Inzikhistn. Dropkin's "The Hammock" transposes the poet's own meaning onto the Chinese letters she cannot read:

> I lie in the hammock
> Through branches the sun shines hot
> I close my eyes
> And see a blue Chinese script
> On a golden page.
> Light blue Chinese letters
> Sparkle up and down
> Like small fantastic windows,
> On a golden tower's wall.
> I don't understand the script
> Only something presses my heart,
> I recollect:
> "I love you, I love you,"
> Like that I read the blue
> Chinese script.[65]

Dropkin's poem can be read as a comment upon the way in which cosmopolitan moderns (such as Amy Lowell and Pound) read their own poetic projects into the Chinese texts they translated. The poem reflects as well Yiddish poets' own uncertain position vis-à-vis the Chinese texts they accessed only indirectly, mediated through English translators.

Shriftn 6 (1920), which included Ignatov's Indian chant translations, also included a collection of primitivist woodcuts, many of which resembled Pacific Northwest Native totem poles, by the artist Max Weber, who had studied with Matisse and introduced Cubism to American painting, along with some of the artist's poetry, which was in turn reminiscent of some of Indian chants that appeared in *Path on the Rainbow.*[66] "Rain" begins: "Tip, tep, in rhythm. / One drop, a million drops the rain" (13). Another, "Love," begins:

> My spirit plays
> My soul sings
> My heart gives thanks
> When she comes,
> She comes,
> She comes to me.[67]

And yet, lest the reader misunderstand these poems as merely imitative Indianesque chant, the group reinforces its Jewish theme with a concluding poem titled "Hannukkah Lights."

Poems by Melekh Ravitch, Mani Leyb, and David Ignatov, among others, that also appear in this issue are composed in a style that, seen alongside the translations of Indian song that followed them, can only be read as Yiddish "interpretations" of Indian poetry. Ignatov's poem "Jews, Brothers" ("Yidelekh, briderlekh") reads:

> Jews, brothers, ha-ha-ha!
> We dance, we jump, ha-ha-ha!
> We raise hands, va-va-va!
> Clapping, clapping, pa-pa-pa!
> Jews, brothers, ha-ha-ha!
> Again, again, ha-ha-ha![68]

The internal rhymes of the poem's lines, the repetitive, rhyming use of the diminutive—yidelakh, bridelakh, hentelakh—and the nonwords that conclude each line, all contribute to the feeling of Indian song-mimicry at work in this poem, especially compared with Ignatov's translation that appears later in the issue of the following Indian chant:

> Hi-ihiya naiho-o! Let us begin our song,
> Let us begin, rejoicing. Hitciya
> yahina-a.
> Let us begin our song, let us begin rejoicing
> Singing of the large corn. Hitciya
> yahina-a

Singing of the small corn. Hitciya
yahina-a.[69]

Ignatov's 1920 issue, in his juxtaposition of translation and interpretation of Native verse, can be read as his answer to *Poetry*'s 1917 Indian issue. Monroe's Indian issue had been comprised, in her words, of "not translations, but interpretations," and Cronyn's anthology had famously begun with a poem by Carl Sandburg titled "Early Moon," which purported to be a translation but was in actuality his own creation.[70] Monroe had herself written in her editorial: "Suspicion arises definitely that the Red Man and his children committed direct plagiarisms on the modern imagists and vorticists," and she offered examples by Carl Sandburg to illustrate her point.

Ignatov's Indian issue of 1920 meant to infiltrate Indian/imagist verse with a Jewish terminology and sensibility, producing an unresolved tension between native Americanness, modern cosmopolitanism, and Old World Jewishness. In similar fashion, the 1921 issue, which began with Zishe Landau's Strikover poems, dedicated to his grandparents and recollecting eastern Europe, also featured Y. Y. Shvarts's epic poem *Kentucky* and a translation of Tagore's *Chitra*. The counterpoint of Old World elegy, modernist poetry about the most American of subject matter, and Poundian translation resulted in a creative but precarious dynamic, one that would have difficulty sustaining itself. The next issue of *Shriftn* would not emerge until four years later, and that issue would be Ignatov's last.

Shriftn 8 (1925–26) contained an anthology of non-Western translated verse, which included Shtiker's Indian chants from *An American Rhythm*, a section of the Finnish epic the *Kalevala* (which, because it had served as inspiration for Longfellow's epic *Hiawatha* clearly held some American significance for the journal), Arabic, and Egyptian verse, as well as Japanese haiku and a selection of Chinese poems by the eighth-century poet Li Po. Much Chinese and Japanese verse had already appeared in *Poetry*; and one of Li Po's poems—one of the same that appeared in *Shriftn*—had been translated by Moon Kwan in *Poetry* in June 1921 under the title "Good Fellowship." Li Po's poems, through the translations of Ernest Fenollosa, had also formed the bulk of Pound's *Cathay* (1915), which featured one poem in common with the *Shriftn* translations, and Amy Lowell had published *Fir-Flower Tablets*, which featured eighty-five poems by Li Po. The source for the rest of Shtiker's translations of Li Po was a book of translations by Shigeyoshi Obata that had been reviewed in *Poetry* in September 1923. This issue, *Shriftn*'s last, also featured an essay on the life of Buddha.[71]

Shriftn clearly continuously operated within the modern, transnational literary sphere delineated in and by *Poetry.*

Native Claims

Shriftn was the first Yiddish journal to prolongedly explore the multiple and often ambivalent ways in which becoming modern(ist) could be argued to be synchronous with going native. Monroe's brand of modern American art adopted, as its defining, authenticating quality, its indigeneity. After World War I, this equivalence of the indigenous and the new would be elaborated upon further by such writers as Waldo Frank, Sherwood Anderson, and Hart Crane. Ignatov, like Monroe, argued that "we here in America must free ourselves from the hegemony of European Yiddish literature. They should look towards us, rather than us towards them."[72] In this moment, the defining character of Yiddish American modernism was its insistent claim on native Americanness, where Yiddish poets, like Mary Austin, without being "expert" in things Indian, could nevertheless, through discursive and translatory exercises in self-transformation, succeed in *being* Indian.

Indianness, in the climate of early American modernism, was a flexible and unfixed signifier that signaled, at once, nativeness and cosmopolitanism, and could interpolate Whitman, ancient Eastern and modern imagist poets as well as Native American verse-makers. *Shriftn*'s (trans)nationalism adapted and transformed the poetry fashionable in U.S. literary circles, and specifically the poetry featured in Harriet Monroe's magazine. The inclusion of *Shriftn*'s emergent modernism in a larger narrative of American literary modernisms not only troubles any clear demarcations between native and alien, East and West, Yiddish and "American," but also highlights the fragility, instability, and artificiality of these categories as they became increasingly central in consolidating a sense of a national literary culture.

Shriftn was not the only Yiddish publication to feature translations of Native American chants. In fact, the Yiddish Communist monthly *Der Hammer*, published by the Communist weekly *Frayhayt*, featured an entire Indian issue in July 1928. The cover portrait image features the caption "A true one-hundred percent American. An Indian from the Navajo tribe." The first feature was a cluster of "Indian songs" (*Indianishe gezangen*) translated by A. Prints. The editors write: "A. Prints is a young Yiddish writer who is strongly interested in the poetry of other languages, chiefly with Black and Indian poems. These poems published here, were taken from *The Path on the Rainbow* anthology

"A True One Hundred Percent American: An Indian from the Navaho Tribe." *Der Hammer*, July 1928. Reproduced with permission by the New York Public Library.

of Indian literature and from other sources. The translations were rendered from English. We omit the name of the English translator. A. Prints is also the author of another article, 'Indian song and culture,' published elsewhere in the current number."[73]

Later in the issue, sharing space with Isaac Raboy's story "Somewhere in North Dakota," is Hersh Rozenfeld's translation of a modern poem: Alice Corbin Henderson's "Parting: An Indian Song," originally published as an "interpretation" in *Path on the Rainbow*. In addition, Sheen Dayksel contributed "Indianishe mayselekh" ("Indian tales"), which consisted of two pieces, "The Land of Lakes" (an origin story about the forming of Minnesota's lakes, source unacknowledged) and a retelling of the "The Lost Arrow," identified by Dayksel as Ahwahneechee (Yosemite California region). And finally, A. Prints's Mary Austin–inspired discussion of Native American poetry, "Indianer gezang un lebn," draws on the work of "pioneers" like "Dr. Baker, Miss Fletcher, Miss Curtis, Burton, Gilman, Dr. Boas," and others in describing the attitudes of Indians toward art, the "character" of their songs, and the influence of Indian song on modern American literature:

> Indians—a fading, dying race. Great and immortal however is the Indian's song, that has been passed down from generation to generation and cherished with great care. And great is the influence of the "Red Man's" song on American literature. If we will understand the way of life, world-view, the thought, the emotion, and the primitive wildness in the blood of the Indian, we must turn to his song, for the Indian and the song are one. With his song the Indian walks the "path of the rainbow" to the land of the "rising-son" [*sic*].[74]

Der Hammer, despite its more explicit politically radical agenda, thus still shared *Shriftn*'s modernist literary and anthropological sources in its appraisal of Native poetics. *Der Hammer* also exemplifies the reengagement with Indianness in the context of political radicalism that is the focus of the next chapter.

⟨ 3 ⟩

Red Jews

Whose America?

Lament for the aborigines . . . the word itself a dirge . . .

No picture, poem, statement, passing them to the
    future:
Yonnondio! Yonnondio!—unlimn'd they disappear;
To-day gives place, and fades—the cities, farms,
    factories fade;
A muffled sonorous sound, a wailing word is borne
    through the air for a moment,
Then blank and gone and still, and utterly lost.

                —Walt Whitman, "Yonnondio"

The title of Tillie Olsen's novel *Yonnondio: From the Thirties* (begun in the 1930s
but published in 1974) and its opening dedication are both borrowed from Walt
Whitman's 1888 poem "Yonnondio." Whitman understood the Iroquois word
yonnondio to mean a lament for the dead.[1] Unlike Whitman's poem, however,
Olsen's novel does not mourn vanishing "aborigines" but rather calls upon "the
cultural memory of the First Nations of the Americas to represent the voices of
the dispossessed proletariat."[2]

Olsen's invocation of the vanishing Indian in giving a voice to her desperate protagonists, the Holbrooks and those like them, suggests a Depression-era radical left wing literary culture's fascination with the figure of the Indian.[3] More attention has been paid to Jewish-authored novels and poems from the Left that featured African American protagonists.[4] However, I suggest that a closer examination of some of a handful of novels from the Left written by "red Jews" and either foregrounding or alluding to Native Americans complicates what we might immediately assume to be simply a somewhat paternalistic sympathy with additional targets of historical oppression and racism.[5] These novels include Michael Gold's *Jews without Money* (1930), Nathanael West's *A Cool Million* (1934), Isaac Raboy's *Der Yidisher Cowboy* (The Yiddish cowboy, 1937; 1942), Howard Fast's *The Last Frontier* (1941), and John Sanford's *The People from Heaven* (1943).

In Michael Gold's *Jews without Money,* Indians are both evoked and suppressed: "The red Indians once inhabited the East Side; then came the Dutch, the English, the Irish, then the Germans, Italians, and Jews. Each group left its deposits, as in geology."[6] As in Olsen's *Yonnondio,* Indians exist in Gold's Lower East Side not as people but as traces. Little Mike's gang is led by Nigger, thus nicknamed because of his "squashed" nose, "dark hair," and "murky face," who "rode the mustangs, and shot the most buffalo among the tenements. He scalped Indians, and was our stern General in war" (37). The children conceive of their urban street life as a variation of Buffalo Bill's Wild West, bolstered in part by the stories of another character, Jake Wolf, a "great man" who "belongs to Tammany Hall and runs the elections every year" (and is thus, to the attentive reader, obviously corrupt). Jake "spent a year in the west, in Chicago, and saw the Indians. They looked like Jews, he said, but were not as smart or brave. One Jew could kill a hundred Indians" (53). Gold describes a rival gang, the Forsythe Street Boys, who in a street fight "whooped down like a band of Indians. . . . They proceeded to massacre us" (47). Later in the novel Mike begins to read the "gaudy little paper books that described [Buffalo Bill's] adventures." He fantasizes:

> I walked down Hester Street toward Mulberry. Yes, it was like the Wild West. Under the fierce sky Buffalo Bill and I chased buffalo over the vast plains. We shot them down in hundreds. Then a secret message was sent us from a beautiful white maiden. She was a prisoner in the camp of the Indians. The cruel redskins were about to torture her. Buffalo Bill and I rode and rode. In the nick of time we saved her. Two hundred cruel redskins bit the dust before our trusty rifles. We escaped with the white girl, and rode and rode and rode. (187)

Mike is then jumped by a group of Italian boys, "whooping like Indians," calling him a "Christ-killer." Mike asks his mother who Christ is, and she tells him he is "their false Messiah." When the real Messiah comes, she says, "he will save the world. He will make everything good" (189). Gold writes, "I needed a Messiah who would look like Buffalo Bill, and who could annihilate our enemies" (190).

The true Messiah of the novel is, of course, revolutionary socialism. The novel ends with Mike's awakening: "O workers' Revolution, you brought hope to me, a lonely, suicidal boy. You are the true Messiah. You will destroy the East Side when you come, and build there a garden for the human spirit" (309). Gold, like Olsen, was a Jew active in the Communist Party and an orthodox Marxist. After the conversion described in *Jews without Money*, Gold, in his "Worker's Correspondence" poems published in the *Daily Worker*, would invoke the vanishing, dispossessed Indian, who was no longer linked with little Mikey's enemies but rather with the grown-up Gold's commitment to radical protest and interethnic working-class brotherhood:

> Arrested as a picket in a recent strike
> I have found my cellmate here an Indian Chief
> His name John Thunder of the Ottawas
> Once his father owned America.[7]

In another poem, Gold writes:

> The Indians marched in bright blankets and war feathers
> That night lit a bonfire and leaped us a war dance
> Swedes, Danes, Norse, we remembered the Sagas
> We sang of the heroes, the Sioux drummed, and the Yanks
> Shouted the John Brown song of the marching on
> Skoal! skoal, O wonderful light of Lenin!
> Come again! again! Bring hope to the lost Dakotas![8]

Like the modernists of the 1920s, Left writers of the 1930s also called upon the figure of the Indian in order to articulate their political and aesthetic programs.[9] However, these Left writers operated in a complicated cultural matrix in which they were not alone in invoking the imagined Indian. I use Nathanael West as a significant touchstone here in that he continually addressed the ways in which the imaginary Indian served as a site in which the discourses of high and low culture, Left and Right politics, problematically converged. A close reading and historical contextualization of West's 1934 novel *A Cool Million* therefore comprises the heart of the following discussion.[10] I read the novel as a satire on the commodification of, specifically, Native and ethnic identities in America. *A Cool Million*'s satirical treatment of ethnicity, the marketplace, nativism, fascism, and communism works as a commentary upon such cultural spaces as world's fairs and ethnic and historical villages, where Jews and Indians performed specialized roles, as well as upon the literary culture of the Left.[11]

West's position vis-à-vis the Left was rather more complicated than that of either Gold or Olsen. As West wrote to Edmund Wilson in 1939:

> Somehow or other I seem to have slipped in between all the "schools." My books meet no needs but my own. . . . [I] go on making what one critic called "private and unfunny jokes." The radical press, although I consider myself on their side, doesn't like it, and thinks it even fascist sometimes, and the literature boys, whom I detest, detest me in turn. The highbrow press finds that I avoid the important things and the lending library touts in the daily press think me shocking. The proof of all this is that I've never had the same publisher twice—once bitten, etc.—because there is nothing to root for in my books and what is even worse, no rooters.[12]

West described his Jewishness in similarly unstable terms. While at Brown, West had described himself as a "Jewish outsider," a "Jew and a not-Jew at the same time."[13] My discussion of West aims to read his preoccupations with Indians, Jews, and the marketplace through the ambivalent and unfixable Jewishness that I suggest is dramatized in *A Cool Million*, whose modernist parody of racial and ethnic typologies succeeds in thoroughly undermining and ultimately destabilizing them.

West repeats, in order to undo, the typologies that Waldo Frank affirms in his 1919 survey of American literary culture, *Our America*. Frank, a writer and critic of German-Jewish descent, argued that the racial qualities of Indians and Jews, and their resulting contributions to American culture, were as antithetical as the imagined physical landscapes they inhabited. Frank describes the Jews as modern America's Puritans: "There was no fortuity in the New Englander's obsession with the Hebrew texts, in his quite conscious taking on of the role of Israel in a hostile world. . . . And as with the Puritan, so with the Jew, once free in a vast country, the urge of power swiftly shook off its religious and pietistic way, and drove untrammeled to material aggression."[14] In America, Frank asserts, secularism had deadened the Jews' spiritual mysticism. Frank is particularly critical of Felix Adler's Ethical Culture society, which he describes as a substitute religion, "completely commercialized . . . a religion, in other words, which was no religion at all, since all the mystery of life, all the harmony of sense, all the immanence of God were deleted from it: and in their place a quiet, moral code destined to make good citizens" (87). The result is the "anaesthetic Jew," who is "bitter, ironic, passionately logical. . . . They become critics of the arts. They consort with artists: study the anatomy of aesthetics: and from the strategy of close acquaintance subtly inspire the distrust of art, prove art is dying, teach how trivial an affair art has become" (88–89).

Frank's chapter on the Jews, "The Chosen People," is immediately followed by a chapter titled "The Land of Buried Cultures," in which Frank addresses the Indians of the Southwest, whom he describes as the inverse of the materialistic, aggressive Puritan-Jew: "The Indian art is classic, if any art is classic. Its dynamics are reserved for the inward meaning. Its surface has the polish of ancient custom. Its content is the pure emotional experience of a people who have for ages sublimated their desire above the possessive into the creative realm" (114).[15] Twelve years later, Oliver La Farge, a novelist, ethnographer, and Indian rights activist, would echo Frank when he wrote that the Indian artist "deserves to be classed as a Modernist, his art is old, yet alive and dynamic. . . . His work has a primitive directness and strength, yet at the same time it possesses sophistication and subtlety. Indian painting is at once classic and modern."[16] Frank thus articulates, along with a chorus of American literary moderns, an opposition between Indian and Jew, between "classic," modern, emotional, and spiritual Native artist, uncorrupted by materialist desire, and "anaesthetic," sterile, and commercial Jewish critic.[17]

Our America coincided with Mabel Dodge's 1917 move from New York to Santa Fe and then Taos, where she established "Greenwich Village's western adjunct."[18] Her visitors and friends eventually included Georgia O'Keefe, Mary Austin, Willa Cather, D. H. Lawrence, and Frank's friend Jean Toomer, and Dodge herself would become a well-known advocate of Native arts. Despite the fact that it was painter Maurice Sterne, Dodge's Jewish Russian-born husband (whom Dodge later left for Tony Lujan, a Native American and Taos local), who visited the American Southwest first and urged his wife to "save the Indians, their art-culture—reveal it to the world," Jewish artists, particularly those of recent eastern European extraction, were not included in an emerging arc of native modernist American literary product.[19] Jews were not "American" but rather, to use the term coined by Mary Austin, thoroughly "New Yorkish."

Our America, arranged by geographic region, was, as Frank himself would write later, "not an objective portrait of a real land, but an appeal for it *to be.*"[20] The America that his book calls into being, however, is in spite of itself an America atomized, fragmented geographically, culturally, and ethnically. Frank writes in his introduction, "Our America is already the discovery of adumbrating groups. But it is true no less, that there are many Americas to-day. The concept to which adheres the greatest strength, the widest truth, must some day *be* America" (10).

Pageants of America

A Cool Million satirizes not only the Indian and Jewish "types" invoked by literary moderns but also the collection and display strategies of museums, expositions, world's fairs, historical villages, and "pageants of democracy" in the first half of the twentieth century that also called an idealized America into being. Barbara Kirshenblatt-Gimblett distinguishes two approaches in the display of objects, *in situ* and *in context*: "In situ approaches to installation tend toward environmental and re-creative displays." In context displays, on the other hand, use "particular techniques of arrangement and explanation to convey ideas. . . . Objects are also set in context by means of other objects, often in relation to a classification or schematic arrangement of some kind, based on typologies of form or proposed historical relationships."[21]

Henry Ford's Greenfield Village, for instance, could be read as a curious variation on the "in context" approach to object display. He began his "salvaging" efforts at the turn of the century by collecting Edisonia and McGuffey readers, among other artifacts, and 1929 marked the dedication of Ford's Edison Institute, which quickly grew into the Greenfield Village and museum. Ford purchased the homes of Noah Webster, William Holmes McGuffey, and the Wright brothers, restored them, and moved them to Greenfield Village. Joining these were an Illinois courthouse where a young Abraham Lincoln once practiced law, the circa-1830s Eagle Tavern, and Mrs. D. Cohen's late-nineteenth-century millinery shop. Nearby, the Ford Museum eventually featured twelve indoor acres of Americana.[22] Ford brought together buildings and artifacts from all over the United States, and from different historical periods, and reconstructed them to forward a narrative of America as engaged in a uniform and harmonious march into modernity.[23] As one visitor wrote on a comment card after viewing the complex, "I never knew that Henry Ford, Thomas Edison, and the Wright brothers all lived on the same street."[24]

Ford's village and museum, however, despite its celebration of such modern inventions as the steam engine and the automobile and the loving reconstruction of Edison's laboratories, displayed a certain nostalgia for an imagined pastoral American past, one that, it could be argued, Ford had helped to eradicate through his affordable automobile.[25] Ford reimagines early industrial America as pastoral, arranging as a village set piece, for example, a picturesquely rusting plow in the verdant front yard of his reconstructed boyhood farmhouse.

Ford was not the only industrialist to parlay his personal nostalgia into a nationalist celebration of America's past. John D. Rockefeller bankrolled the restoration of Williamsburg, Virginia, in 1927, after Ford, apparently, had turned down the project. Colonial Williamsburg had just opened to the public when West wrote his parodic *A Cool Million,* and it could be read as representative of an "in situ" approach. Ford's and Rockefeller's roles in creating these historical villages are significant, in fact, because of the insistence with which Ford and Rockefeller are continually invoked by West in his novel. Colonial Williamsburg, unlike Greenfield Village, was marked by an attention to accurate historical detail, with archaeologists working from court records, governmental archives, libraries, historical societies, military records, and family papers in the reparation and restoration of nearly one hundred colonial structures.[26] In the narrative of Colonial Williamsburg, the story of the restoration of the city is at least as important as the city's own history; it is even included in the historical timeline provided by the guidebook. Like Greenfield Village, Colonial Williamsburg celebrated both a national past and modern innovation, both colonial Williamsburg and "Colonial Williamsburg, Incorporated."

Yet despite the attention to historical detail, the daily life of colonists as performed in Colonial Williamsburg was filtered through the racial fantasies of its twentieth-century creators. The lives of African Americans, women, and the working class were not represented in Colonial Williamsburg.[27] The interwar "colonial revival" movement of which Greenfield Village and Colonial Williamsburg were part, further consolidated through "eighteenth century tract houses, pseudo-colonial shopping streets, celebratory school pageants, and forests of nostalgic books and magazine articles," owed its popularity to growing anxieties about increased immigration and to racialized national fantasies that increasingly imbricated primitive peoples with immigrants.[28]

Beginning in the early sixteenth century, when indigenous peoples of the Americas were brought back to Europe for display, the exhibition of humans blended the "theatrical" and "zoological." As Kirshenblatt-Gimblett suggests, museum exhibitions transformed how people looked at their own immediate surroundings. Suddenly, the ethnographic eye could be turned upon the streets of one's own city, and indeed, in the late nineteenth century, as those streets became increasingly clogged with the immigrant poor, "slumming" began to acquire the patina of serious ethnography as well as constitute a kind of "tourism": "Slumming, like tourism more generally, takes the spectator to the site, and as areas are canonized in a geography of attractions, whole territories become extended ethnographic theme parks. An ethnographic bell jar drops over the terrain. A neighborhood, village, or region becomes for all intents and purposes a living museum in situ."[29]

Fairs, expositions, and historical and tourist villages were all, as Walter Benjamin asserted about nineteenth-century expositions, "sites of pilgrimage to the commodity fetish."[30] If the historical village indirectly referenced modernity through the re-creation of the past, often with the aid of modern technological advances in such fields as archaeology and construction, the international exposition's explicit purpose was to display and manage visions of modern progress. World's fairs, from the first world's fair in the Crystal Palace in London, featured ethnographic displays that presented examples of "primitive peoples" alongside futuristic exhibits that most often featured the "products of tomorrow."[31] The contiguity and interaction of these displays were crucial to the message of the fair. Ethnicity, that is to say, was central to the visions and versions of modernity imagined by world's fairs.[32] Robert W. Rydell observes that the "culture of abundance" constructed and promoted by early twentieth century expositions "pivoted on dreams of empire."[33] Rydell terms this peculiar mix of modernism and imperialism "Coloniale Moderne"; it drove not only the selection, content, and arrangement of fair exhibits but also the very architecture of buildings erected for the fairs' purposes.[34]

In West's *A Cool Million*, Shagpoke Whipple, on a cross-country train with his friends Jake Raven, Lem Pitkin, and Betty Prail, urges all to visit the world's fair during their stopover in Chicago. West was inspired and informed in the writing of his novel by his visit to the 1933–34 Century-of-Progress Chicago World's Fair.[35] Jay Martin writes that West's purpose in visiting Chicago's Century-of-Progress Exposition was to see the American schoolbook exhibit; he was interested in collecting information on "success" books, many of which, such as Horatio Alger's stories, were standard fare in the classroom.[36] The novel, however, parodies and critiques the Century-of-Progress Exposition in any number of ways. I argue that it is the fair's specific preoccupation with ethnicity and the relationship it envisioned between ethnic identities and American modern and progressive culture that animate the satire of West's novel.

As Kirshenblatt-Gimblett observes, "Display not only shows and speaks, it also *does*." Display, that is to say, "constitutes its subject."[37] Given the opposition between Indian and Jew exploited and satirized by West, it is instructive to examine the distinct and specialized roles performed by both Native Americans and Jews at the Century-of-Progress Exposition, which is in many ways representative of the ways in which Natives and Jews were exhibited and thus constituted throughout the early twentieth century. Ethnic exhibits at fairs and expositions were generally featured along the midway, alongside food concessions, souvenir stands, mechanical rides, and animal exhibits. As these ethnic villages generally represented newly colonized peoples, such as, in the wake of the Spanish-American War, peoples from the Philippines, their placement "gave the impression that empire-building could be fun."[38]

As America's first internally colonized population, Native American displays formed a staple of world's fairs, both in "scientific," ethnographic displays and in the Wild West shows that quickly came to be embraced as part of the official programs. At the 1933–34 Chicago fair, five "living groups" of Native Americans were housed in an "Indian village," adjacent to an exact replica of a Mayan temple and between the concessions and the automobile manufacturing exhibit. The Indians were supposed to "live primitive existences as their ancestors did before them"; a publicity release makes explicit the intended effect: "The General Motors tower rises, a bright orange tribute to Modernism, over the wigwams and tepees and hogans of the oldest Americans, over the dances and feathers and beads in the Indian stadium. . . . 'What a distance we have come,' is the theme of the World's Fair, but nowhere does it come home so sharply to the visitor as when he attends the Indian ceremonials."[39] Thus, the "Indian village," in which individual tribes were jumbled and reconstituted as undifferentiated from one another, meant to represent American Indians as frozen in time, still living their ancient, "primitive existence" and thus highly differentiated from the "we" of the modern fair visitors implied by the official literature.

Jews, on the other hand, played multiple roles at the Chicago Century-of-Progress Exposition. As Kirshenblatt-Gimblett has noted, between 1851 and 1940 "Jews represented themselves at international expositions in Europe and America in a wide range of ways."[40] As she also notes, however, their participation was "elusive": "There is no obvious place to look for Jewish participation, no national pavilion (before Jewish Palestine pavilions made their debut) on the international avenue and no foreign village in the amusement zone." Jews were "avid visitors" to international expositions and were also "entrepreneurs and impresarios, helping to raise money for fairs and managing whole divisions of them."[41]

In Chicago, Jews were visibly present most notably in a spectacular Zionist pageant called *The Romance of a People,* which employed thirty-five hundred actors, dancers, and singers and which was staged in Soldier Field. Chaim Weizman, the most internationally prominent promoter of a Jewish state (and later Israel's first president), gave a speech before the pageant. The fair's organizers had asked the Chicago Jewish community to participate in the

Century-of-Progress Exposition, and months of discussion within the Jewish community had ensued. Meyer Weisgal, executive director of Zionist Activities for the Midwest and the creator of the pageant, called for Jews to represent themselves not in a "building, not an exhibit, but a *spectacle*, portraying five thousand years of Jewish history; it would have everything, religion, history, the longing for Zion, the return to Zion, and it would be called *The Romance of a People*. It would have something for everybody, Zionists, non-Zionists, the religious, the nationalists, everybody."[42] The pageant debuted in the evening of Jewish Day, one of two dozen "special days" designated by the fair committee to celebrate the many immigrant groups of Chicago.[43] In addition to Jewish Day and to the pageant, a Jewish exhibit, to be housed in the Hall of Religion for the duration of the fair, was organized by non-Zionist Reform Rabbis Louis Mann and Gerson Levi. It consisted of a display of Jewish artifacts and portraits of famous Jews through the ages, illustrating their contributions to the fields of social science, education, religion, literature, medicine, philanthropy, agriculture, statesmanship, music, art, drama, and child welfare.[44]

Yet Jews were alluded to and invisibly present in other ways, most notably in the eugenics exhibit, housed among the genetics exhibits in the Hall of Science. The exhibit was small but popular.[45] If *The Romance of a People* proposed a progressive view of Jewish civilization, culminating in the incipient creation of a Jewish nation-state, the eugenics exhibit implied the immutability of racial "types." Jews may also have been invisibly present in the fair's foreign villages, as they were in the 1893 Chicago exposition. The 1933–34 fair featured a "Foreign Bazaar," Tunisian village, Oriental village, and Moroccan village. In 1893, it was openly acknowledged that "about four-fifths of the inhabitants of the Turkish village on the Midway Plaisance at the Chicago Exposition were Jews. Merchants, clerks, actors, servants, musicians, and even the dancing girls, were of the mosaic faith, though their looks and garb would lead one to believe them Mohammedans." On Yom Kippur, the Turkish mosque served as a Jewish house of worship, where Jews from "all parts of the Orient"—presumably representing their countries of origin on the Midway, but as "Orientals," not as Jews—gathered for Kol Nidre.[46]

As Kirshenblatt-Gimblett writes of the 1893 fair, "Taken together, the diverse forms of Jewish participation . . . illuminate the paradoxes of diaspora and the theatricality of race, which needed to be staged to be seen. That staging also offered a place to hide."[47] Jews certainly exerted more agency than Native Americans in the 1933–34 fair, both as spectacle and spectators, and yet nevertheless were caught up in some of the same dilemmas. Were Jews immutable "types" or racially unfixable? Citizens of the United States, or the Diaspora, or of their own nation in Palestine? A religion, a nation, or a race? And finally, were Jews modern or ancient?

The ethnological villages of the world's fair served multiple purposes. They were not only entertaining spectacles but also offered environments for anthropological study. Beginning with the 1893 Chicago World's Columbian Exposition, "every American international fair held through World War I included ethnological villages sanctioned by prominent anthropologists who occasionally organized university summer school courses around these displays."[48] As Rydell has written elsewhere, anthropology and world's fairs came of age together. By the 1930s, however, anthropologists and ethnographers, most notably Franz Boas, were protesting both eugenics and the eugenicist logic that informed, both explicitly and implicitly, racial exhibits. At the same time, interwar ethnography and social reform aimed to document, preserve, and ameliorate the situation of living Indians.

John Collier's Indian Reorganization Act, which drew on the ideas of modernist campaigners such as Mabel Dodge Luhan and was supported by them, had as its first aim "the conservation of the biological Indian and of Indian cultures." The act, passed in 1934, aimed to restore to individual tribes sovereignty and autonomy over reservation life. It was a dramatic success for Indian rights, though the act was terminated in the 1950s before much of what it promised came to pass. From the perspective both of romantic melancholy and hopeful preservation, the Indian represented the artistic, spiritual, antibourgeois values that a commercially obsessed America had lost, as Oliver La Farge's Pulitzer Prize–winning novel of 1930, *Laughing Boy*, demonstrates.[49]

La Farge was himself a trained ethnographer and later Indian rights activist. In his novel, Laughing Boy and his wife, Slim Girl, are artists: Laughing Boy creates silver and turquoise jewelry; Slim Girl weaves Navajo blankets. Slim Girl, however, is an Indian who was taken as a child and sent to a government boarding school, where she learned successfully how to be "an American." She hopes to return to the ways of her people through her union with Laughing Boy, but white culture has, the novel implies, corrupted her deeply. This corruption is primarily communicated through her obsessive materialism: she prostitutes herself to a white man for money. Capitalist fantasies of accumulation, the novel argues, contaminate the aesthetic purity of the Indian. Unsurprisingly, one of the Native American ceremonies that most fascinated modernist ethnographers was that of the potlatch, in which prominent figures in the community periodically and ritualistically gave away or destroyed all of their material possessions.[50]

Tourism, souvenir shopping, and the accumulation of knickknacks encouraged by the "culture of abundance" on display at fairs and expositions served to define, by way of contrast, the value of the "genuine" art object, particularly those created by Indian artists. La Farge and John Sloane wrote in their guide to the 1931 Exposition of Indian Tribal Arts in New York:

> The casual tourist who goes out to the Indian country likes to bring back some knickknack as a souvenir and proudly displays it as a "genuine Indian" article. Unhappily, Americans know the art of the Indian chiefly through such cheap curios made for the gullible white man. Looking upon the Indian himself as a curio, and with this cast of mind failing to recognize the high artistic value of the best Indian products, if indeed he ever sees them, the tourist will not pay the price which any craftsman must ask for the mere time, labour, and materials involved in his work. Thus the whites have forced the Indians, often extremely poor and in need of money, to meet their demand for little, sweet-grass baskets, absurd bows and arrows, teapots, candlesticks, and any number of wretched souvenirs which they never made until white men decided that these, and these only, were "genuine Indian souvenirs."[51]

These culture critics thus set up an opposition with the role of the tourist's expectations in the manufacture and purchase of kitschy souvenirs versus modernist suppositions in the creation of valuable and "genuine" Indian artistic product. The Indian artist, continue La Farge and Sloan, "deserves to be classed as a Modernist, his art is old, yet alive and dynamic; but his modernism is an expression of a continuing vigour seeking new outlets and not, like ours, a search for release from exhaustion. . . . His work has a primitive directness and strength, yet at the same time it possesses sophistication and subtlety. Indian painting is at once classic and modern."[52]

La Farge and Sloan echo Frank, who also calls Indian art "classic" and whose content is "pure emotional experience," that is to say, uncorrupted by "possessive" desire. Thus, the aesthetic, cultural, and political sympathies and desires of the Left found expression through a fascination with the Indian, a figure who in the 1930s came to signify resistance to the crass capitalism of Western culture. It was not accidental that a "red" of one stripe would identify with a "red" of another.[53]

Nathanael West and the Parody of *A Cool Million*

Nathanael West, born Nathan Wallenstein Weinstein in 1903 into a family of Lithuanian Jewish immigrants who resolutely taught their children German and not Yiddish, was thirteen years younger than Waldo Frank but attended the same high school, and, Susan Hegeman argues, was deeply influenced by the criticism of Frank and his circle.[54] However, in his 1934 satirical novel *A Cool Million, or the Dismantling of Lemuel Pitkin,* West would both exploit and undo the neat antitheses of *Our America.*[55] The novel envisions a United States that is, like the Germany under the newly appointed chancellor, in thrall to fascism, whose exploitation of an imagined and manufactured folk national culture plays with Frank's identification of Puritans and Jews as "material aggressors," as well as upon the series of dichotomized oppositions between Jews and Indians that Frank forwards as *Our America* continues. In West's critical vision, the slippage of a mythic America into fascism and of the "primitive" into cultural commodification are articulated through the exaggerated enactment of a racialized opposition between Indian and Jew.[56]

In the song "I'm a Yiddish Cowboy," intermarriage between the "newest of the new Americans" and the "oldest of the old Americans" results in an American union that, whatever possibilities it suggests for a successfully integrated American identity, is formalized and consummated by an ecstatic assertion of consumerist activity: "Go buy cigarettes." As in that 1907 lyric, acts of consumption and performance in *A Cool Million* have the specific function of yoking, if not uniting, the two ethnic groups that in early-twentieth-century popular, intellectual, and artistic imaginations had come to reside at two opposite poles on the spectrum of native Americanness. Through a pastiche of passages lifted wholesale from Horatio Alger novels, the novel chronicles the "adventures" of Lemuel Pitkin.[57] Lem is the son of the Widow Pitkin of Ottsville, Vermont, and a descendant of Revolutionary War heroes; he is persuaded by Nathan "Shagpoke" Whipple, former U.S. president and current Rat River National Bank president, to go out in the world and seek his fortune, "like Ford and Rockefeller," to save the family home from foreclosure.[58] The bank wants to sell the Pitkin homestead to a Jewish collector and interior decorator from New York, Asa Goldstein, who collects "Colonial Exteriors and Interiors." In short order, Lem is robbed, thrown in jail, and deprived of his teeth and one eye. He is reunited in New York with Betty Prail, his friend from Ottsville, who has been kidnapped by white slavers and forced to serve a stint in Wu-Fong's "one hundred percent American" brothel, whose suites are decorated in various American regional styles by the same Asa Goldstein. Lem and Betty join Shagpoke Whipple, who is headed out West with his Indian friend Jake Raven to raise funds for his new, fascistic National Revolutionary Party. Out West, Lem loses his leg and is scalped by Indians, led by the Harvard-educated, proto-Marxist intellectual Indian chief Israel Satinpenny.

The novel's satire of race, culture, and commerce acquires an increasingly sinister political inflection. Lem and Shagpoke then join a traveling show, titled *Chamber of American Horrors: Animate and Inanimate Hideosities*, managed by the confidence-man poet Sylvanus Snodgrasse.[59] The show, although it appears to be a museum, is actually a "bureau for disseminating propaganda of the most subversive nature" and is financed by both the Communist Party and the International Jewish Bankers (in the demented logic of the novel, as in German and American fascist discourse, the two organizations are working together). When they arrive in the South, Shagpoke stages a violent revolt with newly recruited members of his fascist organization: the heads of Negroes are paraded on poles; a Jewish salesman is nailed to the door of his hotel room; the housekeeper of the local Catholic priest is raped. In the chaos, Lem escapes to New York, where he finds employment with a vaudeville act. Persuaded by Shagpoke to make a political speech on stage, he is assassinated. The novel closes with a parade of Whipple's Leather Shirts, who now rule the nation, in which Lem Pitkin is memorialized as a martyr for the cause.[60]

West wrote *A Cool Million* at the height of the Depression, hoping to capitalize on the critical success of *Miss Lonelyhearts*. He was motivated both by a desire for material success and by the disappointment of the commercial failure of *Miss Lonelyhearts*, which was directly attributable to the financial collapse of Liveright, the publishing house that had issued it. Just as favorable reviews of the just-published novel had begun to come in, one of Liveright's creditors seized two thousand of the first press run of twenty-two hundred and refused to release them until he had been paid. Liveright also refused to give West back the copyright. What is more, the publication of *Miss Lonelyhearts* coincided with a national crisis: Roosevelt's declaration of a national bank "holiday," which West mentions in *A Cool Million*, making sure to remark the life savings his hero has once again lost.[61] A letter to Minna and Milton Abernathy demonstrates West's keen awareness of the ways in which the circulation of art was dependent on the vagaries of a fragile and unpredictable market:

> The book surprised everyone including me—it got swell reviews and even more it started to sell very well, making Macy's best seller list and selling 2000 copies in less than 10 days right in Manhattan without salesmen or

promotion of any kind. Liveright has not been functioning as a publishing house for the past six weeks and the book had to make its way by itself.

Everybody, Knopf, Harrison Smith, etc. says that with normal exploitation it might have sold 15,000 copies.

I've been heartsick over the thing as you can imagine, and I'm still sick.[62]

West's "heartsickness" over the fate of *Miss Lonelyhearts* resulted in the writing of *A Cool Million,* an account, writ large, of the subordination of art, history, ideology, sexual relations, and ethnic identities to the marketplace.

At the same time that he endured this initiation into the painfully enmeshed relationship between art and commerce, West served as associate editor and contributor in 1932 and 1933 to two magazines, *Contact* and its satirical counterpart, *Americana. Contact,* with William Carlos Williams as editor and Robert McAlmon and West as associate editors, was to affiliate itself with romantic notions of authenticity, Americanness, and primitiveness, announcing its intent on its title page to "attempt to cut a trail through the American jungle without the use of a European compass."[63] West considered the second issue of *Contact,* in May 1932, a "primitive America" issue, but in it, mysteriously, he planned to print, in addition to original contributions, a sermon by Jonathan Edwards, a sketch of Benjamin Franklin by one of his contemporaries, and an excerpt from an old Sears, Roebuck catalog, as if it were a poem.[64] West, that is to say, was evolving a vision of a "primitive" modernism that quoted Puritanism, the gospel of success and the language of advertising. His interminglings of art, commerce, and the rhetoric of "America," however, were not included in the final product, which in its ultimate incarnation included several pieces of short fiction that, like the regionally organized *Our America,* featured Mexico, Texas, New England, upstate New York, and the South.[65] In the editor's "Comment," Williams writes earnestly that the project of the American Primitive issue is to "reveal the object" and as a result "touch authentically the profundity of its attachments." West's relentless parody of the "authentic" in *A Cool Million,* however, seems to militate against Williams's reading of "primitive" America.[66] West expressed his disappointment in *Contact'*s sincere vision of an "authentic" America when he wrote to Milton Abernathy after the second number had come out:

I don't like *Contact* much. We had an idea in the beginning, but it looks as though we'll drift into the old "regionalism." You know the Blue Denim stuff they print in Pagany and Hound and Horn. No. 1. *Lem Harrington*

at Cross Purposes: Sally was sweating like a horse at her weeding and Lem
had an erection behind the hydrangea bushes. No. 2: *The Paint Horse:* The
Indian came across the meadow leading a restive horse and old Mrs Purdy
remembered her youth in the circus with no little regret. No 3: *The White
Church:* The old county church looked like a prim little girl in a starched
white dress as Jetsy drove by in the Ford on her way to the movies.[67]

Lem Pitkin, an Indian, the circus, and Ford all make appearances in this
declaration of the failure both of *Contact*'s regionalism and its modernism.
Indeed, this reads both as a critique of the magazine and as a rehearsal for *A Cool
Million*'s brand of satire, which is marked, like this passage, by its abundance
of ironic lists, catalogs, and revues.

T. R. Steiner describes *A Cool Million* as an "encyclopedia of mythic
'America,'" and a key feature of that mythic landscape was the Indian, who in
the 1930s, as we have seen, was the object of nativist, modernist, leftist, and
popular fascination.[68] According to West's brother-in-law S. J. Perelman, West
was "much impressed with the Indian and the bad deal he had received."[69]
West wrote a seventeen-page screen treatment, probably around 1935, about
Osceola, which he described as "a story of one of the greatest heroes in American
frontier history. The story of a soldier who never lost a battle, of a statesman
who never made a mistake, of a lover who was always generous and loyal, yet,
in the end, lost everything . . . who was destroyed, like an ancient Greek hero,
by inevitable destiny."[70] Osceola, Martin believes, was for West the "Indian Lem
Pitkin," that is, "another dismantled innocent."

Osceola's innocence, however, was precisely what made West's story a
potentially profitable one; after all, what West proposed was the transformation
of Osceola into a subject fit for mass consumption. If Osceola represents West's
attempt to exploit commercial culture, the Indians of *A Cool Million* reify his
complicated and even ambivalent critique of it. Lemuel Pitkin, Jake Raven, and
Israel Satinpenny all perform, at different moments, alternative and profitable
versions of popularly circulated visions of the Indian. Lem and Shagpoke's
"red-skinned friend," Jake Raven, after disappearing in the aftermath of Chief
Satinpenny's massacre, turns up alive, performing as "Chief" Jake Raven in
Snodgrasse's revue and peddling a secret "Indian elixir." At the same time,
Whipple exhibits Lem for money as "the last man to have been scalped by the
Indians and the sole survivor of the Yuba River Massacre."

The Harvard-educated Satinpenny represents most specifically both early
Puritan myths that swirled around Indians and Jews and Frank's identification
of Puritans with Jews. His name evokes both the popular Puritan hypothesis

that the American Indians were descended from the ten lost tribes of Israel, as well as, with "Satinpenny," the old familiar charge of the Jew as both material-ist aggressor and Communist. The intellectual, Spengler-quoting Satinpenny, in his catalog detailing the detritus of modernity, articulates high culture's preoccupation in the thirties with the authentic, pastoral, premodern way of life represented by the Indian:

> "Red men!" he thundered. "The time has come to protest in the name of the Indian peoples and to cry out against that abomination of abominations, the paleface.
>
> "In our father's memory this was a fair, sweet land, where a man could hear his heart beat without wondering if what he heard wasn't an alarm clock, where a man could fill his nose with pleasant flower odors without finding that they came from a bottle. Need I speak of springs that had never known the tyranny of iron pipes? Of deer that never tasted hay? Of wild ducks that had never been banded by the U.S. Department of Conservation?
>
> "In return for the loss of these things, we accepted the white man's civilization, syphilis and the radio, tuberculosis and the cinema. We accepted his civilization because he himself believed in it. But now that he has begun to doubt, why should we continue to accept? His final gift to us is doubt, a soul-corroding doubt. He rotted this land in the name of progress, and now it is he himself who is rotting. . . .
>
> "In what way is the white man wiser than the red? We lived here from time immemorial and everything was sweet and fresh. The pale-face came and in his wisdom filled the sky with smoke and the rivers with refuse. What, in his wisdom, was he doing? I'll tell you. He was making clever cigarette lighters. He was making superb fountain pens. He was making paper bags, doorknobs, leatherette satchels . . . the land was flooded with toilet paper, painted boxes to keep pins in, key rings, watch fobs, leatherette satchels. . . .
>
> "Now even the Grand Canyon will no longer hold razor blades. Now the dam, O warriors, has broken and he is up to his neck in the articles of his manufacture." (156–57)

Israel Satinpenny, however, not least in his invocation of Spengler, exposes the ways in which the critique of the commercial in favor of the "authentic" becomes increasingly and troublingly articulated through racial and ethnic typologies. Both progressive and nativist entities, after all, made similar ap-peals to the values represented, it was imagined, by the Indian. The character of Shagpoke Whipple was modeled not only on Calvin Coolidge but also on

William Dudley Pelley, the leader of a fascist organization in the 1930s called the Silver Shirts, which was modeled on the Nazi Party.[71] In the novel, Shagpoke cultivates a friendship with Jake Raven, declaring: "I am happy to welcome you into our organization. We 'Leather Shirts' can learn much from your people, fortitude, courage, and relentless purpose, among other things" (113). The real-life Pelley made overtures to Indians: he recruited a "redskin" branch of his legion to stamp out communism on the reservations. Throughout *A Cool Million*, West addresses the irony involved in the way a number of political and cultural attitudes, seemingly at odds with each other, all used the figure of the Indian as an ideological and metaphorical touchstone. The critique of commodity culture articulated by the Jewish Indian Satinpenny was, the novel suggests, a site in which the discourses of modernism, Marxism, and fascism converged.

At the same time, Jewish characters in the novel are the manufacturers, appropriators, and purveyors of artifacts meant to reference an imagined national past, which is itself constructed around and invested in fantasies of Indianness. Asa Goldstein is the proprietor of the Fifth Avenue antiques store Colonial Exteriors and Interiors, appropriator and marketer of Lemuel Pitkin's "authentic" Vermont cottage, and decorator of Wu-Fong's brothel. Ezra Silverblatt is mentioned briefly as the official tailor to the National Revolutionary Party, whose costume consists of "coonskin hats with extra long tails, deerskin shirts with or without fringes, blue jeans, moccasins, squirrel rifles, everything for the American Fascist at rock bottom prices" (101, 113). The Jewish merchant outfits Whipple's Fascists in an "American" costume that, with its deerskin shirt and moccasins, is an appropriation of Indian garb.[72]

The conflicted nature of West's critique of the marketplace inheres in the ironic fact that while West sought to expose and parody American materialism, he also openly hoped the novel would prove successful and provide him, finally, with an income. West had, Martin writes, "the instincts of a good businessman: he was disciplined and well organized, with a love for moneyed life. He looked, Arthur Kober remarks, 'like someone out of Wall Street,' 'very formal indeed.'"[73] *A Cool Million* was a business venture for West even as it is a satire, among other things, of America's most prominent businessmen.

Nathan "Shagpoke" Whipple, whose name is very close to Nathan Weinstein/ Nathanael West's own, repeatedly mouths Coolidge-like aphorisms that recall the latter's famous "The business of America is business." Shagpoke declares to Lem after he has refused to lend Lem enough money to save his home: "The story of Rockefeller and of Ford is the story of every great American, and you should strive to make it your story"; Lemuel resolves to "go and do as Rockefeller and Ford had done" (137). The novel's critical anatomy of business and businessmen, however, is informed by and a critical component of West's discussions of race, nationalism, and nativism.[74] Ford and Rockefeller are reincarnated as Goldstein and Silverblatt; in all likelihood, neither Ford, whose anti-Semitic barbs in his newspaper the *Dearborn Independent* were notorious, nor Rockefeller, who had funded the Eugenics Committee of the United States in the early 1920s, would have appreciated the joke.[75] The novel critiques, at once, Rockefeller and Ford as the exemplars of the American material success that eluded West and Rockefeller and Ford as the guardians of American national culture.

The Jewish Goldstein's determination to purchase Lemuel's boyhood home from Widow Pitkin's mortgage holder leads directly to the foreclosure on the house and, subsequently, Lem's misadventures; Goldstein's store, in the window of which he displays the Pitkin cottage, parodies Ford's method, in creating Greenfield Village, of purchasing, dismantling, and then reconstructing such Americana as "authentic" New England cottages. Lem, like his house, is systematically "dismantled" throughout the novel, and through his death at its conclusion is finally reconstituted (like Greenfield Village or Colonial Williamsburg) as a symbol of an America "delivered from sophistication, Marxism, and International Capitalism," thus "purged of alien diseases" (179).

Wu-Fong's brothel both emblematizes this corruption of native America that Ford's Greenfield Village sought to correct and replicates Greenfield Village's importation and prostitution of Americana.[76] When Betty Prail is first brought to Wu-Fong's establishment, initially a "House of All Nations," she is meant to "round out his collection," for he is still missing a "real American girl." Betty Prail's suite, a "perfect colonial interior," is decorated by, of course, Asa Goldstein (92–94). Betty's most avid clients are "orientals, Slavs, Latins, Celts, and Semites," who bring to mind the ethnic makeup of the masses of immigrants that, in their likeminded eagerness to consume authentic American "product," were perceived as a threat to native American culture in the early part of the century.

Later in the novel, his business suffering under the pressures of the Depression, Wu-Fong realizes that "the trend was in the direction of home industry and home talent, and when the Hearst papers began their 'Buy American' campaign he decided to get rid of all the foreigners in his employ and turn his establishment into an hundred percentum American place" (126). Many families of "genuine native stock," in desperation, have "thrown their female children on the open market," and it is with these that Wu-Fong stocks his brothel, after hiring Asa Goldstein to design a series of American interiors (Pennsylvania Dutch, Old South, Log Cabin Pioneer, Victorian New York, Western Cattle Days, California Monterey, Indian, and Modern Girl) described by West with obvious relish.

West would later recycle this brothel of American culture, conceived of, designed, and managed by two "aliens," in his proposal for an "American Chauve-Souris." When it became apparent, after critical reviews, that *A Cool Million* would not be the money-maker that West had apparently hoped it would be, West hit upon a "surefire commercial idea" for a theatrical revue based on American folk materials.[77] His "American Chauve-Souris" was named after Nikita Balieff and the Moscow Art Theatre's "Theatre de la Chauve-Souris," which was a hit in Paris and Berlin and later imported to the United States in the 1920s. West imagined a series of musical sketches depicting "Nantucket during the great days of the whaling industry," "Natchez-Under-the-River at the time of the land pirates," "the Erie Canal at the time of its construction," "a gathering of mountaineers," and finally, "a Harlem rent party, using real scat music."[78] West even wrote to the Leland Hayward Agency that "the material should be as authentic as possible . . . in no case should it be permitted to deteriorate to the 'folksy' or 'arty' in a Cape Cod Tea Shop sense."[79]

"I could keep this sort of thing up forever," writes West in the middle of his list of projected scenes. He imagines, moreover, that "this material, arranged chronologically and combined with the history of an American family as the plot, would make an excellent moving picture."[80] The revue was meant to be a performance of a series of American set pieces united through one family's history; what it was, rather, was a representation of the national "family" fragmented by and through American mytho-history. That the ideal American family was consistently imagined, particularly in "Fitter Family" contests, as native, white, and continually endangered by undesirable elements such as blacks and Jews, lent West's satire a sharper edge.[81] The family of West's "Chauve-Souris" was, it seems, rather more typically and "authentically" American—if deeply unsettling to the racially "responsible" spectator—than the "fitter family" imagined by mass culture. West's multiracial, multiethnic "family," after all, could count as its members both Nantucket whalers and inhabitants of Harlem.

While *A Cool Million*'s failure immediately prompted the fitter family satire "Chauve-Souris," West continued to affiliate Indianness, Jewishness, and the marketplace. In the fall of 1933, West contributed a short story titled "Business Deal" to the Hollywood issue of *Americana*; it was a satirical sketch in which the head of Gargantual Pictures engages in a battle of wills with a screenwriter who has come into the office to discuss his contract.[82] During the tense exchange, the producer, Eugene Klingspiel, decides that "a good joke would clear the atmosphere. 'Vas you dere, Sharlie?' He regretted it immediately; Charlie's frigid stare made his remark almost indelicate."[83] West would repeat this offending line several years later in his novel *The Day of the Locust,* which West worked on for three years before it was published in 1939. That novel also, famously, features an Indian who recalls both "Chief" Jake Raven in his incarnation as walking advertisement and Israel Satinpenny as Jewish Indian. He is referred to as Chief Kiss-My-Towkus and repeats the accented line from West's earlier story: "Vas you dere, Sharley?"

West puts this gag line first in the mouth of a successful Hollywood producer and then in the mouth of a Hollywood Indian, an Indian performing a commodified, and commodifying, version of himself. Tod Hackett meets him outside a Sunset Boulevard saddlery store, wearing a sandwich board that reads:

TUTTLE'S TRADING POST
for
GENUINE RELICS OF THE OLD WEST
Beads, Silver, Jewelry, Moccasins,
Dolls, Toys, Rare Books, Postcards.
TAKE BACK A SOUVENIR
from
TUTTLE'S TRADING POST.[84]

Rita Barnard describes this Hollywood Indian as a "symbolic summation of West's critique of commodity culture."[85] Chief Kiss-My-Towkus represents the reduction of the American West to a collection of knickknacks and souvenirs for sale; these objects are signs, for Barnard, of "the loss not only of 'a fair sweet land' but of authentic experience."[86] What *A Cool Million* seems to suggest, however, is that West does not lament the loss of authentic experience as much as problematize its very possibility.[87] West's "authentics" seem always to refer to their own satirical possibility, or, as in his treatment of Osceola and the "Chauve-Souris," their potential profit.

Klingspiel, a Jewish Hollywood producer, and Chief Kiss-My-Towkus, a "Jewish" Hollywood Indian, then, are connected through the utterance of a punch line popularly associated with a Jewish comic: "Vas you dere, Sharley?"[88] In both cases the line underscores the commodification of ethnic identity and the transmutation of commodity culture into American myth (and vice versa) that West continually exposes in *A Cool Million*, dramatizing the way in which a preoccupation with native identities results in ethnic and national fricture and fracture. Waldo Frank and Mary Austin argued the irreconcilability of the Jew and the Indian; for these moderns, the unbridgeable divide between Indian and Jew was due to the spiritual, cultural, and aesthetic "authenticity" of the first and the manifest inauthenticity of the second. West could not conceive of an "authentic" that could exist within the machine of America's commodity culture. Both modernism's trust in authentic possibility as articulated by Williams and commodity culture's exploitation of it were to West deeply suspect.

Red Jews

Writers on the Left were themselves potential targets for West's satire, as Sylvanus Snodgrasse, the fake poet in *A Cool Million* who becomes a propagandist for the Communist Party, suggests. In the early 1930s, West was, according to Jay Martin, "interested in Communism because his friends were, because he was interested in them."[89] By the mid-1930s in Hollywood, where many writers employed by the studios were attracted to the Communist Party, West attended, by his own admission, one meeting, but he "found it all too easy to laugh at the second-rate minds the Party was attracting."[90] West was invited to join the dues-paying periphery of the party, but not its decision-making core. West's interests were "with people rather than programs, and what appeared to his associates to be a liberal leaning was really a feeling for human tragedy."[91] Leftists regarded him, Martin writes, "as a laughing anarchist," and felt there was a "kind of bohemianism about West for which the 'serious' Marxist should show contempt."[92] He was not invited to speak at the League of American Writers School. By the time of the Hitler-Stalin nonaggression pact, when, split by internecine turmoil, "one by one social-action Hollywood groups exploded or ground to a halt," Martin argues that West had already "recognized the tragedy of deception from the beginning." Quoting John Bright, he writes: "Whereas the Marxists emphasized the revolution, West emphasized its betrayal."[93] John Sanford, in his memoir, recalled of West, "During the several years of your friendship, he'd shown no interest in reforming the system he lived under; indeed, any reference to politics, particularly to socialism, had evoked almost always derision or disdain."[94]

In 1940, however, influenced by his wife, Eileen McKenney, and her sister Ruth McKenney, whose husband edited *The New Masses*, West had agreed to revisit the party, of which he had never become a member. He also planned a fifth novel, which, he wrote, "I intend to keep extremely simple and full of the milk of human kindness, and I am not joking, I really mean it."[95] Again, however, in his encounters with party functionaries, West ran up against rigid ideology and the party's position on the war. West had been attracted to the party because of his antifascism; in 1940, this was severely strained. West died young and tragically in a car accident in 1940. It is impossible to say how he might have repositioned himself in and around Left politics had he lived to see the invasion of the Soviet Union, Pearl Harbor, and the subsequent reenergizing of the American radical Left in the antifascist struggle, as well as the increasing governmental repressions of suspected Communists.

If in the 1930s, both the Left and the Right associated Native Americans and their art with authenticity and cultural purity, then in the 1940s, for Jewish writers on the Left, the fate of the Jews in Europe served increasingly as the lens through which to revisit Native history. From January 1937 through December 1937, the Yiddish writer Yitskhok (Isaac) Raboy, famous in American Yiddish circles for his fictions about eastern European immigrants on the American frontier, serialized a novel in the Yiddish Communist monthly *Der Hammer*. *Der Yidisher Cowboy,* meaning, alternatively, the Yiddish, or Jewish, Cowboy (the term "Yidish," in Yiddish, means both) was loosely based on Raboy's own experience as a hired ranch hand in North Dakota. The novel follows the adventures of an immigrant named, like his creator, Isaac who goes to work on a North Dakota horse ranch. The novel quickly evolves from a Yiddish picaresque western to a drama about labor injustice, disempowerment, and displacement. Isaac, the hero, is shocked by his employer's bad treatment of his wife and his ranch hands, by his racism and anti-Semitism, and by his dishonesty in business. *Der Yidisher Cowboy* becomes a socialist drama set on the prairie instead of a Lower East Side sweatshop. The novel features a multiethnic cast of characters: German and Norwegian settlers, Isaac the eastern European Jewish immigrant, and finally, suffering Native Americans. When Indians appear in the novel, they further serve to highlight the injustice of Hildenberg, the employer (a German employer, no less), and by extension European colonization and U.S. imperialist policies directed against its own native populations.

The complete novel was published in 1942, against a backdrop of war and news of Nazi atrocities. Raboy's protest against the reservation system seemed to acquire an additional field of reference:

> This was how they treated him, the man with the feather in his hair, here in the land of his birth, that land that truly was his America! . . . What was the reason for the incredible injustice of taking their land away and forcing them onto reservations? Compelling people who had lived for generations on the broad prairie to squeeze into tiny settlements, cut them off from their own kind and with no way of perpetuating their own values. Of course, these weren't the only injustices Isaac had ever had to contemplate. An immigrant Jew, he was familiar with all kinds of restrictions and injustices.[96]

Raboy was not the only artist to invoke the imagined links between America and Europe, reservations and ghettos, and Native and Jewish dispossession and displacement in the era of Nazi rule. John Sanford (born Julian Shapiro) and Howard Fast, both, we could say, self-described "red Jews," also published novels in the 1940s that foregrounded Native American and Jewish struggle.[97] Sanford, like West, was the child of Lithuanian Jewish immigrants, was a boyhood friend of Nathanael West's, was inspired by West to begin writing, and changed his name on West's suggestion. Although they had had a falling out before both moved to Hollywood, Sanford dedicated his 1943 novel *The People from Heaven* to West.[98]

Fast, ten years younger than West and Sanford, was, like them, interested in revisiting and revising historical narratives that had long since hardened into myth. His novels of the 1940s were works of American history and Jewish history that celebrated personal and national liberation.[99] Of *The Last Frontier* (1941), anticipating Leslie Fiedler's arguments about "New Westerns," Oliver La Farge wrote in his review:

> This novel is something new in Americana. At first sight one recognizes that it comes out of the healthy, increasing trend to rewrite the history of our frontier with a new honesty which has tended, first, to be reasonably truthful at last about the Indians on whose dead bodies American was founded, and more recently to perceive that the Indians, too, are a part of American society, and that our treatment of them was and is a part of our democracy's success or failure. . . . Mr. Fast puts his finger on the fact that where the servants of democracy violate its essential principles in a small matter, the way be opened to greater violations.[100]

Described by Fast as an "absolutely true" story, *The Last Frontier* narrates the desperate flight by a group of about three hundred Northern Cheyenne men, women, and children from the desolate Oklahoma reservation upon which they have been forced to live to their ancestral homeland in Montana.[101] As the army pursues them and is increasingly baffled by its inability to halt the Indians' progress, the government responds by adding troops to the pursuit. Half of the band, closed in by troops, is defeated, imprisoned, starved, and finally massacred when they attempt a final, desperate escape to freedom. Demoralized and embarrassed, the government decides to permit the group that reaches Montana to stay there.

La Farge thinks that the argument of the novel is weakened by "subtle references to Nazism" that are "anachronistic and forced." However, the novel is meant to be a parable, as is Sanford's *The People from Heaven*. Like West's *A Cool Million*, these novels, about racism in the United States, are meant to evoke the rise of fascism and racially motivated oppression and mass murder in Europe, which reflect back in turn upon the ominous possibilities contained in American racial injustices. Carl Van Doren, in his foreword to *The Last Frontier*, makes the historical analogy explicit:

> In 1942 the experience of millions of men held in wretched subjection by invaders has taught the world at large what this small remote tribe understood. Here is a story that is tremendous in its application to our day: a story to hearten all grieving exiles, all languishing victims of alien tyrants, all imaginative, sympathetic men and women who have had to revalue freedom in the dread prospect of losing it. Against incomparable odds an incalculable heroism once rose up, and led to an unpredictable triumph. . . . And not till today could the story have had the powerful impact it has in the light of daily happenings in occupied countries. The facts lie buried, waiting to be called out of the past when there should be a present waiting for them.[102]

Van Doren does not once single out the Jews of Europe; nor does he mention Fast's own Jewishness. But Fast himself does indeed make the connection between the Jews and the Cheyenne of his novel, oppressed and yet fiercely devoted to liberty and to the reclamation of their territorial patrimony. Fast does this across texts: the same year that he published *The Last Frontier,* he also published a history book aimed at young readers, called, after Meyer Weisgal's pageant at the Chicago 1933–34 World's Fair, *The Romance of a People*.[103] Like the earlier pageant, Fast's *The Romance of a People* tells "a story of a people who have existed for more than four thousand years, not as a nation—such as the English or the French, but as a people, bound together by a common belief in a good and just and merciful God."[104] By the end of the book, Fast has implicated both himself and his reader as members of this people: "You are part of the story." His conclusion links Zionist struggle in Palestine with antifascist struggle in Europe:

> It would be a good thing if this story could end here, leaving a picture of strong, young pioneers returning to build their homeland anew.
>
> Yet this is a story that has no end. It will go on and on, through your life and your children's lives, and you are part of the story.
>
> The suffering of the Jews was not over. Not even in Palestine. For Palestine, while promised to the Jews very graciously, was not given graciously.

The British, hoping to appease the Arabs, who had let the land sink into desolation and ruin, made the Jews fight for every new immigrant. When the Arabs turned to attack the Jews, the British would neither defend them nor allow them to defend themselves.

For this, the British are paying dearly, even now as this is written, and the Jews may have to pay even more dearly.

For only a few years ago, a new monster rose up. An evil force, marked by a hooked cross, had adopted all the old horrors of anti-Semitism. The Nazi party in Germany, led by its debased leader, Hitler, rose to re-inflict all the old persecutions upon the Jews. . . .

Yet the half a million young Jews in Palestine will not give up easily. With their bare hands they built their homes and wrested the soil from the desert, and they will die fighting before they give it up.[105]

Throughout his two books, Fast uses similar language to describe the Cheyenne and the Jews, particularly around the notions of homeland, exile, freedom, and resistance. When the doomed band of Cheyennes is held prisoner at Fort Robinson, they are told, through an interpreter, that they must go back to Oklahoma. The interpreter conveys their response: "If they can never reach [their land], they'll die here. They say they were dead a long time ago; they say a man is dead when his home is taken away from him, when he becomes a slave in jail. They say it's good of you to make council with them, but if the president want them to die, they'll die right here."[106] Throughout the novel, characters marvel at the Cheyennes' love of liberty so profound that they would die before relinquishing it.

Like the Cheyennes, Fast's Jews, both in the present and in the past, are determined to die before giving up their homeland. Fast describes dry, desert Palestine, which he had never seen, as a land of "tumbled mountains, green meadows, and tall forests," terms that resemble the language he used to describe the Cheyennes' northern homeland in the Black Hills of Wyoming.[107] Describing the Jewish uprising against the Roman Empire in 66 C.E., Fast writes:

The Jews were fighting mad. Perhaps never before in all our history had so many Jews been ready to die fighting for what they believed. They understood what they were doing—that they were pitting themselves against the greatest military power on the face of the earth, that there was almost no hope for success. . . .

The memory is sad, but it is not a memory to be ashamed of. We were fighting for freedom them, teaching the world how to die for freedom.[108]

The hopeless yet courageous Jewish uprising against the implacable Roman Empire is described in precisely the same terms as the Cheyenne resistance against the U.S. government: "They never forgot that they were Jews. They never forgot that they were exiles. They lived only for the day when they might return to Palestine."[109]

In the absence of a Cheyenne language, which Fast soon realized he could never fully access, Fast clearly drew upon the language of Jewish exile, diaspora, and longing for Zion to describe the Cheyennes in *The Last Frontier*.[110] Fast's novel thus invokes the shadow of fascism and the struggle against it but also suggests parallels between Native and Jewish exile, nationhood, and longing for liberation and homeland.

Moreover, Fast uses much of the same language, many years later, to describe his feelings about communism in the 1940s and 1950s: "This was the party of Bill Foster and Big Bill Haywood and Elizabeth Gurley Flynn, the party that organized the French Resistance and fought the Nazis to the death and taught the world a new lesson in courage and honor, the party that had created the Abraham Lincoln Brigade and never stinted at the price placed on freedom."[111] For Fast, that is to say, Indians and Jews are like one another insofar as they are both, really, Communists and Zionists.

For Sanford too, to be Red is to be Indian, Jewish, and Left. This is suggested in his fiction first in his novel *The People from Heaven*, which takes place in Warrensberg, the small upstate New York village in the Adirondacks where he and West had rented a cottage in the summer of 1931.[112] Additionally, when he writes of the period of the writing and publication of *The People from Heaven* in his autobiographical novels, Indianness, Jewishness, and radicalism become more firmly entwined with one another in relation to the novel. As Alan Wald writes, this is a novel by "an unrepentant Jewish-American Marxist about anti-Black and anti-Native American racist culture."[113]

The Warrensburg narrative takes place over about a week. A local grocer and thug, Ed Bishop, runs the town; a small handful of dissenters include the preacher, Dan Hunter; the doctor, Dan Slocum; the local prostitute; and the man who is in love with her. There is also a local Jew—Abe Novinsky, an immigrant from Russia and survivor of a czarist pogrom—and an Abenaki Indian named Bigelow Vroom and his son, Aben. All exist in a kind of tense, precarious peace until an itinerant black woman comes to town and is taken in by the preacher and protected by his friends. The townspeople name her, significantly, America Smith. Racism and violence bubble to the surface: Ed Bishop terrorizes her, the other racial "others" who have up until then been ostracized by the community, as well as the progressive cohort who ineffectually protect them. Ultimately,

Bishop rapes America Smith, and, in the final, climactic chapter, as he turns his murderous terror upon the Jew and the Indian, America shoots him among the ruins of the burned down church.

The scenes of present-day Warrensburg alternate with poetic passages that describe the roots of present-day racism in the colonial violence of America's past.[114] As Wald writes, these lyrical passages, which were compared by some to Williams's *In the American Grain,* are in fact impressed with a sophisticated and Marxist-influenced historical revisionism, as these "known episodes" of history are reinterpreted and "refracted through the individual sensibility of the author."[115]

The novel is thus both formally difficult as well as overtly revolutionary. Sanford had joined the Communist Party in 1939, at about the same time that he began *The People from Heaven,* amid news of *Kristallnacht* and boatloads of Jewish refugees being turned away from safe harbors and forced to return to Germany, events that he explicitly connects with both the novel and with his decision to join the Communist Party.[116] Sanford links violent anti-Semitism, through Novinsky's recounting of the pogrom in which his sister was killed, with colonial conquest, slavery, and fascism. The novel also suggests, decades before this became a position embraced by radical nationalist groups, that oppressed peoples have the right to arm and defend themselves. America Smith and Bigelow and Aben Broom take violent revenge upon their tormentors.

Aben Broom's act of violent resistance foreshadows that of America's in the last scene of the novel. Aben is called upon in school to explain the causes of the Civil War, and as he recounts the arguments over states' rights and the expansion of slavery into newly conquered territories, his classmate Marvin Piper whispers various racial insults, including, "Aben, the dog-eater," and "Aben is a red-skin son-of-a-bitch."[117] Aben threatens to "do the same thing to him that Crazy Horse done to Custer," and indeed, the argument climaxes with Aben leaping onto Marvin, and, "as history repeats himself," scalping him. His father, telling him, "us Indians have gotten whaled enough, son," takes up a gun to defend his son. Later, he gives that gun to America Smith. Thus, African American and Native American oppression and resistance are linked and allied. In the novel's climax, which is played out in front of the whole community during Sunday services in the burned out remains of the church, Bigelow Vroom challenges Eli Bishop's threats to America Smith, and he is knocked unconscious:

> Bishop wheeled on the crowd and stood poised, but only a killdeer, on the wing, broke the silence with its two-word fiat. "An hour after he can walk," he said, nodding back at Vroom, "we're going to have a parade in this town,

and he's going to head it." He stooped to pick up a pine-cone. "It'll start at the Post Office, and it'll keep on moving till it's out of sight. There'll be four people marching in that parade: this Indian here, the Indian's boy-bastard Aben, the nigger-woman, and one more." He cracked a few scales from the cone and let them fall. "The Jew." He looked now at Novinsky. "The Jew son-of-a-bitch: he goes too. This use to be a white man's town, Warrensburg, and it won't be long before it's white again." A butterfly beat past, its speckled wings applauding.[118]

It is at this moment that America calmly shoots Eli Bishop and is then tacitly pardoned by the sheriff and entire town.

In his memoir, Sanford describes the reactions to the manuscript first by the party, to whom he had "been directed to submit the current version of *The People from Heaven* for the approval of a literary committee," and then by potential publishers and reviewers. During his meeting with party readers, Sanford was told that the book problematically advocated violence and that it was "obscure": "'This is *Daily Worker* bullshit!' you said. 'The party line from party parrots! It doesn't come off, says you—I write the wrong thing and even the wrong thing is written wrong. What gall, from slobs who can't write at all!'"[119]

Potential publishers rejected the manuscript, saying it was "too difficult to read, to understand, and to sell."[120] Wrote another, "I am afraid the material is just too strong to find a market."[121] And another, "But I can't for the life of me see how we could reach any considerable audience with it. You've combined so many experimental techniques that I am afraid even a better than average reader would come up with a feeling of frustration."[122] When the book was finally published in 1943, reviewers were puzzled and divided.[123] Sanford recounts his despondency in this moment, not over the reviews of the book, but because he has volunteered for the army several times and has been turned down: "I feel left out," you said. "I feel as though I'd been passed over by my own generation. Being a Jew, I thought I knew what rejection was, but this is worse. My country has no use for me."[124]

Sanford again invokes his identity as Jewish outsider in two encounters with his friend Lynn Riggs, which bracket this volume of the autobiography and are thus intimately linked with the writing of *The People from Heaven*. Riggs, who was Cherokee, is perhaps best known today for having authored the play *Green Grow the Lilacs,* which later became the musical *Oklahoma!* (1943). As the volume opens, Sanford has just arrived in Hollywood and is teamed with the playwright Riggs by the studio. Riggs is soon let go, though they remain friends. He presents a gift to Sanford:

From the seat beside him, he produced a book bound in red and black: it contained two of his plays, *Russet Mantle* and *Cherokee Night*. Opening it, you found an inscription on the flyleaf:

> John—
> "Some day the agony will end"
> for you Cherokees.
>   —Lynn
>   Hollywood Sept. 4 1936

> *Some day the agony will end,* you thought. You'd learn one day that the line was from the final scene of the second play, the one he'd written about his people.
> You looked up at him, saying, "it never does end, though, does it?"
> And he said, "Who should know that better than us Jews?"[125]

Nine years later, Sanford again meets Riggs, this time when Riggs comes to his house and indicates that he would also like to join the party:

> It was nine years since he'd given you his book of plays, but you knew the inscription by heart: *Some day the agony will end for you Cherokees.* On a shelf almost within reach, you could see a black spine and its gold stamping.
> You waved at the book, saying, "When I read what you'd scrawled in that, I said the agony never ended, and you said, 'Who should know that better than us Jews?' I've never forgotten that."
> "Then maybe you're beginning to understand why I'm here."
> "Peculiar about us: a Jew likes the Indians; an Indian likes the Jews."
> "Not so peculiar. Think of our histories."[126]

The writers described here varied in the degree to which they were involved with or determined the cultural program of the Communist Party, but all considered themselves to be writing from the Left. If West satirized the ease with which ideologues from both the Left and the Right were invested in rigid typologies and performances of Jewishness and Indianness, Fast and Sanford demonstrate the ways in which Jewishness, Indianness, and the radical Left were to be thought of as identical and interchangeable. But their disagreements with the party specifically over the questions of nationalism and armed resistance is significant, for it is precisely with these terms that New Lefts would emerge out of the civil rights struggles and define themselves against their antecedents.

《4》

Henry Roth, Native Son

"Bing! I'm an Innian": Henry Roth, Eda Lou Walton, and Native Modernism

America you don't really want to go to war.
America it's them bad Russians.
Them Russians them Russians and them Chinamen. And them
Russians.
The Russia wants to eat us alive. The Russia's power mad. She
wants to take our cars from out our garages.
Her wants to grab Chicago. Her needs a Red Readers Digest.
Her wants our auto plants in Siberia. Him big bureaucracy
running our filling stations.
That no good. Ugh. Him make Indians learn read. Him need
    Big black niggers. Hah. Her make us all work sixteen hours a day. Help.
America this is quite serious.

                    —Allen Ginsberg, "America"

Allen Ginsberg's poem "America" satirizes cold war paranoia through the Pidgin English of the stereotypical Indian. The voice of Ginsberg's Indian fantasizing a Russian takeover of Chicago and filling stations, however, emerges out of a cacophony of Yiddish cadences ("Scott Nearing was a grand old man / a real mensch Mother Bloor made me cry I once saw / Israel Amter plain"), unapologetic radicalism ("America I feel sentimental about the Wobblies. / America I used to be a communist when I was a kid I'm not sorry"), prophetic warning ("America how can I write a holy litany in your silly mood?"), and assertions of sexual difference ("America I'm putting my queer shoulder to the wheel").[1] Ginsberg inaugurated the ethos of the New Left with his *Howl and Other Poems* (1956); his poem "America" introduces a seething mix of ethnic, political, and sexual difference in an "Indian" voice, out of which emerges a deeply comical and scathing national critique.

Henry Roth's *Call It Sleep,* whose afterlife and subsequent rebirthing of its author is the subject of this chapter, thus unfolded in a New Left aesthetic and political culture that newly valorized tribalism and difference. Here, I reread Roth's modernist aesthetic developed in *Call It Sleep* as itself emerging from the Indianness espoused by his mentor and lover Eda Lou Walton. *Call It Sleep* was, in turn, "rediscovered" in a moment characterized by its countercultural fascination with all things Indian. And finally, I suggest that the passionate Zionism of Roth's second career emerged from and was mediated through his continuing engagement with tropes of Indianness and nativeness.

The year 1934 saw the publication of both Nathanael West's *A Cool Million* and Henry Roth's *Call It Sleep.* The story of the writing, reception, disappearance, and rediscovery in the 1960s of *Call It Sleep* is at this point rather familiar to students of twentieth-century American literature.[2] Roth has become famous not only for his novel but for the thirty-year-long silence that followed it, during which Roth began and abandoned several projects; burned many of his manuscripts in apparent fear of being investigated for Communist sympathies; worked, among other jobs, as an attendant in a mental hospital and as a Maine waterfowl farmer; and finally, with the proceeds of the novel's 1964 paperback reprinting, moved to New Mexico and began to work on a massive, multivolume autobiographical novel (four volumes of which were published between 1994 and 1998) until his death in 1995.

Conjecture about the cause of Roth's famous writer's block have fueled much commentary upon the novel. The novel's final phrases—"One might as well call it sleep. He shut his eyes"—were read by many of the novel's later critics as presaging Roth's inability to write a second novel. His silence was, in alternative readings, that of the second-generation Jewish immigrant who has exhausted his material; that of the proletarian writer paralyzed by the narrow scope of ideological writing; or, as suggested by his latest volumes of memoir, thinly disguised as fiction, the result of an intense self-loathing produced by a childhood of abuse and incestuous activity.[3]

It is not Roth's silence with which I am concerned as much as the conditions that accompanied his reemergence into American literary culture in the 1960s. In 1956, the *American Scholar* asked a number of critics and scholars to name the most "undeservedly neglected book of the previous twenty-five years." Both Alfred Kazin and Leslie Fiedler mentioned *Call It Sleep.* In 1960, Pageant Books reissued a hardbound edition of *Call It Sleep,* and in 1964, the paperback edition of the novel became the first paperback to merit a front-page review by Irving Howe in the *New York Times Book Review.* In 1960, shortly before the reissue of the novel, a long essay by Leslie Fiedler, the first substantial critical appraisal of the novel to appear in print, appeared in *Commentary.* "Henry Roth's Neglected Masterpiece" was accompanied by a short piece by Roth himself, the second in a year to appear in *Commentary.* The first, "At Times in Flight—a Parable," concerned Roth's courting of his wife, composer Muriel Parker, whom he had met at Yaddo in 1938 and for whom he left Eda Lou Walton, the muse of *Call It Sleep.* The second piece, coming as it did after Fiedler's essay, effectively confirmed Roth's reemergence as a writer. Titled "The Dun Dakotas," the brief and cryptic piece was part personal reflection and part parable, the latter of which had been meant to comprise the prologue for an aborted second novel. The subject of "The Dun Dakotas," according to Roth, was the "loss of a sense of history."[4] It begins with Roth's description of his blocked years:

> There was something ruinous about the time, or fatal to creative gusto, or so I feel. I have my inklings about its nature, my brief illumination, but just what it was I leave to others more competent at defining abstractions or rendering something definitive out of the multitude of eddies and appearances. . . . I have spent a great deal of time wondering about it; I don't spend so much now.[5]

Roth then launches into a "a yarn," concerning a surveying expedition into the Dakotas that was to serve as the material for a prologue for a second novel.[6] "You can imagine," Roth writes, "the gnarled terrain, or consult an encyclopedia, or consult Mr. Eliot—the wrenched and contorted land, the lopped pillars, and the grinning gullies" (108). Suddenly, the captain, scout, and their party find themselves surrounded by Indians. The scout placates the chief and proposes a game of poker. After the chief has won all of their money, the scout asks if the party will be permitted to pass:

> The chief folded his arms across his chest and dreamed a long dream or a long thought—whether of bison, or the bright tepees of childhood, or the game birds of youth I do not know.

But that was as far as I got for over twenty-five years, waiting for the decision of the chief who had turned into stone or into legend, waiting for a man to decide what history was in the dun Dakotas, waiting for a sanction; and oddly enough it would have to be the victim who would provide it, though none could say who was the victim, who the victor. And only now can I tell you, and perhaps it's a good sign, at least for my generation, who waited with me—though perhaps it's too late.

"Will the chief let us pass?" the scout repeated. "Always remember Great Chief."

And the chief unfolded his arms and motioned them the way of their journey. "Go now," he said. (109)

The belated passage granted by the Indian chief signifies the release of Roth the writer from his long silence, decades spent, so to speak, wandering in the American wilderness, or, given his mention of "Mr. Eliot," a modernist wasteland. Roth imagines a writer frozen by history at the beginning of the piece, a blockage that is both signified and broken by the Indian chief. Roth, in a 1986 conversation, makes this symbolic function of the Indian chief explicit:

There, as I originally intended, was to be a realistic encounter between a band of Indians and the surveyors for a railroad. It was to be a realistic job, done as realistically as I would know how. . . . But since it became a block, for me, in the course of time it moved out of the realistic realm and became a symbolic block that I had to go through, somehow or other—I had to get by, I had to get past. Because this whole thing seemed, in retrospect, to be what had blocked me way back in 1936, you might say. So it became a symbol—and the symbol, these two characters facing each other, in which I suddenly became the petrified figure, the immobilized figure, waiting for an answer.[7]

Although Roth in the next breath claims not to know "who this chief is, or what he represents," this discussion seeks to articulate and expose the presence throughout Roth's writing of the Indian, who, I argue, acts as a link between the modernist, bohemian, politically radical, self-consciously American milieu of Eda Lou Walton, who mentored the young Roth and was his lover, and the messianic underpinnings of Roth's later preoccupation with Spain, Marrano Jews, and Zionism.[8]

Born in 1894 in Deming, New Mexico, Walton earned her PhD in English and anthropology at Berkeley and wrote a groundbreaking dissertation titled

"Navajo Traditional Poetry: Its Content and Form."[9] She published two books of poetry: *Dawn Boy: Blackfoot and Navajo Songs* (1926), heavily based on her translations and interpretations of Indian poetry, and *Jane Matthew and Other Poems* (1931; dedicated to "H.R."). Her poetry anthology *The City Day: An Anthology of Recent American Poetry* (1929) acknowledged and thanked Henry Roth "for assistance in proofreading and other clerical help."[10] Walton cultivated relationships with many prominent poets, anthropologists, academics, and intellectuals of the 1920s and 1930s.[11] "Eda Lou," Roth explained, "mothered, initiated, and otherwise befriended young writers, poets, and artists. You might say that she would take on these people who needed strong maternal affection, because she herself had a strong maternal urge. Now that's all very well up to a certain stage, but to continue beyond that stage becomes very bad. And I think I continued too long."[12]

Werner Sollors has pointed out that Roth consistently describes Walton as maternal or mothering; he stresses their age difference of twelve years; and he continually casts himself as a child, passive and naive.[13] Roth commented during an interview that he had "exchanged a Jewish mama for a native American mama."[14] Walton initiated Roth the writer, introducing him not only to the members of her circle but to modernist literature, represented by T. S. Eliot and James Joyce and also by her own poetry and by the poets she selected for *The City Day.*[15] Walton's modernism had a decidedly Americanist tinge, her affiliation in Roth's narrative with Eliot and Joyce notwithstanding. Her attitude toward Indian songs, and in particular translations of them, seems to have been heavily influenced by Mary Austin. Her preface to *Dawn Boy* begins:

> I have presented here the re-created songs of two Indian tribes: the Blackfoot and the Navajo. By "re-created" songs I mean not literal, not even free, translations of Indian texts, but rather interpretations of Indian poetic material. . . . And yet, despite these various alterations, I have, I am sure, been closely true to the essence, the heart and spirit of the Indian poetic conception. I have presented these poems simply and directly, without artificiality of diction, letting the beauty of the idea or symbol stand clean-cut. This method of presentation harmonizes best with Indian texts.[16]

In her introductory arguments to *The City Day,* which arranged poems "as to picture the full cycle of a city day," Walton, like Austin in *The American Rhythm,* ties the question of literary experimentation to that of place. The anthology was conceived as a collection of recent American poetry for American students, who as a group, according to Walton, had become heavily urbanized.[17]

Given Walton's interest in Indian poetry, her Southwest origins, and her position as guardian of American culture and literature, to which she could grant or block access, it is not much of an imaginative stretch to associate her with the Indian chief of "The Dun Dakotas."[18] Indeed, "Edith Welles" (Walton) and the Greenwich Village context within which Roth encountered her, which he reproduces so strikingly in the volume *From Bondage* of *Mercy of a Rude Stream,* is continually associated throughout *Mercy* with her earlier work among the Navajos. Her dissertation and published translations of Navajo poetry are mentioned with some frequency, as are the presence in her apartment of "Navajo rugs."[19] She entertains Ira and Larry (figures that stand in for Roth and his friend Lester Winters) with Indian legends, stories of her encounters with the Navajos, and discussions of her anthropological, literary, and political interest in Indians.

During one of these conversations, in which Edith tells the story of Zaru, the "last wild Indian of California," the young, shy Ira reveals an ability for word play, in which the word "Indian" becomes the terrain upon which Ira's incipient modernist literary abilities emerge:[20]

> "I was thinking," Larry said diffidently. "They call them Indians, and they're not Indians."
>
> "No, of course not." Edith regarded him indulgently. "Anthropologists have tried many other names. 'Aborigine' is one. But there's been an objection to that. On the part of the Indians themselves in some cases, yes. It makes them feel as if they were considered some sort of wild creature. And of course they're anything but that. They have—or had—a highly developed culture. 'Native' is a good term, probably the best, certainly the most legitimate. But our one hundred percent Americans, fourth- or fifth-generation super-patriots, object. They consider themselves the only native Americans. Which is absurd. 'Amerind' is one term that's been tried."
>
> "Tamarind," Larry chuckled. "Tamarind is a tree, isn't it?"
>
> "Yes, I think so. I don't know what kind."
>
> "A wooden Indian," Larry quipped.
>
> "And about as awkward as 'Amerind,'" said Edith. "I don't believe the name will last. Do you have a name to suggest, Ira?"
>
> "No," he said, with lingering bashfulness. "But I was thinking of 'Indigen.'"
>
> "'Indigenous' or 'indigent'?" Larry bantered.
>
> "It could be both."
>
> "As in fact most Indians are," Edith commented.[21]

Edith's observation of the double associations of the word "native": that is, the way it which it can be used to describe, alternately, both white, privileged, "one hundred percent" Americans and the indigenous people of the Americas, is played upon later by Roth, who has his alter ego and narrator Ira Stigman reflect of Edith: "She was your equal, and better than your equal: native stock, the Ascendancy, John Synge called it."[22]

The Indian comes to signify, in Edith's and Ira's comments, both nativeness and modernism, or rather more precisely, talking *about* Indians becomes an opportunity to reference immigrants (that is, the implicit antipathy toward them on the part of "one hundred percenters") and exercise an inventive, modernist attitude toward language. "Your feeling for words," Edith tells Ira in this episode, "is remarkable."[23] Walton's own "feeling for words," her predilection as a poet for "parallelistic repetitions," was considered by at least one critic and friend, David Greenhood, an inevitable by-product of her Navajo studies: "I do not mean she made any conscious applications of the Indian's poetics. She did not have to. The parallel recurrences, for example, which she analyzed as a scholar, tallied with what she must have sensed throughout her girlhood as a listener with a superb ear, even though she knew not many of the Indian words."[24]

Greenhood connects Walton's interest in Indians to her later endeavors as the editor of *The City Day*:

> It is only when we go from one country to another that change becomes more notable than accordance, the new landscape's own "language" is a different one, and the "ritual" of the old seems abandoned. But in a true poet, the old scene sings in a strange land. This is what happened with Eda Lou Walton when she went East. And when, before that, she made an anthropological study of Indian prosody, hoping to know it as she did the English, it was not for erudition but for kinship. The contact points of affinition were what she was always seeking everywhere in everybody.[25]

Greenhood echoes Roth's description of Walton, whose relationships with other poets and writers were adoptions of sorts, as maternal. Walton searches for "kinship," "everywhere in everybody," with Indians on the one hand, and with Roth, it seems, on the other. Roth has claimed that what he learned from reading Joyce's *Ulysses* was that the materials for a great, literarily innovative novel were close at hand, that Roth's own native scene, as Joyce's own, could provide him with the materials for a modernist tour de force: "What I gained was this awed realization that you didn't have to go anywhere at all except around the corner to flesh out a literary work of art—given some kind of vision, of course."[26] But he could have learned this from Walton, who in her own poetry and in her comments on contemporary American poetry consistently emphasized the aesthetic possibilities of the poet's native scene.

In *Call It Sleep*, Roth borrowed and quoted from the poets featured in Walton's anthology *The City Day* as well as from Walton's own prose and poetry.[27] Echoes of Walton's work in *Call It Sleep* range from fragments of phrases, repeated and enlarged, to structural and thematic concerns. In Walton's introductory essay to *The City Day*, she uses the phrase "The men walked like scissors" as an example of what she terms "associative imagery" in modern poetry.[28] Could it be that Roth references this when he names his protagonist David Schearl ("scissors" in Yiddish)? Walton discusses Yvor Winters's poem "The Street," in which appear lines that startlingly prefigure *Call It Sleep*:

> I met God in the street car, but I could not
> pray to him, and we were both embarrassed; and to get away I chose
> the first finality—black streets like
> unlit windows, coffee hour by hour,
> And chilling sleep.[29]

David Schearl searches for God in the streetcar tracks; he, like the poet of "The Street," seeks refuge in sleep at the end of the novel. Walton goes on to describe the first stanza of Hart Crane's "To Brooklyn Bridge," which in her reading "presents the image of the sea gull in flight (true freedom) as against the image of the Statue of Liberty (false freedom)":

> How many dawns, chill from his rippling rest
> The seagull's wings shall dip and pivot him
> Shedding white rings of tumult, building high
> Over the chained bay waters Liberty—[30]

Roth's description of the Statue of Liberty in the prologue to *Call It Sleep* likewise works deliberately against the statue's conventional associations:

> The spinning disk of the late afternoon sun slanted behind her, and to those on board who gazed, her features were charred with shadow, her depths exhausted, her masses ironed to one single plane. Against the luminous sky the rays of her halo were spikes of darkness roweling the air; shadow flattened

the torch she bore to a black cross against flawless light—the blackened hilt of a broken sword. Liberty.[31]

In Crane's poem, Walton writes, the "bridge becomes an eternal symbol, a religious symbol," its language that of "religious exaltation."[32] Its "guerdon" is as "obscure as that heaven of the Jews"; it represents the "terrific threshold of the prophet's pledge / Prayer of pariah, and the lover's cry." It is possible to discern here the faint outlines of some of *Call It Sleep*'s associative images: David's "vision" in the streetcar tracks, which replaces Crane's bridge as religious symbol, and the dimly understood passages of Isaiah. Roth could be quoting Crane's "terrific threshold of the prophet's pledge" when he twice describes the electrification of the rails, which David, informed by Isaiah, reads as prophetic and mystical, as "terrific" in its power.[33]

Not merely E. E. Cummings's poem, but also Walton's comments about the poem may have dictated the form of Roth's final sequence, which is frequently called Joycean.[34] In the section titled "Rhythms of Modern Poetry" in her introductory essay to *The City Day*, Walton writes: "If, as Robert Graves thinks, the time has come when poetry is for the eye rather than for the ear, Cummings in his so-called eccentricities of typography is in decided advance of other poets using eye-rhythms."[35] The final sections of *Call It Sleep*, as Sollors has pointed out, recall the syntax and word divisions of "Chansons Innocentes I":

> in Just-
> spring   when the world is mud—
> luscious the little
> lame balloonman
> whistles   far   and wee.[36]

Compare *Call It Sleep:*

> ed his right foot—
> Crritlkt!
> —What?
> He stared at the river, sprang away from the rail and dove into the shadows. (417)

The funeral procession witnessed by David in the section titled "The Cellar" in *Call It Sleep*, a moment which is revisited several times throughout the novel, might have been inspired by the Wallace Stevens poem "Cortege for Rosenbloom," which Walton discusses following her comment on Cummings, a poem in which, Walton writes, "a small man is mockingly made godlike for the purpose of satire."[37] The possibility that the Jew is the object of this satire might have prompted Roth to rewrite this moment as one of rather serious psychological trauma for his boy-protagonist.

It is not only the poems featured in *The City Day* that may have provided Roth with material—images, vocabulary, syntax, technique—for his novel but also Walton's discussions of them: her judgments, her interpretations, her pronouncements of which poets were in "decided advance" over others. If *The City Day* provided Roth with a sense of what was "modern" in American poetry, Walton's own poetry could provide him with a sense of the "native." Walton's use of Native materials is explicit in her first volume of poetry, *Dawn Boy,* but no less significant in her second volume, *Jane Matthew and Other Poems,* which she dedicated to Roth.

For Greenhood, Walton's use of her "native scene" inheres in her use of landscape. Roth may very well have taken note of Walton's landscape descriptions in *Jane Matthew and Other Poems,* adapting them for his urbanscape (having David call telegraph poles "Mr. High Wood" [93], for example). But the poems' use of incest and Indian themes also furnished Roth with a sense of the native.[38] "Jane Matthew" describes a love triangle between Jane, a poet, Dale, an artist, and a surrogate daughter, Kate, in persistently incestuous terms: the girl has an affair with her adopted "father" and Dale and Jane's own relationship is likened to that of mother and son.[39]

In "The Blue Room," set among the Organ Mountains in Las Cruces, New Mexico, the relationship between a girl and her father slides into the taboo: "She wished her father's love, she tearfully / Desired his coming. Every night the latch / Was locked against desire, her timid way, / But barriers were breaking: she would catch /His hand against her breast!" (98).[40] Margaret flees her father's house and moves to the desert, where she lives out the rest of her days in despair and self-loathing. The poem's climax comes when Margaret comes upon an Indian ceremony on Tortugas Mount, which involves the beating of "uninitiate boys" by priests, while girls dance naked before them. Suddenly, Margaret appears in the midst of the dancers, urging the priests to "take this sacrifice." The presence in the ceremony of an "Indian Cross" and Margaret's desire for self-sacrifice together recall the climactic final chapters of *Call It Sleep,* when David offers his father, who is enraged by the rosary David has in his possession, his whip with which to beat him.

There seems, in Walton's poetry, to exist a confusion, or at a least a connection, between literary expression, the incestuous, and the Native, which is reflected in the way she is memorialized by Greenhood and Roth. According to Greenhood, Walton searched for kinship everywhere and in everyone, but most particularly in the Indian. Roth describes all her dealings with initiate poets, himself included, as maternal as well as sexual. If the character of Genya, considered retroactively through Roth's comment that she is a mix of Walton and his own mother, can be read as an expression of Roth's desire for a bilateral line of descent, both Native and Jewish, then Walton's poetry too reveals her own, similar wish.

Maxwell Geismar, in his critical introduction to the 1960 edition of *Call It Sleep*, called the relationship between David Schearl and his mother at the center of the novel "a classic example of the oedipal relation—described so beautifully, so completely, that one realizes that the author, too, wrote this classic fable in all innocence of spirit."[41] That oedipal relationship, however, as readers of *Mercy of a Rude Stream* have discovered, may have been a way of displacing another incestuous relationship, or at least the desire for one. Nativist modernism, Walter Benn Michaels argues, continually reimagines national relations in terms of blood relations: national identity thus becomes a matter of racial identity. Marc Shell, in *The End of Kinship*, argues that "in the United States, where fraternity is 'the first objective, ethically . . . of the democratic way of life,' the link between a radically egalitarian democracy and incest potentially plays a remarkable ideological role."[42] That is, if democracy promises "universal siblinghood," in which all countrymen are brothers, then "siblings and spouses are one and the same."[43] The incestuous liaisons in Walton's poems, as read and transformed by Roth, are not merely efforts to explore the transgressive or the taboo but ways of reimagining and resituating kinship and, thus, native American identity.

Messiahs, Mystics, and Marranos

The publication in the 1930s and the rediscovery in the 1960s of *Call It Sleep* paralleled that of another, not so very different text. *Black Elk Speaks* was originally published in 1932 and, like *Call It Sleep*, drew some critical praise and then, despite a tiny but devoted readership, sunk from view until the 1960s.[44] *Black Elk Speaks* is a Native American autobiography as told to, and mediated through, the anthropologist John G. Neihardt. Much of it focuses on Black

Elk's childhood, during which, like David Schearl in *Call It Sleep,* the young boy experiences a series of mystical visions.

The book of Isaiah comprises one of the central subtexts, or pre-texts, for *Call It Sleep;* coincidentally, Black Elk's first vision, experienced, like David Schearl's, when he is a child in some ways also recalls Isaiah's:

> The two men with the spears now stood beside me, one on either hand, and the horses took their places in their quarters, looking inward, four by four. And the oldest of the Grandfathers spoke with a kind voice and said: "Come right in and do not fear." And as he spoke, all the horses of the four quarters neighed to cheer me. So I went in and stood before the six, and they looked older than men could ever be—old like hills, like stars.[45]

Compare Isaiah:

> In the year of King Uzziah's death I saw the Lord seated on a throne, high and exalted, and the skirt of his robe filled the temple. About him were attendant seraphim, and each had six wings; one pair covered his face and one pair his feet, and one pair was spread in flight. They were calling ceaselessly to one another,
>
> Holy, holy, holy is the Lord of Hosts:
> The whole earth is full of his glory.[46]

The passages share a certain numerical precision—Black Elk's six old men correspond to the seraphim with six wings; the old men are attended by horses, where the Lord is surrounded by seraphim. Both visions are accompanied by song: the seraphim chant to one another; the old men sing Black Elk a song: "They are appearing, may you behold! They are appearing, may you behold!" (27). Isaiah is purified with a burning coal; Black Elk experiences his vision in a "flaming rainbow tepee" (46). Isaiah is charged with the task of warning his people of impending tragedy;[47] Black Elk has visions of his nation's suffering: "My boy, have courage, for my power shall be yours, and you shall need it, for your nation on earth will have great troubles" (30).[48]

Black Elk is certainly quite aware of the biblical prophetic tradition within which he inserts himself. This is not surprising, given that Black Elk, later in his life and before he recounted his life story to Neihardt, had converted to Christianity, which Neihardt does not reveal in his narrative.[49] The Ghost Dance religious movement, which Black Elk describes and participated in, was in great part messianic, influenced by Jewish and Christian messianic texts, of which the book of Isaiah is one. Given Walton's interest in Native American literature, it is possible that Roth read *Black Elk Speaks* in 1932 as he was working on *Call It Sleep;* it could be that David's visions are rewritings of Black Elk as well as Isaiah or, rather, Black Elk *through* Isaiah. Both texts reference past messianic movements and yearnings in the 1930s, a time of fervent expectation of Michael Gold's messiah: the workers' revolution. The 1960s were also, like the 1930s, a decade of global turmoil and political movements with messianic undertones. Just as the republication of *Call It Sleep* was co-emergent with the publication of Irving Howe's *World of Our Fathers* and a revival of interest on the part of Jewish Americans in their socialist, immigrant origins, *Black Elk Speaks* became belatedly popular in a climate in which Indians became the object of renewed political as well as spiritual and mystical attention.[50] It is in this climate that Roth's novel too reemerged into popularity.

Michael Castro, in *Interpreting the Indian: Twentieth-Century Poets and the Native-American,* explains the generation of the 1960s and its "interest in things Indian" thus:

> Younger people here, as elsewhere, tended to think of themselves as "tribal" and "communal." We saw ourselves as "counterculturists," and were active in the antiwar movement. We were reading poems in public—in many cases, before we had published any. We were collaborating with other artists in "intermedia situations." We were developing our own communities and educating one another by reading aloud our own poems, and those of the "real poets" we liked, in social and political contexts. For many of us, such communal activities were more relevant than formal classroom study to our felt needs and actual development as poets. Allen Ginsberg, Charles Olson, and William Carlos Williams had pointed us toward a poetics rooted in the rhythms of body and breath and the music of the human voice talking American speech. For us, the actual involvement in physical, oral poetics distinguished our own evolving aesthetic sharply from what was being promoted in the academies; it linked us, however superficially, with the poetics of tribal peoples.[51]

Leslie Fiedler, who was so instrumental in the rediscovery of Henry Roth, dedicated *The Return of the Vanishing American* (1968) "with thanks to the Blackfeet tribe who adopted me." In this inadvertent echo of Roth's dedication of *Call It Sleep* to Walton, his adoptive "native American mama" who translated, as it happens, Blackfoot poetry, Fiedler suggests yet another expression of the ethnic writer's wish for bilateral descent. Fiedler locates his study squarely within a revivalist moment. He observes that not only are "descendents of Eastern European Jews or Dublin Irish" feeling the "stirrings in him [*sic*] of a second soul, the soul of the Red Man" but also Native Americans themselves are in the throes of a nationalist, spiritual, and literary renaissance.[52] The bulk of the book anatomizes the presence or influence of the imaginary Indian throughout American literary mythology: The "Myth of Love in the Woods" (i.e., Pocahontas); the "Myth of the White Woman with a Tomahawk" (i.e., the Indian captivity tale); the "Myth of the Good Companions in the Wilderness" (Natty Bumppo and Chingachgook); the "Myth of the Runaway Male" (Rip Van Winkle) (51–52). The ultimate concern of the book, however, is the New Western, that is, an emergent genre that Fiedler sees as unique to the cultural moment in which he writes:

> But in the last several years, beginning somewhere around 1960, John Barth and Thomas Berger and Ken Kesey and David Markson and Peter Mat-thiessen and James Leo Herlihy and Leonard Cohen, as well as the inspired script writers of *Cat Ballou*, and I myself twice over, have, perhaps without being aware, been involved in a common venture: the creation of the New Western, a form which not so much redeems the Pop Western as exploits it with irreverence and pleasure, in contempt of the "serious reader" and his expectations. (14)

Nathanael West was, according to Fiedler, an early practitioner of the genre, and in the postwar period Truman Capote, Norman Mailer, and William Burroughs also promised to join the swelling ranks of the writers of the New Western. What New Westerns seem to share, according to Fiedler, is "the notion of madness as essential to the New World" (185). The "westering impulse" is transformed from geographical trip to acid trip: "insofar as the New Western is truly New, it, too, must be psychedelic" (175).

Fiedler continually binds together the Indian and the Jew, observing both the prominence of the Jewish writer in the creation of the 1960s New Western, and also the metaphorical and mythographical ties between Jew and Indian. Christopher Columbus was a Marrano, a Spanish Jew practicing his religion secretly during the throes of the Inquisition.[53] Pocahontas and her father, Powhatan, are the American variants of Shakespeare's Jewish merchant Shylock and his daughter, Jessica, and Sir Walter Scott's Ivanhoe: that is, "the Tale of the Jew's Absconding Daughter" (69).

The 1960s and 1970s saw a crop of films and novels that would come to be called by John Cawelti and Leslie Fiedler "New Westerns," which both associated with Jewishness.[54] John Cawelti wrote in 1976:

> The striking thing about the more recent Indian westerns is that they move beyond sympathy for the plight of individuals toward an attempt at a reconstruction of the Indian experience itself. . . . In its treatment of violence as an expression of aggressive drives toward destruction in the pioneer spirit, in its negative and guilt-ridden assessment of the winning of the West, and its reversal of traditional valuations of the symbolic figures and groups of the western story this new formula has a great deal in common with another recent form that I have labeled, rather facetiously, the legend of the Jewish cowboy. The hero of this type of western is not literally Jewish, though often played by Jewish actors. Actually, I suspect that Jews are likely to be the last of the ethnic groups to insist on donning the mantle of the cowboy hero. The heroes of *Butch Cassidy and the Sundance Kid* and *McCabe and Mrs. Miller*, however, behave more like characters transported from the pages of a novel by Saul Bellow or Bernard Malamud into the legendary West than they do like the traditional western hero. They win our interest and sympathy not by courage and heroic deeds but by bemused incompetence, genial cowardice, and the ability to face the worst with buoyancy and wit. They are six-gun schlemiels and existentialists in cowboy boots.[55]

Arthur Kopit's play *Indians* (1969, later the basis for the film *Buffalo Bill and the Indians, or Sitting Bull's History Lesson*) is a representative example of these revisionist Westerns with a so-called Jewish sensibility. Kopit's play is an effort both to create effective countermyths about the West and to protest U.S. actions in Vietnam. Kopit was explicit about his play's anti-Vietnam protest, saying that he "wanted to expose the madness of our involvement in Vietnam."[56] He even puts the words of General Westmoreland into the mouth of his character Colonel Forsyth after the massacre at Wounded Knee.[57] Kopit links past and current conflicts in suggesting the ways in which "we" are always "creating a history for ourselves."[58] With westward expansion came a "romantic literature [that] was being written to justify and ennoble a very unsavory, violent, and horrible process" and, Kopit adds, then, as now, there was a "desperate need to justify what was happening in terms of national pride, in terms of goodness."[59]

N. Scott Momaday, reviewing Kopit's play, wrote: "We have in Kopit's conception of Buffalo Bill a sensitivity of tragic proportions; the old scout is alive to himself at last, and the hard irony of his situation is not lost upon him."[60] As the ghost of Sitting Bull says to Buffalo Bill, implicating the nation: "We had land. You wanted it. You took it. That . . . I understand perfectly. What I cannot understand . . . is why you did all this, and *at the same time* . . . professed your love" (72). Buffalo Bill responds, "Funny. For a while, I actually thought my Wild West Show would *help*. I could give you money. Food. Clothing. And make people *understand* things . . . better" (72).

Kopit's subject, however, is not only the damage wrought by American national myths but also the thwarted national aspirations of Indians themselves, which are both articulated and rendered powerless through acts of performance. Chief Joseph, for instance, appears in this Wild West, contracted by Buffalo Bill to recite, "twice a day, three times on Sundays," his now famous words said upon his surrender to General Howard near the Canadian border (52). When Buffalo Bill sadly asks Sitting Bull's ghost, "We had . . . fun, though, you and I . . . Didn't we?" Sitting Bull responds: "Oh, yes. And that's the terrible thing. We had all surrendered. We were on reservations. We could not fight, or hunt. We could do nothing. Then you came and allowed us to imitate our glory. . . . It was humiliating! For sometimes, we could almost imagine it was real" (73). Like Mordechai Noah's play *She Would Be a Soldier*, the most radical assertion of resistance to power is put in the mouth of an Indian chief—that is, Sitting Bull. As the talks between the Sioux and the Senate delegation fall apart, just as Noah's Indian chief compares himself to the king of England, Sitting Bull challenges the authority of the Great Father in Washington: "If the Great Spirits have chosen anyone to be leader of their country, know that it is not the Great Father; *it is myself*" (62).

Kopit inherits the theatrical traditions of both Mordechai Noah, whose concern with myth, history, and nation he shares, and the vaudeville-Broadway musical, which is highly aware, as is *Indians*, of its own stylized fakery. Both these influences had emerged in moments that, like the 1960s, were characterized by ethnic and political disorder and anxiety.[61] In Kopit's play, it is a guilt-wracked Buffalo Bill, rather than a maniacal Jewish comic, who mediates, quite literally, between non-Indian and Indian national interests and performed identities. But, as N. Scott Momaday notes in his review, Kopit's play might have come a bit too late. That is to say, a mediator is no longer needed, when "of late, and like the Sitting Bull of Kopit's play, the Indians have begun to bring themselves on. They have become remarkably visible on the national scene—and audible as well. It would seem that they have found a voice at last, and it is the voice of protest by and large."[62] Momaday's review indicates how any non-Native interpretations of Indians would come to be severely challenged by an emerging Native political activism.

Fiedler does not mention by name any of the Native writers who in the 1960s were enjoying their own renaissance.[63] There were in addition other New Left Jewish poets and writers unmentioned by Fiedler who invoked Indians. In 1966, for instance, Joanne Greenberg published a collection of short stories that included one titled "L'Olam and White Shell Woman."[64] Joanne Greenberg, who is now perhaps best known for her novel *I Never Promised You a Rose Garden*, would in fact go on to teach cultural anthropology. Her story's narrator is a young Jewish student who finds a summer job waiting tables in a restaurant on Arizona's Navajo reservation as its "first 'Anglo' waitress" (178).

Initially, the narrator imagines her encounter with the Navajos in terms of the cachet it might lend her back at the university: "I jumped at the chance to learn some Navaho. . . . It would be a wonderful tongue to 'lapse into' at school" (178). But her efforts are frustrated by the difficulty of the language and the indifference of her fellow waitresses. Throughout the story, the distance at which the Navaho characters keep the narrator exists in tension with her claims of tribal kinship:

> Alice only shrugged. "Anyway, I am not Christian."
>
> "Not me too," Bessie echoed.
>
> Lita and the two cooks who had come out to watch me laugh, shook their heads. I had to laugh again.
>
> "Well," I said, "neither am I."
>
> "You ain' no Navaho." And the girl looked at me as though I had stained something borrowed. The People and the Enemy, brother or stranger.
>
> I couldn't let things stay that simple for them. "No," I said, "and not Tewa or Zuni. I'm something else, something called a Brooklyn Jew."
>
> "I never heard of that tribe," Alice answered skeptically.
>
> I looked out the window over the dry reaches of the land. "Our two people would have understood one another. My people once came from a land like this, and they herded sheep too. You name everything on your land for some event in the past, a miracle or wonder that happened there. My fathers did that too. Navaho don't disappear into the people of the pueblos or the white man. My fathers kept their ways too." They were quiet, skeptical.
>
> Then one of the cooks said, "You Anglo; you talk Anglo."
>
> So I rared back and hit them with the "Shema," and then "Kol Nidre," which was what came to mind.

> They listened in complete silence and, afterward, Bessie Tsosie said, "That sound like Tewa."
>
> The fat cook snorted. "I speak Tewa, and that ain't Tewa."
>
> "What did you say them people was?"
>
> "In the beginning, Israelites, then Hebrews, then Jews."
>
> I saw a sharp glance go between Alice and Bessie, and the two cooks were looking at one another. Having more than one name meant something to them. (180–81)

Finally, at the end of the summer, the narrator is invited to the last day of the tribal fair, a gesture of inclusion that serves to highlight both her affinity with the Navajos and her working-class, Jewish immigrant difference: "I stumbled over everything: white hummocks, ruts, stones. They walked easily. I was an Anglo, all right, a stranger" (188). But at the same time, "In the American city of my birth I was a stranger too. I learned the city's ways until I passed, 'assimilated' but for the strange intonations of my prayers, out of the ghetto. . . . I didn't know the Navaho, not their language or beliefs. They didn't know Abraham or Isaac, but I wasn't lonely, stumbling over what they knew and expected. Why should I be; it was the biggest ghetto I had ever seen" (188).

Another poet of the New Left, Jerome Rothenberg, edited the anthology of global poetry *Technicians of the Sacred* (1968), which included many contributions by Native poets, and much later in his career, *Shaking the Pumpkin: Traditional Poetry of the Indian North Americas* (1993). In 1974 Rothenberg published a poetry collection, *Poland/1931*, whose final poem, "Cokboy," is, like "L'Olam and White Shell Woman," a meditation on Native-Jewish collisions and intersections:

> saddlesore I came
> a jew among
> the Indians
> vot em I doink in dis strange place
> mit deez pipple mit strange eyes
> could be it's trouble.[65]

Rothenberg's Yiddish-accented "Cokboy," an almost-but-not-quite cowboy, affirms his Jewish difference even as, as the poem continues, he conquers and possesses America.

Not only, Fiedler writes, do "Jew and Indian tend to fall together in the world of myth," but it is no wonder that Jews "have played so large a role in creating the New or anti-'Upman' Western Novel; though, as a matter of fact, they did not begin to do so until, in America and especially in the field of the arts, they began to move rapidly into the establishment, i.e. to go 'up.'"[66] That is to say, the Jewish writer, once he has entered the establishment, is free to critique it; the Jewish author of the New Western thus becomes both emblem of successful American assimilation into the "establishment" and of opposition and challenge to that establishment.

Fiedler does not connect any part of his argument with Henry Roth and the novel Fiedler helped to reintroduce. He does, elsewhere, identify Roth with Nathanael West, writing that Roth "is ideologically in much the same position as Nathanael West, whose *A Cool Million* appeared in the same year as *Call It Sleep,* and whose technique, different as it was, also baffled the official "proletarians."[67] More important, however, is Fiedler's assertion that *Call It Sleep,* like the New Western generally, is "finally and astonishingly a religious book":

> David Schearl . . . is portrayed not only as a small boy and a Jew but also as a "mystic," a naive adept visited by visions he scarcely understands until a phrase from the sixth chapter of Isaiah illuminates for him his own improbable prophetic initiation. . . . Turning the final pages of Roth's book, one realizes suddenly how in the time of the Great Depression all the more serious fictionists yearned in secret to touch a religious note, toying with the messianic and the apocalyptic but refusing to call them by names not honored in the left-wing journals of the time.[68]

The New Western is likewise mystical in its valorization of the mad, drug- or schizophrenia-induced hallucinatory state, as exemplified in Ken Kesey's *One Flew Over the Cuckoo's Nest* or Leonard Cohen's *Beautiful Losers.* Fiedler flirts with the theory that some schizophrenics have, like mystics Black Elk and David Schearl, "'broken through' rather than 'broken down.'" He cites further an English psychiatrist who "suggests that Columbus's stumbling upon America and his garbled accounts of it provide an illuminating parallel to the ventures of certain madmen into the regions of extended or altered consciousness, and to their confused version, once they are outside of it, of the strange realm in which they have been."[69]

Roth himself acknowledged the theological and mystical aspects of his novel, which have not received quite as much attention as its modernist aspects or its proletarian context. Roth, in fact, describes the leftist political fervor of the 1930s as fundamentally religious in sensibility. "Bellow," mused Roth during a 1979 interview, "wrote his first novel, I think, around 1944. So he never went through that terrible trauma that many of us went through in the thirties, that swept Jewish intellectuals into this messianic, mystical kind of . . . trance (I was about to say) [laughs] . . . out of which *Call It Sleep* was written."[70]

Roth moved gradually from being Communist Party member and committed Marxist, an "atheist internationalist who scorned religious and ethnic sectarianism," to being a passionate Zionist committed to secular, nationalist expressions of Jewishness.[71] He himself wondered at the dramatic philosophical and political conversion, writing in his journal in 1967 of Israel's conduct and ultimate victory in the six-day war earlier that year:

> He sat back. I won't go into it, he thought, I'm neither neither [*sic*] military strategist, nor competent analyst of cause & forces, only that I approve & that victory is dear to me, Necessary to me. What has become of him? He still sided passionately with the Viet Cong in their struggle vs. the U.S. still grieved at their losses, gloated at their victories; he still sided with Cuba & Che Guevara's efforts in rallying guerrillas in South America against native capitalists, against U.S. imperialism, of whom they were the henchmen. But when it came to Israel, his sentiments underwent a drastic change. He was opposed to the Arabs who were also the enemies of U.S. imperialism; he championed Israel who was its ally—if not its ally then its protégé, the recipient of U.S. aid. Nothing could shake him in his conviction that Israel should survive—though there were times, many, when he wondered whether it would survive; times when he despaired over its survival, seeing who its friends were, and who its enemies were.[72]

But Roth does not repudiate his former Marxism as much as attempt to adjust it to accommodate the contradiction of his new faith:

> Eliot had become an Anglican Catholic, the thought occurred to him, and he himself now had formed a strong spiritual attachment with Israel. Were both aspects of the same thing? Both a reactionary retreat? Probably. Neither had anywhere to go. . . . Eliot had made the sacrifice, the conversion on behalf of his writing, in order to have what to write about, the man & the author one. The necessity to write—or create—was paramount, and any conviction, faith, creed that enabled the writing justified itself, however absurd. What if he tried an identification, re-identification with Judaism? No, it wasn't necessary. He had already experienced a strong identification with something more tenable, Israel, which probably was as doomed as Eliot's Anglo-Catholicism. Capitalism was still capitalism, and though its fate did

not mean the end of a state, it would mean the merger of Israel with the Arabs, just as the different socialist republics of the S.U. were merged into a unit, s. union. Well, worse could happen. In fact, perhaps that should be the goal of any pro-Israeli Marxist.[73]

The modernist, the politically radical, and the mystical are in Roth's mind intertwined. In his 1979 interview with William Freedman in Jerusalem, Roth again describes the ideological shift that he had experienced surrounding Israel's 1967 war. He again compares his new sense of Jewish nationalism with Eliot's political and religious conversion, defining both as sites of specifically literary regeneration:

> Eliot had gone through a transformation by accepting Classicism, Royalism, and Anglo-Catholicism; and I thought: the lucky bastard! But that sort of thing was absolutely beyond me, impossible. There was no outlet for me, at least not until the '67 war. But even before that war I was in a way crystallizing. I was beginning to become curious about this place; and then the war seemed to crystallize it. From then I realized I had bridged this awful chasm, this awful discontinuity, by the identification with Israel. And this continuity made another possible. I could feel, arising again, a kind of literary urge. But it takes quite a while, at least for my slow kind of mind, to move from commitment to its literary expression. I began to write in a rather confused and haphazard way about what I did feel—about what communism meant to me, what I felt about Israel, and so forth. I have the notebook somewhere, and I imagine that will become part of the raw material for what I expect to write.
>
> But what the war and the newly solidified identity did most was to liberate the youthful period. That may be both ambiguous and interesting. It liberated me to examine and write about the whole youthful sexual awakening in relation to Walton, which I had previously felt inadequate for. The kind of thing I did, the kind of person she was—I just felt completely unable to treat that sort of thing. Maybe what I'm representing or attempting to represent is not Walton, but there is a character there. . . . (16)
>
> . . . What did Israel do to me? Well, that guy Eliot must have known he was at the end of his rope, that unless he found a way to regenerate himself he was through as a poet. So he found a way. (17)

Freedman responds: "Perhaps this all ties in. Perhaps what I'm hearing from you now is a reflection of the same mysticism that energized *Call It Sleep*, the same quest for redemption at a preternatural source" (20–21). Roth agrees: "There is the same mysticism, I'm sure, and now it has to tax itself here" (21).

Israel, after its victory in 1967, was, for some, at the center of a swirl of messianic, nationalist, and mystical ideas.[74] As Steven S. Schwarzschild wrote in 1968, "In a more technically theological sense the Israeli victory in the Six Day War has produced an immensely aggravated danger of pseudo-faith and pseudo-Messianism. It is by now a cliché how Israeli as well as galut Jews without religious faith suddenly came to believe in miracles (performed by a nonexistent God) and thought they were witnessing the '*Atchalta d'Geula*'—the beginning of redemption."[75]

The links among Columbus, Spain, Native Americans, Jews, and various kinds of nationalisms were on Roth's mind in the 1960s. During a stay in Mexico in 1965, Roth wrote in a letter: "As for me, I have dreams, cuckoo dreams of writing another 'great' novel. (I'll keep dreaming that till I die). And the loci of my present fiction, my present envisionings, are and have been for some time Mexico and Spain. I see a wonderful connection between the Inquisition and the conquistadores."[76] In 1965 and 1966, Roth spent six months in Spain researching a prospective novel about a "crypto-Jew who, contrary to edict, managed to slip through the Inquisition's net and land with the conquistadores in the New World."[77] This novel was not written; Roth instead wrote a short story titled "The Surveyor," published in the *New Yorker* in 1966, just as, according to Roth himself, Roth was beginning to "crystallize" his feelings of Jewish nationalism.

"The Surveyor" describes an American tourist in Seville who attracts attention from the Spanish police as, with surveying equipment, he plots out a spot of land with grim precision and then lays a wreath on the site—a flower bed in a traffic oval. Stigman, the same figure who narrates Roth's autobiographical *Mercy of a Rude Stream*, is questioned by police, who are persuaded by a state attorney to let him go. The lawyer invites Stigman and his wife to a cafe, where he reveals that the site is the *quemadero*, where heretics, including lapsed *conversos* (Jews who converted to the Catholic faith) found guilty by the Inquisition were burned. The lawyer then reveals that he himself also has a personal interest in the site, because his great-grandfather had a custom of lighting a candle every Friday night. The two men hold a brief discussion about ethnic, national, and religious identities:

> "I knew where the *quemadero* was because I feel the same way about the people who died there that you do. Because I cannot forget their heroic constancy, as you call it. It was the heroic constancy of Spaniards who were also Jews."

"Spaniards!" Stigman looked at the other man with a startled expression. "It was the heroic constancy of Jews who were also Spaniards!"

Ortega sat motionless. For once, his uncertain face seemed at rest.

"And do you light a candle on Friday nights?" asked Stigman.

The lawyer shook his head, almost as if disdaining the thought. "A candle in consciousness is enough, is it not? And you?"

"Oh no," Stigman said. "I left the faith of my ancestors many years ago."[78]

Stigman seems to be a writer not paralyzed by history but rather driven by it, obsessed with it, even though it is not necessarily his own history. The assumption of this historical memory has replaced the practice of the ancestral faith. The Spanish Jews, martyrs for their faith, are the absent presence at the center of the story, and Stigman and Ortega engage in a wrestling match in which each stakes a claim on the "heroic constancy" of what one chooses to regard as Spaniards and the other as Jews.

If "The Dun Dakotas" described a writer frozen by history, perhaps because the history described by the story—white incursion into the western United States—is one with which the writer feels a fragile and ambivalent connection, "The Surveyor" concerns the writer-character's claim to history and his desire for an alternative ancestry, that of Spanish Jews rather than eastern European Jews. This, however, may be a way of revisiting the same material as "The Dun Dakotas," for Roth had originally envisioned his subject to be a Spanish Jew who landed in the New World with the conquistadores. To adopt Spanish-Jewish ancestry is, in some way, to stake a claim on America, through, to use Roth's term, the "side door."

Twelve years after publishing "The Surveyor," Roth returned to his Spanish materials and wrote a nonfiction piece titled "The Wrong Place." Much of the piece details Roth's response to Spain's pervasive and "overpowering" Catholicism. He imagines himself the Marrano youth about whom he intends to write: "It's easy, I muse, as I stand there raptly gazing up at the stained-glass windows that shine like ethereal retablos, it's easy to accept Catholicism. It's beautiful. If only my mother and father would cut out their clandestine observances, I'd forget about Judaism."[79] Roth himself begins to succumb to the seductiveness of Catholicism: "I am aware of a sense of surrender, a sense of religious commitment. I can glimpse Eliot's distress, Eliot's necessity, Eliot's compulsion—without being persuaded."[80]

Finally, however, as he stands on the spot of the *quemadero* in a scenario that he fictionalizes in "The Surveyor," Roth arrives at a kind of revelation of what his visit to Spain, and his preoccupation with Marrano Jews, is really all about: "I stood there, in the shadow of El Cid, conscious that I was treading on the ashes of martyrs—I had closed the doors myself: on the business Diaspora, the acquisitive Diaspora, the observing Diaspora. What door was open? Idiot, I thought: the same door that was open to those Marranos's descendants who but yesterday fled from Arab persecution: Israel!"[81]

In this essay, as in his interview with Freedman the following year, Roth identifies his rediscovery of Judaism through Spain and Israel with Eliot's regeneration as a poet through his conversion. At the same time that Roth articulates his admiration, troubled as it is, for Eliot, he expresses a profound disillusionment with Joyce. Joyce's failing, according to Roth, was that he had remained silent on the issue of Irish nationalism.

In *From Bondage*, the third volume of *Mercy of a Rude Stream,* Roth offers further explanation for his "rupture," as he terms it, with Joyce. Roth/Ira Stigman takes issue both with Joyce's representation of a Jew without historical memory, and Joyce's own refusal to address "the continuing evolution of Ireland."[82] He describes *Ulysses* as an "evasion of history": "The book was the work of a man who sought to fossilize his country, its land, its people, to rob them of their future, arrest their ebullient, coursing life, their traditions and aspirations" (67). For Roth, Leopold Bloom is also a figure lifted out of history:

> On every page, commencing with the scarce nominal Jew that the great Guru foisted on the reader, a Jew without memory, without wry anxiety, exilic insecurity, not merely oblivious of his heritage, but virtually devoid! Of the Kishinev pogrom the year before, nothing, of Dreyfus, nothing, nothing to say to Dlugacz, or whatever his name was, the Hungarian butcher, no sally about the pork kidney: was it kosher? No inference, no connection between a newspaper offering plots in Palestine and the possibility of a Jewish community in Dublin. . . . And despite the lack, daring to depict the Jew's "stream of consciousness," the inner flow of a Jew's psyche, an Irish quasi-Marrano of the year 1904.[83]

The figure of the Marrano turns out to be a useful one for Roth: it increasingly comes to signify not only alienation from cultural origins but also the urgent necessity of return to those origins, which Roth redefines as essentially nationalistic and political. The Marrano is a potent fictive device: an embryonic character, a way of thinking about David Schearl at certain moments in *Call It Sleep,* a way of describing both Bloom and Joyce. It serves also as an autobiographical flourish, as Roth continually imagines himself as, or identifies with, the Marrano. It is an identification continued by his critics. Jonathan Rosen wrote in 1995, after Roth's death, that Roth had told him he had been planning a sequel to the opera *Carmen,* in which Don Jose, tried for Carmen's murder in Seville, has for his defense lawyer a "brilliant converso." "It is a shame," writes Rosen, "he never did write the book about the Inquisition, though his own life as an American Jewish converso is perhaps more remarkable than anything he might have made up about Spain."[84]

"A Place in the World and an Origin"

What Roth wrote about Spain was, he admitted, essentially autobiographical. Marranos, the conquistadores, and the state of Israel are bound together through Roth's particular sense of history. Roth is preoccupied with the question of the native, or "at-homeness," and it is an obsession that grows out of the experience of writing *Call It Sleep* and out of Roth's exhaustive analysis of his own creative stasis. Even the titles of a number of short pieces collected in *Shifting Landscape* reveal a concern with space, home, mobility and homelessness: "Many Mansions," "The Prisoners," "At Times in Flight," "No Longer at Home," "Itinerant Ithacan," "The Wrong Place." Joyce's failing, in Roth's words, is that he "couldn't make it home." In 1983, Roth wrote:

> I do not know Hebrew. I don't have many illusions about the future of Israel. I have very strong reservations about the Israeli politicians. But in Israel I see a Jewish cop running after a Jewish thief, and I see that both are at home there. This is what I mean by "continuity." Because in America the Jew is not at home. He's always the outsider.[85]

Roth has famously subjected *Call It Sleep* to a retroactive reading in which he explains the novel as having grown out of a feeling of not-at-home-ness, specifically, the feeling of dislocation and alienation experienced by the boy Roth when his family relocated from the Lower East Side to Harlem.[86] He has described the East Side as a "Jewish mini-state," describing his time spent there as "the only time he ever felt a sense of belonging to both a place and a people."[87]

Roth marks the renaissance of his writing with the 1967 war in Israel, and he describes his relationship with Israel, like his relationship with Walton, through the metaphor of adoption:

> What I wrote seemed to reflect a peculiar adoption. Israel did not adopt me; I adopted my *ex post facto* native land . . . suddenly I had a place in the

world and an origin. Having started to write, it seemed natural to go on from there, and I have been writing long hours every day since then. I am not yet sure what it is leading to, but it is necessary and is growing out of a new allegiance, and adhesion that comes from belonging.[88]

At the same time, however, Roth himself does not feel at home when he is actually in Israel, saying in 1986, "I felt, essentially, like a foreigner. . . . It's not merely the language. It's the landscape, you know?"[89] It seems Roth, like Walton, searched for kinship everywhere and in everybody, and yet unlike Walton, ultimately despaired of ever finding it.

Roth was not the only ethnic writer to argue a kinship between Columbus, Jews, and American Indians as a way of working through his sense of home and belonging, as we have seen in Gerald Vizenor's *Heirs of Columbus*. Vizenor was, not coincidentally, another of Walton's protégés.[90] Vizenor's fantastical treatment of history, aesthetics, nationalism, and ethnic identities could not, on the surface, be further away from Roth's fictional autobiography, the first volume of which was published only a few years after *The Heirs of Columbus*. *Mercy of a Rude Stream,* however, does issue a challenge to the reader on the level of historical truth. The autobiographical veracity of the novels has been the primary subject of discussion among Roth's commentators. *Mercy* at frequent moments invites readers to read it as a postmodern novel.[91] Indeed some have, interpreting the confession of incest at the center of the novels as a fiction that, in the words of one critic, "symbolically expresses the cultural bondage toward which Roth felt a paralyzing ambivalence," and "not to be construed" as "autobiographical."[92]

Mercy of a Rude Stream's postmodernism inheres in its determination to elide, rather than render transparent, the distinction between fact and fiction: that is, between Henry Roth, the writer, and Ira Stigman, the protagonist of the autobiography. The novels are all written, for the most part, in the third person, but occasionally a section will appear that is written in the first person.[93] As Hana Wirth-Nesher has noted, the names or initials of Stigman's wife, children, and relatives are identical to those of Roth's family; the present-day interludes refer to information that is public knowledge, such as Muriel's musical career or Roth's illness, and include details about the writing of *Mercy,* the "haunting presence" of *Call It Sleep,* and Roth's writer's block. The inside cover of each volume displays photographs of Roth's own family and friends.[94]

There is, moreover, a complex layering of texts and time frames: the sections that take place during Ira's childhood and adolescence are interspersed with present-day musings, most addressed to Ira's computer, which he has named Ecclesias. However, the present-day commentary, the metanarrative, often corrects and counters the narrative and offers additional autobiographical information, recounting events that took place in the past but after the time frame circumscribed by *Mercy* (for example, the writing of Stigman's great novel, clearly *Call It Sleep,* and the courting of his wife). The narrative, in addition, seems to be a revision and expansion of an earlier version to which Stigman often refers. Roth also incorporates some previously published material, such as the short story "Somebody Always Grabs the Purple."[95]

Call It Sleep haunts both the narrative and the metanarrative: Stigman explicitly refers to the traumative effect of the writing of the novel during his metanarrative, and the narrative itself is rife with quotes and references to *Call It Sleep,* as scenes, images, and phrases are reproduced, and often implicitly explained, in the sections that recount Ira's childhood and young adulthood. These moments have the effect of revealing to the reader Roth's sources for much of *Call It Sleep,* but this is only an effect, as this text was written well after *Call It Sleep,* and indeed, it is unclear which text is meant to serve as the "original."[96]

Just as the exemplary modernist texts presume readerly acquaintance with a subtext, or source text—The *Odyssey* in *Ulysses; Isaiah,* or the Passover *Haggada,* or even *Ulysses* in *Call It Sleep*—*Mercy* presumes a readerly intimacy with *Call It Sleep,* as Roth sets out to both clarify and, as it turns out, undermine his earlier work. Wirth-Nesher writes: "Henry Roth, wrapped in a long silence and admired by a readership enamored of the innocent boy depicted in *Call It Sleep,* confesses his sins, his abnormality. He wants to set the record straight by shocking his readers into the realization that he was victimizer, not only victim, that the innocent only child of *Call It Sleep* is an elegant evasion."[97] Accordingly, not only does Ira Stigman (the "stigma" embedded in his name refers to the burden of his sins) commit incest with his sister; he also entices his friends' sisters and his own cousin into cellars. He recounts moments in which he himself is preyed upon, by a homeless man in Mt. Morris Park and by his teacher in the classroom after school. He overhears his uncle Louie proposition his mother, and his mother, declining, confesses her unrequited passion for her own brother.[98] In *Call It Sleep,* the shocking confession David overhears and dimly understands is the tale of his mother's transgressive liaison with a Christian organist; indeed, the entire novel is an extended rumination on the encounter between Jew and Gentile, and the inevitable abutment and resulting friction between Jewish and Christian symbols and texts. *Mercy,* on the other hand, again and again, through a number of characters, returns to the transgressive act that is "a perversion of remaining within the fold."[99]

If *Call It Sleep* has been read as the story of the writer's initiation into modernism, then *Mercy* could be read as the writer's distancing of himself from it. Ira's ruinous block, in Jeffrey Folks's reading, results "not merely from personal weakness: it is related to and perhaps 'necessary' to his (and to Roth's) self-conception as a modernist artist in exile from the repression of inherited culture. Incest, in other words, is an effective figure to represent the closed culture, controlled by loyalties to tradition and to family, which Roth imagines in opposition to a 'national' or international culture of modernism."[100] It is Edith's Zaru anecdote that precedes Ira's coinage of the word "Indigen" that perhaps best represents in miniature the threefold purpose of *Mercy*. The tale concerns Zaru, the last surviving member of a tribe of Indians that had vanished from California. After years of surviving in the wilderness with his sister, he gives himself up after her death, "the last wild Indian in California." He is convinced the white men will kill him and is unable to communicate with anyone, until Dr. Wasserman, under whom Edith had studied at Berkeley, who knew some rudiments of Zaru's language, wins the Indian's trust. Dr. Wasserman publishes an account of Zaru's readjustment to civilization and wins international acclaim. Edith becomes his student. Then, in a disturbing coda to the story, Edith reveals that during a field trip, Wasserman "had virtually raped her."[101]

Ira has three responses to this story: one immediate, one delayed and internal, and one told from the writer's vantage point, responding to the experience of rewriting the anecdote as part of his text. Ira's immediate response is, so to speak, "modernist," as he punningly creates a new name for the Indian, "Indigen," prompting Edith's fateful remark about his "feeling for words." Ira's second, internal response is a sense of identification with Zaru and his sister, in which he imagines himself and his sister, Minnie, in exile in the wilderness, free from the dread of being caught: "It was the only pleasure they had. What else were they going to do? He'd slap her if she didn't submit. To whom was she going to complain? The white man? Besides, that was *her* only pleasure, too."[102] Before either of these responses occurs in the text, however, Ira the writer interrupts his narrative and inserts a commentary about modern technology and the act of composition, in which the entire Zaru story's instability in the narrative is highlighted as Ira ponders whether to let it remain or "just delete."[103]

This anecdote prompts, in quick succession, commentaries on aesthetic and ethnic identities. Ira imagines himself an Indian, a figure who in his hiddenness rather recalls the Marrano youth into whose mind Roth had projected himself in "The Wrong Place." Ira calls himself an Indian at least one more time in *Mercy*, intending the term specifically to call attention to his incestuous desires.[104] Zaru is yet another figure who wanders in a wasteland, like Roth's surveying party in "The Dun Dakotas"; Roth described his writer's block as a wasteland. Wirth-Nesher argues that "there are two counterlives that structure the narrative of *Mercy*—Americanization and Zionism."[105] What I suggest here is that for Roth, Indianness, by way of Eda Lou Walton, provided a portal into both. At the time of his literary renascence, I argue, Roth's sense of mystical import and his nationalist stirrings were prompted or at least bolstered by a resurging Native American literary and political visibility. But as we shall see, autochthony and the struggle for national liberation, native claims through which writers like Fast or Roth insisted on reading kinship between Jews and Indians, could also serve as sites of competition for Jews and Indians.

⟨5⟩

First Nations

The Last Mohicans

We were here first,
no ceiling to separate our blue doors from the sky,
no horses to graze where our deer used to graze,
no strangers bursting in on the night of our wives.
O give the wind a flute to weep for the people
of this wounded place,
and tomorrow to weep for you.
And tomorrow to weep for you.

—Mahmoud Darwish, "Speech of the Red Indian"

Jerusalem, 2007: two images, one from a local English-language newspaper and the other from a T-shirt store on Ben Yehuda Street, the pedestrian mall downtown usually thronged with tourists. In the newspaper, a group of Palestinian protestors are dressed in buckskin, fringed shirts, and feather headdresses. The backs of two Israeli soldiers frame the scene. Two signs are visible: "Is this our Reservation" and "Indian wars are not over, Mrs. Rice. . . . We are still here, too!" The caption, titled "Expressing Their Reservations," reads: "IDF troops stand guard as Palestinians, dressed as Native Americans, hold signs addressed to U.S. Secretary of State Condoleeza Rice at the Hawara checkpoint south of Nablus yesterday."[1] The second image, on a T-shirt, depicts Israeli Prime

Photographed by author.

Minister Ehud Olmert and an American Indian, again dressed stereotypically in a feathered headdress and buckskin fringed shirt, superimposed over a map of Israel. The caption reads in English: "Ehud, let me tell you about trading land for peace!" Both images are clearly performing for an American audience, gesturing toward ideas of indigenousness, homeland, and nationhood rooted in a U.S. context. These days, it seems both Israelis and Palestinians can use the figure of the imagined Indian to bolster their competing claims to indigenousness, and thus the status, legal and imaginative, of first nation.

This chapter elaborates upon contemporary Jewish and Native assertions of territoriality and sovereignty as articulated in such identity-making projects as museums in addition to literary texts. Such assertions are exercised in the increasingly competitive and charged landscape of contemporary identity politics.

In other words, Jews' and Palestinians' competing claims of kinship with Indians that have erupted around the Israeli-Palestinian conflict are inseparable from the charged discourse of Holocaust memory and ethnic power in American culture.

Emily Miller Budick and Eric Sundquist have demonstrated the ways in which a potentially competitive relationship between Jewish American and African American fiction has centered on invocations, displacements, and appropriations of the Holocaust.[2] I discern a similar emergent trend between Jewish and Native cultural production. An insistence on alternative Holocausts that supersede and replace the Jewish Holocaust, writes Budick, "may be read as assaults against Jewish history that inherit, in fairly traditional ways, classical anti-Semitism. They may also be understood as defensive responses to what is perceived as an assertion of Jewish power and authority," including perceived Jewish influence over U.S. policies regarding Israel.[3] Edward Linenthal writes of the United States Holocaust Museum that, for many, "the museum would be a symbol of the deft use of Holocaust memory to advance ethnic power, expressed most crassly in a comment made to me that the museum was a way to remind congressmen how to vote on issues regarding the State of Israel."[4]

In tangling together contemporary conversations about Holocaust memory, the place of Israel in the Jewish American literary imagination, ethnic power in American public culture, and Jewish-Native interactions, I am adapting Budick's arguments about black-Jewish intertextuality. The assertion of ethnic memory in the service of a project of cultural autonomy inevitably involves what Budick calls "cultural overwriting": the appropriation and displacement of another group's competing cultural memories. I begin with a discussion of two postwar Yiddish narratives, by Sheen Dayksel and Shia Tenenbaum, that call upon Indian materials to both mourn and re-create a lost "Yiddishland." Turning to Bernard Malamud, I read his unfinished novel *The People* as a text that in its fantasy of a Jewish Indian chief in fact meditates on American Jewish anxieties and ambivalence about Jewish sovereignty as embodied in Israel post-1967. I then turn to contemporary Spokane/Coeur d'Alene writer Sherman Alexie, reading his work in the context of Native and Jewish museums as exercises in sovereignty, ethnic memory, and cultural reclamation. And finally, I suggest that the Jewish territory imagined in Michael Chabon's novel *The Yiddish Policemen's Union* reflects the definitive post-1967 turn in Jewish-Native intersections: tropes of "brotherhood" have given way to a language of irreconcilable tribal and territorial interests.

In 1959 Shmuel ("Sheen") Dayksel published a volume titled *Indianishe dertseylungen* (Indian tales), which combined autobiographical reminiscence, fiction, and ethnography. The book's frontispiece, a design that transposes the

מארלאג.
ש. דייקסעל בוך־קאמיטעט

Sh. Dayksel, *Indianishe
dertseylungen*, title page.

"On a two-year 'span' over the land."
From *Indianishe dertseylungen*.

"From 'My Indian Mother.'"
From *Indianishe dertseylungen.*

Yiddish title and author's name onto a Pacific Northwest Native decorative figure, serves as the model for the tropes of Jewish-Indian kinship, adoption, and resemblance that dominate the stories. In "My Indian Mother," for instance, the one story to have since been translated into English, Dayksel is "adopted" by an Indian woman whom he has cured through his chiropractic expertise. She calls him both a stranger and a kinsman: "I don't know . . . there is something in your face . . . something of our own . . . maybe you yourself also descend from one of our remote ancestors."[5]

The book features photographs of Dayksel dressed as a scout, of Dayksel with Indian friends, of Dayksel in Native costume entertaining a group of similarly costumed youngsters, and finally, of traditional Native dances.[6] The collection is loosely based on Dayksel's own progress across the country as he visited and was adopted into multiple tribes, although Dayksel's actual "tramp" seems to have occurred well before the publication of the stories, probably as early as the 1920s, when Dayksel published his first "Indian tales" in *Der Hammer*.[7] Dayksel, born in 1886 in Kishinev, was seventy-three when these stories were published in New York; the photographs of Dayksel in the volume show a much younger man.

דער שלאַנגען־טאַנץ

אַ פריינט אין סאָענקאָפי

אַ פריינט אין אָראַיבי

פריינט אין יאָסעמיטי

Clockwise, from top left: "The Snake-Dance," "A Friend in Soencopi [*sic*]," "Friends in Yosemite," "A Friend in Oraibi." From *Indianishe dertseylungen*.

אויבערשטע און אונטערשטע: האָפּי שמעטערלינג-פרילינג טענץ, מיטלסטע: ש. ד. דערציילט אַ מעשה

Middle and bottom: "Hopi Butterfly-Spring Dance." Top: "Sh.D. Tells a Story." From *Indianishe dertseylungen.*

In his acknowledgments, Dayksel writes:

> My new book is not only fine literature; not only an altogether new theme in the Yiddish language, but it is also very dear to me in the sad fact that, in a large number of particulars, Indian history is so similar in its fate with our own people.
>
> In each story there are interwoven historical, true chapters in the bloody history of the "Red Men," sad facts of a history of a people, who have been brutally robbed not only of their immense, grand, rich, and beautiful land which now bears the proud name "America," but who, along with their culture and beliefs, have been the targets of an effort to annihilate and destroy.
>
> Perhaps this book will be at least one step in the powerful wave which will certainly sooner or later help erode the present malice and desolation in the world and help build a brotherly future for humankind in a peaceful world.
>
> Again, dear friends, thank you for your help and let us hope that the prophets, who spoke of the holocaust of our language and literature, will be discovered to be false prophets, and that our dear, heart-felt mother-tongue, with our literature, just like our people and our culture, will continue to flourish. (283)

Here, Dayksel defines his project as both tribal and universal: Native and Jewish peoples have both been the targets of efforts to "annihilate and destroy," but the Yiddish language, "just like our people and our culture, will continue to flourish." At the same time, Dayksel invokes a liberal universalism: he hopes his collection will "help build a brotherly future for humankind in a peaceful world."

In the first story, "A takhter fun di tsen farloyrene shovtim" ("A daughter of the ten lost tribes"), an American-born New York Jew traveling across the country falls in love with a beautiful Hopi schoolteacher. The couple passionately discusses Native American and European Jewish genocide at the hands of the Christian world, and then Bayamka, the schoolteacher, theorizes that American Indians are descended from the ten lost tribes. Forged in a shared genocidal history, the union of Bayamka and David signals a triumphant transculturation of Jew and Indian: the New York Jew "goes native," and the Indian maiden becomes Jewish.

The second story in the collection, "Afn tsofn-zoym fun grend-kenyon" ("On the northern edge of the Grand Canyon"), describes an elderly Navajo man living on a remote edge of the Grand Canyon, whose childhood memories are of the decimation of his tribe in the 1860s in the forced internment at Fort

Sumner in Bosque Redondo (here is one moment among many when Dayksel interweaves historical information and ethnography into his fiction; he describes He-ra-ra's hogan and interjects words and sentences in Native languages. Other stories address in great detail, for instance, the battle of Little Big Horn and the massacre at Wounded Knee, Indian boarding schools, and the involvement of Native Americans in the Communist Party). He-ra-ra remembers the death march to Bosque Redondo, during which a thousand people died. His father, before his death, tells him never to forget and to avenge the violence done to his tribe. Dayksel writes: "Bosque-Redondo in New Mexico—was the first concentration camp in America" (73).

In the third story in the collection, Dayksel befriends a Sioux family, who recount to him in dramatic and emotional detail their traumatic national history. The narrative of the elderly grandfather is an astonishing account, in its devastating anti-imperial critique, of Sitting Bull's and Crazy Horse's resistance against Custer, of Ghost Dance religion, and of the slaughter of innocents at Wounded Knee. Sheen, the narrator, quietly listens, at only one point telling his interlocutors about Hitler's effort to exterminate his own people, the Jews.

Dayksel's radical left-wing politics are thus in abundant evidence throughout the narrative: these stories are committed to an ethos of brotherhood across the working classes that transcends race and ethnicity but that also, for Dayksel, does not erase particular national narratives. He offers a consistent critique of genocidal and imperialist policies against American Indians by the U.S. government and everyday, casual, and violent racism among ordinary Americans. This is linked with the tragic fate of the Jews in Europe, even as, however, Dayksel frames his collection as a triumphant affirmation of the continued flourishing of his mother tongue after the devastation of the Holocaust.

More than a few post-Holocaust collections of Yiddish literature made similar claims of cultural vibrancy. One anthology in particular, a collection titled *New Yorkish and Other Yiddish American Stories* (1995), featured a story that had first appeared in Yiddish in 1977, in the journal *Tsukunft* (Future).[8] Shia Tenenboym's short fictional memoir, originally titled in Yiddish "Tsvishn Indianer" ("Among the Indians"), was translated in the collection as "Among the Indians in Oklahoma." It is an ironic choice for this optimistic collection, which attempted to affirm the liveliness of Yiddish literature in the late twentieth century, when Yiddish readers were rapidly dwindling not only because of the Holocaust but also, in an English-language context, through American assimilation. The preface states, "The Yiddish literature presented here is not to be considered as an heirloom of a bygone age but as a guidepost to a thriving self-conscious Jewish community life in North America" (i). The predominant tenor of Tenenboym's story, however, in contrast to that of the preface, is absence and loss.

"Among the Indians" pretends to be memoir, narrated by a writer in the present remembering the time he spent as a new immigrant in Oklahoma in 1935. The twenty-four-year-old writer has moved to Norman to work on his autobiography and to trace the last days of his older brother Jonah, who died there some years previously, leaving his Indian sweetheart, his prayer book, and his watch with an engraved Star of David. The story culminates with the narrator's extended visit to Seminole, where his vision of recovering his dead brother's fiancée, Pocahontas, terminates in failure. The story is preoccupied with historical memory; in the very first paragraph we are told that the narrator's landlady recounts stories about "our first President, stories that were told to her by her grandfather, the captain of a slave-ship, when she was a little girl" (192). By thus immediately imbricating mytho-heroic American history (stories of our first president) with the darker, more shameful, imperialistic aspects of that history (narrated by the captain of a slave ship), Tenenboym's story introduces its themes of communal and individual memory, nostalgia, and dispossession. An old Indian chief talks about "the war with the White Man at the end of the 19th century as though it had happened only yesterday." Seminole, "attacked by a storm of red dust," reminds the narrator of the biblical city of Sodom, and he fantasizes that he himself is Lot's homesick wife, transfixed by memories of his Polish hometown.

Oklahoma, in this story, is reimagined as sovereign Jewish-Native territory. Tenenboym refers to Seminole, whose inhabitants seem to only consist of Indians and Jews, as a shtetl, whose Jewish inhabitants are obsessed with the artifacts of their European past. The Seminole doctor, a Jew from Kiev who treated Jonah, the narrator's brother, boasts of his collection of Yiddish volumes; the Tanzmans, the narrator's hosts, proudly display their century-old sacramental wine cup and their 120-year-old candlesticks. The Tanzmans complain that their son Charlie, a desirable match for the daughters of the local Jewish families, is enamored with an Indian woman, whom the narrator glimpses:

> Her diminutive face was yellow and pockmarked, making her look like an old woman. When she laughed, it sounded to me as though she were crying. From her small brown eyes peered an ancient sorrow, the sorrow of her old, weary, and aggrieved people, which had once owned an enormous territory—all of America. . . . One day, as I studied her face, I suddenly noticed Jewish features of ancient days when King David ruled the Jewish country. She sang sad songs filled with a kind of Jewish nostalgia. (195)

Even as Tenenboym imagines Seminole-as-shtetl, the collapse of difference between Jew and Indian in fact signifies a vanished eastern European civilization and its replacement with nostalgia among America's Jews. The story is a meditation on loss, longing, and disappearance. Two traumatized and displaced peoples are linked through the mourning figure of Pocahontas as well as through the totemic power of objects as residues of memory: candlesticks, Yiddish books, and watches.[9] "Tsvishn Indianer" thus introduces the new terms of the Jewish-Indian encounter, now mediated through objects, relics, museums, and memorial and mourning spaces.

Dovid Katz, in his history of the Yiddish language, repeats what has perhaps become a persistent metaphor among both Holocaust survivors and aging Yiddish speakers in titling one of his final chapters about the decimated post-Holocaust Yiddish world "Mohicans."[10] This metaphor can be traced to Bernard Malamud's story "The Last Mohican," the first of his Fidelman stories published in his 1958 collection *The Magic Barrel*. It is not obviously about America's Indians but rather about Europe's Jews, as encountered by an American Jew in Rome, a failed artist who now intends to complete a critical history of the Italian painter Giotto. Upon his arrival, Fidelman meets Susskind, who Malamud unambiguously constructs as his double as well as a racialized other: the last Mohican of the story's title. The "dark" Susskind, a Holocaust survivor and refugee, initially wants Fidelman's only spare suit but eventually steals Fidelman's manuscript, forcing Fidelman to search for him in Rome's Jewish ghetto, where the American for the first time confronts a scarred and diminished post-Holocaust Jewish community. In search of Susskind, Fidelman visits a synagogue, where he meets a father who, like Chingachgook, is grieving for his dead son, and Rome's Jewish cemetery, filled with the burial places of those who had died in the "late large war." "The Last Mohican" exposes and interrogates what James Fenimore Cooper's *The Last of the Mohicans* represents as natural and inevitable: a national landscape haunted by a vanishing people. *The People's* engagement with the imaginary Indian, in turn, draws upon these linked genocides in grappling with what was emerging in the early 1980s, with Israel's unpopular incursion into Lebanon, as the "problem" of the Jewish nation.

In 1968 Malamud visited Israel as a guest of the Merkaz Latefutsot and gave a reading at the Jerusalem Kahn Theatre. Telling the audience that he was reading in celebration of Jerusalem, the "thriving, vibrating, beating city of our people," he read "The Jew Bird," "The German Refugee," "My Son the Murderer" (a short story about the Vietnam war), and "Black Is My Favorite Color," all stories dealing on some level with race and racism. Later during his visit, speaking to a Hebrew University seminar, Malamud commented on the idea of a school of American Jewish writers, on his own use of Jewish materials, and finally addressed the presence of Israel. An article described his talk:

> There is also Israel. The emergence and development of the State of Israel has created a new picture of the Jew. And there are so many things in Israel Americans feel they share. Those who have lived the American adventure see this land as an adventure too. They share a common idea of the seeking of a frontier and a wholeness of the land. There is also the sense of being a melting-pot nation. In the opening, [Mr. Malamud] had said that he was "glad to be in this magic country" (this is his first visit) saying by this he meant that he saw Israel as "a triumph of human imagination." It was Thursday, the day of Israel's action against Fatah bases across the Jordan, and helicopters carrying the wounded frequently flew over the campus on the way to and from the Ein Karem Medical Centre. And Mr. Malamud added, after a helicopter had passed as he was speaking of "magic" and "imagination": "Though, when you hear the helicopters overhead you realize that something else is needed, too."
>
> However, Israel also symbolizes "the tragedy of the victories—the victory that is never final." [11]

These comments about Israel rehearse the conflicts of *The People,* which Malamud left unfinished when he died in 1986. Malamud admires the adventure of the frontier, the mystical properties ("wholeness") of the land, and reluctantly admits the necessity of an army ("something else is needed too"). He sees Israel as a "melting-pot nation," a nation of immigrants, but leaves open the question whether it, like the United States, had yet to fully acknowledge the claims to indigenousness of other groups. Finally, Malamud offers a vision of Israel as a tragic and unfinished victory—"a victory that is never final," its state of unfinishedness curiously paralleling that of the novel he would eventually write about the tragedies and victories of tribalism.

In 1983 Malamud wrote:

> I may have done as much as I can with the sort of short story I have been writing so long—the somewhat mythological, biblically oriented tales I have been writing. These become more and more difficult to do and I feel I must make a change. What I see as possible is another variation of the comic-mythological—possibly working out the Chief Joseph of the Nez Perce idea—in other words, the Jewish Indian. [12]

These notes would eventually turn into the novel *The People*. He left sixteen chapters, a fragment of chapter 17, and notes for four more chapters, all published together in 1989. Janna Malamud Smith, in her memoir, notes that her father began *The People* after he had suffered a stroke that affected his language "resettled his words so they rested together more limply."[13] She writes:

> A man of exorbitant will, he returned to his desk and pen and daily fought to retrieve what he could find. He began with very short stories and gradually worked his way to a novel he'd wanted to write about a Jewish Indian, called *The People*. Long before he became ill, he sometimes told a joke that began, "once there was a Jewish Indian." He would grin at the outset, kid-delighted with the silly concept. And, of course, it mirrored his own foreign/native being perfectly—Yozip, the novel's protagonist, seems loosely based on Max Malamud [Bernard's father].[14]

The People functions first of all as an intervention in a tradition of white representations of Native histories and cultures: specifically, in this case, the story of Chief Joseph of the Nez Perce, who in the nineteenth century became something of a national celebrity. When Joseph became chief of his Northeastern Oregonian tribe, he had to confront increasing pressure exerted by the federal government upon the tribe to move to a reservation in Idaho. Chief Joseph engineered one of the most famous and tactically brilliant retreats in military history, leading his band of about seven hundred people on a fourteen-hundred-mile march over three months toward Canada, engaging in numerous skirmishes with U.S. soldiers on the way. He formally surrendered in 1877, reportedly with a speech that concluded with the now famous sentences: "Hear me, my chiefs! I am tired. My heart is sick and sad. From where the sun now stands I will fight no more forever." Chief Joseph and what remained of his people were moved to Oklahoma and before he died in 1904 were eventually permitted to return to the Pacific Northwest, though not to their ancestral lands.

Drawing upon both the lost-tribes myths of "red Jews" as well as vaudeville traditions of Jewish redface, Malamud reimagines Chief Joseph as a Yiddish-accented immigrant Jewish peddler named Yozip Bloom, perhaps named after that most famous detribalized Jew, Leopold Bloom. Yozip is kidnapped, then adopted by a Northwestern tribe—called only "the People" in the novel—made their chief, and renamed Jozip, in an intentional echo of Joseph, his adopted father and chief's name. In the face of increasing violence and incursion by federal troops, Jozip decides to flee with the People northward. Only days from the Canadian border, the tribe is forced to surrender, and its members are shipped to a reservation in Missouri. Malamud's last completed chapter ends on a haunting note reminiscent of concentration camp–bound cattle cars: "The moaning of the Indians began as the freight cars were moving along the tracks" (97).

In Malamud's notes for the remaining chapters, Jozip leaves the reservation and goes to Chicago, where he joins Buffalo Bill's Wild West show as a "white Indian." He enrolls in night school and decides to become a lawyer "for the Indians." In his notes for the final chapter Malamud wrote cryptically: "Last scene: 'Hasidic' dance of the recovered self. A rejoicing of life when the self seems annealed. Leave with an Indian talking" (99).

Pirjo Ahokas, in one of the few interpretive treatments of the novel, places *The People* in a context of revisionist Westerns. Arthur Kopit's *Indians*, because it also imagines Chief Joseph joining Buffalo Bill's Wild West show, probably served as one source for Malamud, as did, perhaps, films like *Little Big Man, Butch Cassidy and the Sundance Kid, Blazing Saddles,* and *The Frisco Kid,* which with their "six-gun schlemiels" and "existentialists in cowboy boots" explicitly aimed to critique the gender, ethnic, and racial hierarchies of earlier frontier narratives.[15] *The People* departs from the revisionist Western, however, in that it does not really seek to correct the historical record, but rather to complicate it through the layering of different kinds of narratives, such as that of Moses and the Holocaust, atop that of Chief Joseph.

Malamud's notes for the novel reveal not a disregard for the historical realities of the Nez Perce and Chief Joseph but rather a profound engagement with and then a self-conscious distancing from them. Malamud is not only rewriting various histories but also other fictions, from the familiar genre of the captivity narrative to the postmodern pastiche of Kopit's play, and most immediately Robert Penn Warren's long narrative poem lengthily titled *Chief Joseph of the Nez Perce: Who Called Themselves the Nimipu, "The Real People,"* published in 1983. Like Kopit's play, Warren's poem interfuses fiction with history, alternating quotes from nineteenth-century journals, memoirs, interviews, and newspaper reports—that is to say, official histories—with Chief Joseph's imagined interior monologue. Warren, like Kopit, imagines Chief Joseph at the end of his life riding alongside Buffalo Bill, whom he calls the "clown, the magician who could transform / For howling patriots, or royalty, / The blood of history into red ketchup, / A favorite American condiment."[16] Malamud's Jozip too calls Buffalo Bill's Wild West show a "circus." If Kopit's Indians are really Vietnamese, Warren's Indians are really Southerners, hounded by Union soldiers, both representing for Warren "the rooted victims of an abstract, implacable destiny."[17] Malamud's version of the Chief Joseph story competes with even as it echoes these sources in Judaizing not only Chief Joseph but his people as well: Chief Joseph tells Yozip that the People (which echoes the Hebrew formulation *Am Israel*, the "people of Israel") are "children of Quodish" (which recalls the Hebrew Kadosh—holy), "descended from the first tribe" (14).

This Indian-Jewish doubling, however, becomes an increasingly strained exercise as the narrative continues, for although the tip of Yozip's nose, a trope of Jewish identity, is accidentally clipped during his initiation ceremony, and his hair, significantly, turns red during his sojourn with the People, he also continually grapples with his difference from his adopted tribe, not least because he has American citizenship papers waiting for him in Chicago. "I am white," he meditates to himself at one point in the narrative:

> but I think like I am red. The old chief told me this when I went in his tribe, that I was an Indian. I said if you think so; then he asked me who I was and I couldn't answer him with the right words. When I told him this he said to me, "I will tell you that you are a red man. Feel your face," and when I felt my face I felt it was a red face. But I said, "I am an Indian who is a Jew." "And I understand that too," he said. And I said to myself, "Why should an Indian give me this particular lesson?" (75)

Jozip is himself doubled: he is Yozip and Jozip, Indian and Jew, red and white. It is not only Jozip's whiteness and Jewishness, however, that keep erupting as a measure of his difference but also his pacifism, which Malamud's notes call the "necessary axis" of the book.[18] "What kind of warrior chief," Jozip asks himself, "was a Jew who lived among Indians with peace raging in his heart?" (75). Jozip's efforts to negotiate rather than fight are coupled with his anxious self-consciousness over what he calls his speech impediment. His Yiddish-accented English prompts the American soldiers, with whom he tries to negotiate peace, to equate "Jew talk" and "Indian talk": "'Sounds like Jew talk to me,' said the colonel in the capacious cape. 'Nobody can trust these goddamn Indians in any way at all'" (46).

Evelyn Avery asks, "Why should this 'shtetl' loner fall in love with Native Americans? Why should this immigrant commit himself to tribal life? Perhaps, suggests Malamud, Indian life appeals to Yozip as a member of the lost tribe of Jewish Americans searching for their identity in the new world, a quintessentially American quest."[19] I would argue in addition that where Malamud's novel *The Tenants* (1971) plumbs the anxieties generated by the Black Power movement of the late 1960s and early 1970s, *The People* marks a covert engagement with American Jewish ambivalence about Zionism, and the moral choices and confusions that necessarily accompany the assumption and defense of territory.[20] Malamud conceived of Jozip's story as the narrative of a fall, marked by Jozip's descent into violence during battle, followed by a recuperation of the self. Malamud's vision for the end of The People, in which Jozip performs a Hasidic dance of the recovered and "annealed" self, is made possible by the People having essentially vanished by the end of the novel. Jozip's final dance, a dance of displacement by a pacifist warrior who is both Jewish and Indian, both native and alien to the land, foregrounds what I read as the covert anxieties with which this embryonic novel grapples: that of Jewish territory, power, and nationhood. The People, that is to say, presages the moment in which post-Holocaust Jewish assertions of kinship with Indians would come to be increasingly challenged, both from within and without.

Dances of Displacement

> The two funniest tribes I've ever been around are Indians and Jews, so I guess that says something about the inherent humor of genocide.
>
> —Sherman Alexie, "What You Pawn I Will Redeem"

> We do not want to make the National Museum of the American Indian into an Indian Holocaust Museum.
>
> —J. Richard West, Director of the NMAI

Sherman Alexie's long poem "Inside Dachau," published only three years after the opening of the monumental United States Holocaust Memorial Museum in Washington, DC, begins to suggest the ways in which Jewish Holocaust memory, especially as performed in the memorial museum, works in charged ways to resolve the fraught historical relationship between Native peoples and museums with the growing centrality of ethnic museums/memorials as identity-making projects in today's public culture.[21] In Alexie's poem, the indigenous poet imaginatively enters Jewish history through an encounter with relics and museum spaces. The poet and his wife are the tourists, visiting another people's death site: "The camp was austere. The museum was simple." But who is whose metaphor? "Once there, I had expected to feel simple/emotions: hate, anger, sorrow. That was my plan. / I would write poetry about how the season/of winter found a perfect home in cold Dachau. / I would be a Jewish man who died in the camp. / I would be the ideal metaphor." The poet's German hosts "are truly ashamed of Dachau." But, they ask, "'what about all the Dachaus/ in the United States? What about the death camps / in your country?' Yes, Mikael and Veronika, you ask simple / questions which are ignored, season after season" (117–18).

Having introduced the "American Holocaust" alongside the Jewish one, a poetics of displacement thus begins to jostle Alexie's poetics of Jewish-Indian identification:

> 4. THE AMERICAN INDIAN HOLOCAUST MUSEUM
> What do we indigenous people want from our country?
> We stand over mass graves. Our collective grief makes us numb.
> We are waiting for the construction of our museum.
>
> We too could stack the shoes of our dead and fill a city to its thirteenth floor.
> What did you expect us to become?
> What do we indigenous people want from our country?
> We are waiting for the construction of our museum.
>
> We are the great-grandchildren of Sand Creek and Wounded Knee.
> We are the veterans of the Indian wars. We are the sons and daughters of
> the walking dead. We have lost everyone.
> What do we indigenous people want from our country?
> We stand over mass graves. Our collective grief makes us numb.
> We are waiting for the construction of our museum. (119–20)

"If I were Jewish," Alexie writes in the poem's sixth section, titled "After we are free," "how would I mourn the dead? / I am Spokane. I wake" (121). Through the call and response of this poem Alexie contrasts his Spokane identity against a hypothetical Jewish one. Being Spokane, the poem asserts, entails ways of mourning, remembering, dancing, singing, loving, feeling, storytelling, sleeping, and homecoming that are distinctly *not* Jewish, which itself remains undefined in the poem. Finally, in the last section of "Inside Dachau," the poet concludes: "I am not a Jew. I was just a guest / in that theater which will never close" (122). In the contemporary moment, Alexie's poems suggest, it has become possible for the Native poet to become "American" by simultaneously invoking and distancing himself from the Jews and their Holocaust.

Read alongside "Inside Dachau," Sherman Alexie's short story "What You Pawn I Will Redeem" thus evokes Jewish-Indian entanglement in complicated and ambivalent ways. Jackson Jackson, Alexie's protagonist, attributes Indian and Jewish humor to their similar "tribal" histories of suffering; he also, with his ironic, self-deprecating, tragicomic voice, recalls Malamud's schlemiel protagonists. But most complexly, it is a pawnbroker, that most stereotypically Jewish of American professions, who is the agent both of Jackson's dispossession and his redemption.

"First you have a home, then you don't," Jackson observes, describing both his own and a collective history.[22] Jackson is a Spokane Indian, and despite the fact that his people have lived within a hundred-mile radius of Seattle for at least ten thousand years, he is homeless in a Seattle peopled almost entirely, in this story, by dispossessed Indians: "Homeless Indians are everywhere in Seattle." Appropriately enough in this Malamudian story, Alexie's pawnbroker, who has Jackson's grandmother's regalia hanging in his shop window, is also vaguely magical: the pawnshop appears and disappears, and its owner grows more youthful over the course of the story. The mysterious pawnbroker, who Jackson says sounds sad, as though "sorry for taking advantage of our disadvantages," launches Alexie's hero on a quest for the money to redeem his family regalia. Over the course of the next twenty-four hours, Jackson wanders, Leopold Bloom–like, through Seattle, makes some money, loses it, makes some more, spends it on his friends. But he succeeds in his quest:

> "Did you work hard for this money?" he asked.
> "Yes," I said.
> He closed his eyes and thought harder about the possibilities. Then he stepped into the back room and returned with my grandmother's regalia.
> "Take it," he said, and held it out to me.
> "I don't have the money."
> "I don't want your money."
> "But I wanted to win it."
> "You did win it. Now take it before I change my mind." (179)

Alexie's story is a fable about the theft and restoration of identities and histories: the presence of Jackson's grandmother's regalia in the pawnshop recalls the very real processes by which Native objects were stolen, bought, sold, and acquired by archaeologists, collectors, curio shops, and museums. Just as Jackson reclaims his patrimony from the magical, crypto-Jewish pawnbroker, so too more prosaically, we might say, did the 1989 congressional legislation establishing a National Museum of the American Indian (NMAI) and the Native American Graves Protection and Repatriation Act (NAGPRA, 1990) make possible a Native American reclamation of objects, of bodies, and of the right to narrate their own histories, from that other most crypto-Jewish of professions, anthropology.

Elaine Heumann Gurian, a museum professional who has worked both with the United States Holocaust Memorial Museum (USHMM) and the NMAI, argues that both represent innovations in what we normally consider to be museums' object-centered function. "As the world's population continues to migrate and intermingle," Gurian argues, "institutions called museums that include more active methods of cultural transfer will be created. Sound, smell, and environmental setting will gain ascendancy as methods of interpretation; and objects will become not the raison d'être, but rather just one element in a complex presentation. In this regard, the multiple exhibition strategies of the United States Holocaust Museum and the preferences of indigenous people coincide."[23]

They may coincide, but they do not always agree. From the moment that planning began on a national Holocaust memorial, Native American and Jewish histories became competitively, intimately, and inversely linked. The USHMM was read immediately by many as having displaced a national memorial to the genocide of Native peoples, who had in fact "fared worse" than the Jews of Europe.[24] The USHMM, a monument to Jews' and other victims' powerlessness and world indifference in the face of the Nazi onslaught, and by some accounts the most visited museum in the United States, has in fact come to be read as the very incarnation of Jewish power as well as Jewish self-interest, even by its own visitors.

In the Darfur exhibit at the USHMM, which I visited in the summer of 2008, visitors fill out questionnaires that ask them to articulate similarities between Darfur and the Holocaust, as well as what "lessons" of the Holocaust can be applied to Darfur. Wrote one visitor: "Jews have lobbiest [*sic*]; Africans don't." Wrote another: "I wish the Jews today would focus their energies into helping others who suffer! Remembering the past isn't useful without helping the future." Michael Bernard-Donals, in his study of the visitors' comment book after September 11, 2001, quotes "Rich H.," who writes: "[what happened to the Jews during the Holocaust] is a dark part of human history. However, it is also sad to see today that the jews [*sic*] are passing their experience to Palestinians by bombing homes and killing innocent people. When are they going to learn to be a human being? Now, Jews use the Holocaust to justify their act to the Palestinians."[25]

Michael Berenbaum, the museum's first director, argued that the USHMM was a national institution and as such would have to tell the story of the Holocaust in a way that moved "beyond the boundaries of ethnic memory" and so would be meaningful to a wider American audience.[26] In what Berenbaum has termed the "Americanization" or the "nativization" of the Holocaust, the museum deliberately links Americans to its story and enshrines "American values" of pluralism, democracy, and concern for human rights in its dramatic presentation of their negation in Nazi Germany.[27] But straining against this broadly redemptive understanding of the USHMM as an American, even universal, memory space are critiques of the USHMM as an ominous expression of Jewish power in the American public sphere, especially regarding U.S. policies toward Israel, as well as a symbol of the U.S. government's refusal to acknowledge its own acts of genocide. "In the pathological dynamic of genocidal histories," writes Lilian Friedberg, "the perpetrator culture invariably turns its gaze to the horrors registered in the archives and accounts of the 'other guys.' This is why Holocaust studies in the United States focus almost exclusively on the atrocity of Auschwitz, not of Wounded Knee or Sand Creek."[28] Such readings easily fold Jews into the "perpetrator culture," both as Euroamericans and as allies of a Jewish state, itself associated with an oppressive occupation of native space.

In 2005 Tiffany Midge, of Hunkpapa Sioux and German ancestry, published a poem in the *Cold Mountain Review* titled "After Viewing the Holocaust Museum's Room of Shoes and a Gallery of Plains' Indian Moccasins, Washington D.C.":

> The portrait is clear;
> one is art
> the other evidence.
> One is artifact
> the other atrocity.
> Each is interned
> behind glass,
> with diagrams
> and panels,
> a testament to miles
> walked. Both
> are worn,
> each a pair,
> one is cobbled
> one is beaded.
> At my tour's end
> can I buy a key-chain shoe?
> Will I be assigned the ID card
> of one of the perished
> at Wounded Knee?
> The moccasins
> are beautiful. Seed pearls
> woven intricate as lace.

We don't mourn
the elegant doe skins,
we admire the handicraft.
We don't ask whose soles
do these relic come from.
We don't look for signs of resistance,
or evidence of blood.
Nor do we wonder
if he was old
and passed in his sleep,
or if this child
traded for a stick of candy
or a pinch of dried meat.
We do not make assumptions.
Their deaths were not curated,
Not part of an installation. We
don't absorb their violent
or harrowing ends under soft
lights or dramatic shadows.
We look right
through them,
more invisible
than the sighs
of ghosts.
And then we move
on to the next
viewing,
and the next,
and the next,
to another
collector's trophy
lying
beneath a
veil of glass.[29]

Midge's poem serves to point out the hidden, unspoken horrors of the Smithsonian's Indian collections now on display in the NMAI, but it does so through a critique of the display strategies of the Holocaust museum, particularly its aestheticization of gristly evidence ("We / don't absorb their violent / or harrowing ends under soft / lights or dramatic shadows") and its effort to make visitors identify with the victims of the Holocaust by distributing identification cards upon entry into the museum. Yet Midge depends in some sense on the Holocaust museum's metonymic strategies—its displays of piles of shoes, forks, eyeglasses, suitcases, and the controversial wall-sized photograph of a mountain of hair—for her own reading of the gallery of moccasins. Like Alexie, Midge restages the Jewish-Indian encounter as a collision of memories and histories crucially mediated by the objects/sacred relics on display in the museum space.

On my last visit to the USHMM, I noticed a card that a young visitor had written in response to *Remember the Children: Daniel's Story,* the museum's traveling exhibit about a fictional Jewish boy who experiences and survives the Holocaust: "I know how you feel, Daniel. My ancestors were murdered also in the *Trail of Tears.*—E.L." I imagined that E.L. was in Washington, DC, to visit the NMAI, to perhaps learn about those Cherokee ancestors, though the NMAI does not itself mention the Trail of Tears. I was intrigued by the possibility that the Holocaust museum offered E.L. a space of memory and mourning absent in the NMAI.[30] E.L.'s note also signals the newest dynamic of Jewish-Indian encounter, wrought in the slippage made possible in these Jewish and Native museums between evidence and art, victims and objects.

Philip Gourevitch, in his critique of the USHMM, writes that "the Holocaust museum installs Jews on the Mall as a people identified by their experience of mass murder. If Jews had not had that experience, Jews would not have this museum. This fact points to the centrality of victimology in contemporary American identity politics."[31] In contrast, the NMAI, located only a few blocks away, has been criticized for its failure to fully address the genocidal policies of the American government.[32] The museum deliberately skirts the potentially competitive and displacing discourse of genocidal histories entirely, instead building a narrative about Native individual and communal identities, self-determination, and living cultures. "Survivance" is a key term, meaning cultural persistence and adaptiveness, that resurfaces throughout the language of the museum. The NMAI not only describes historical struggles over Indian sovereignty; it itself is an assertion of cultural sovereignty. The NMAI, writes Amanda Cobb, "not only symbolically represented the reclamation of Indian land but very specifically and literally *reclaims* that land."[33] Its grounds re-create precontact "Indian Country," featuring a forest environment, wetlands, crops of beans, corn, and squash, stones representing cardinal direction markers, and grandfather rocks. The narrative of the museum is constructed around radical assertions of Indian self-definition and self-determination, sovereignty and nationhood, which implicitly involve critiques of government policy, most crucially in the concluding exhibit, *Our Lives.* "We are ancient nations," one text declares, "seeking recognition and respect from modern nations."

One of the final exhibits of the NMAI-DC departs from the insistence upon autochthony in the rest of the museum, however, by describing the portable nature of "Native space" and Native identity with what seems to be a "Jewish" language of diaspora, identity liberated from territorial sovereignty: "Native space is land—and something more. Native space is a way of feeling, thinking, and acting. Even away from our ancestral lands, we carry our Native space with us. . . . This is survivance."

This overlapping of Jewish and Native languages of portable homelands, migration, and adaptation is articulated even more forcefully in New York's National Museum of the American Indian. New York is home to the largest Jewish and Native urban populations in the United States and also to one of the largest, if not the largest, concentration of immigrants in the nation.[34] The New York campus of the NMAI (the Gustav Heye Center) and the Museum of Jewish Heritage: A Living Memorial to the Holocaust (MJH) share space in one of what Jeffrey Shandler terms "the city's—and the nation's—most visible arenas for the performance of . . . 'a newly popular faith—the cult of heritages.'"[35] "In contrast to the grand spaciousness and measured order of American heritage presentations on the Mall in Washington D.C.," Shandler continues, "lower Manhattan epitomizes New York's intense compression of competing voices, agendas, and histories."[36] What is more, the Museum of Jewish Heritage and the Heye Center were literally in competition for space in lower Manhattan: both were floated as possible tenants of the former Customs House, where the Heye Center is currently housed.[37]

Like Ben Katchor's *The Jew of New York,* the MJH and the Gustav Heye Center both retell the story of New York as alternatively Native or Jewish space. A recent exhibit at the Heye Center, *New Tribe New York* (2005–6), for instance, focused on "New York-based Native artists who are part of a "new tribe": "These and other Native contemporary artists form a new tribe, whose members may or may not formally belong to an Indian tribe. The idea encompasses individuals who are often unconventional and nontraditional, and sometimes controversial. . . . These artists move freely in and among many different kinds of environments—between tradition and contemporaneity, between Native and non-Native peoples, between rural and urban spaces, between the center and the margins of society."[38]

Here, and in the exhibit *Remix* (2008), the museum's curators forward a vision of Native identity that is hybrid, postmodern, urban, fluid, and liminal: "individuals who thrive at crossroads."[39] In *Remix,* the focus is on "artists of mixed heritage," who signify a "new articulation of identity that we've come to call 'post-Indian.'"[40] Just as the recent independent film *The Tribe* imagines contemporary Jewish identity as a "remix," this exhibit declares: "Heirs to a rich history, the artists deftly define their moment by dismantling and rebuilding, like DJs borrowing and writing new sounds, beats, actions, engagements."[41] The reclamation of New York, long associated with Jewishness—just think of Mary Austin's condescension toward those "New Yorkish" critics—as Native space, also involves a reimagining of Native identities that begin to coincide with Jewish ones.

At the same time that the Heye Center adopts a Jewish discourse in its emphasis on hybridity, individuality, portability, and modernity, the Museum of Jewish Heritage recollects the NMAI in its fierce assertion of cultural sovereignty. The first and last artifacts that the visitor sees in the museum's permanent exhibit, two Torah scrolls rescued from the Nazi Holocaust, are defined as significantly "emblematic" of the museum's "message." Once slated for display in the Nazi's Jewish Museum in Prague, the first scroll is now exhibited in a "museum created by a living, flourishing Jewish community."[42]

The Torah scroll is unrolled to "The Song of the Sea," the poem that appears in Exodus after the crossing of the Red Sea praising God for having delivered his people and destroyed their enemies. Through such visual tropes, the museum makes compatible its narratives of Americanization and Zionism; today, the museum concludes, both Israel and the United States "have become the pillars of contemporary Jewish civilization." Exodus, in the context of this museum, means, all at once, deliverance to an ancestral land, deliverance from Nazi efforts at annihilation, and deliverance to a new, American Promised Land, confirmed by the museum's dramatic views of the Statue of Liberty and Ellis Island. This "complex and challenging display of heritage and Holocaust joins a crowded neighborhood of heritage productions," including now the site of the World Trade Center, another powerful *lieu de mémoire* that itself recollects and borrows from Holocaust memorial discourse and aesthetics.[43] As Shandler notes, this Jewish heritage is offered to non-Jews as a "public performance of Jewish pride and a universal moral paradigm of intolerance and its consequences": that is, as both a tribal and "universal" space.[44]

The juxtaposing of both Holocaust memorial museums highlights the freedom with which American Jews can use Holocaust memory to negotiate between sameness and difference, power and marginality, liberalism and tribalism. Likewise, in referring to Holocaust museums as that which they are *not,* I suggest that Native museums, like Sherman Alexie, draw upon even as they insist that they reject Jewish models in their assertions of particularistic cultural identities. Read alongside the rise of museum spaces as contested sites of "heritage and Holocaust," the meditations of Roth, Malamud, Dayksel, Tenenbaum, and Alexie concerning Indian/Jewish disappearance or national renewal, apocalypse or redemption, and the tragedy or victory of a national homeland still feel sharply relevant and resonate in the most recent works by Jewish authors.

Imagined Homelands and the Contest of History

In 1969 it was still possible for Vine Deloria Jr. to use the Jewish example of diaspora, peoplehood, and longing for Zion as an analogy for Native nationalism:

> No movement can sustain itself, no people can continue, no government can function, and no religion can become a reality except it be bound to a land area of its own. The Jews have managed to sustain themselves in the Diaspora for over two thousand years, but in the expectation of their homeland's restoration. So-called power movements are primarily the urge of peoples to find their homeland and channel their psychic energies through their land into social and economic reality. Without land and a homeland no movement can survive.[45]

The "Radical Zionist Manifesto," written by American Jews and published in 1970, echoed such indigenous manifestoes in its language of national liberation and its insistence on territorial sovereignty. It declared:

> We call for the liberation of Jewish people and the restructuring of our people's existence in such a way as to facilitate self-determination and development of our own institutions so as to control our destiny as a nation.
>
> To this end, we see Israel as central to the liberation of the Jewish people. The Jewish state, Israel, is the modern expression of a people's right to national life in its own land. As such, settlement in Israel is the primary option facing each Jew in the diaspora. We see the only other viable option as being the struggle for Jewish self-determination in the countries where Jews live.
>
> We are committed to the creation of a socialist society in Israel. We look toward mutual recognition of the national rights of the Jews and Palestinian Arabs, and the cooperation of all people in the area toward the realization of socialism and human justice.[46]

A Jewish insistence upon sharing an indigenous activist language of liberation, self-determination, and the right to a national, spiritual life has persisted despite, or perhaps because of, Israel's 1967 war, a crisis over which the radical Left eventually broke with Jewish nationalism and many Jews broke with the radical Left. This war is often discussed as the moment during which American Jews, faced with what seemed to be Israel's certain destruction and proud of the Israeli triumph, were finally liberated from the stereotype of the weak diaspora Jew and found new pride in Israel and with their sense of Jewishness. However, as much as this may be true, at least according to the personal testimonies of, for instance, Henry Roth, this moment may more accurately be read as the beginning of a crisis of the American Jewish Left, during which it became increasingly difficult to argue compatibility between Zionism and a radical Left that followed the United Nations in characterizing Zionism as racism, resolving to align itself with Palestinian struggle as legitimate armed resistance by a people of color against an "imperialist" presence.[47]

Assertions of Jewish-Indian kinship still fuel the efforts of, for instance, Gordon Bronitsky, an anthropologist and community activist, one of whose recent projects has been to bring together Israeli and indigenous American poets—Navajos in the Southwest and Mi'kmaq in the Canadian Maritimes—around the concept of the "sanctity of land."[48] At the same time, exchanges have taken place between representatives of Palestinian communities and Native communities, accounts of which display similar claims of kinship over land rights. In 2008, for instance, the American-Arab Anti-Discrimination Committee Washington, DC, Area Chapter commemorated the thirty-second anniversary of Yom al-Ard, or Land Day, by gathering at the National Museum of the American Indian on the National Mall to "learn about the culture and history of the indigenous people who were here before and after the United States was founded." "Land Day is held every year in remembrance of the loss of Palestinian lives and land," writes Jamal Najjab of the commemoration. "What better way to remember than to be in a place which tells the story of how the Native Americans lost the same precious gifts?"[49] Popular Internet discourse demonstrates lively conversations about the analogies between Palestinians and Indians that are, sadly, too often characterized by profound and anti-Semitic misunderstandings of Zionism.

Most famously, Palestinian poet Mahmoud Darwish has evoked American Indians as metaphors for Palestinian experience.[50] For some Jewish Israeli writers as well, like Rachel Tzvia Back and Nava Semel, an imagined kinship between Indians and Palestinians has come to displace that which had been imagined between Indians and Jews. As Semel explains of her novel: "I am an Israeli and a Zionist with every bone in my body, but at the same time, and precisely because of my clear Zionist stance, I allow myself to undermine my foundations and defy them. As an author, I aspire to subvert my sense of self.

The idea behind the book is to examine real Israeli identity against a funhouse image of the identity that could have been."[51]

Semel's novel '*I-yisra'el* (2005) imagines a series of alternative histories around Mordecai Noah's vision for a Jewish nation in the United States. In one section of Semel's novel, for instance, Herzl dies obscure and unknown, and many millions of Jews did not die in Europe, having emigrated to Noah's Jewish state of Ararat.[52] Semel's novel imagines what Jewish-Indian transculturation might look like; Mordechai Noah had intended to include Indians in his in-gathering of exiles, and the culture of Isra-Island has assimilated certain indigenous emblems and ceremonies, if not actual people, thus offering a glimpse, in the unironic words of one reviewer, of "utopian" possibility.[53] This transculturation is inspired by Israeli experience:

> Paradoxically, or perhaps it is poetic justice, it is we Israelis who have been influenced by our Arab neighbors and by our blood-brotherhood with the Palestinians. The Israeli identity was forged in the Mediterranean crucible, both in our temperament and in the fabric of daily life, as in our food and music. In the Israeli experience there is a great measure of "Arabization" that clashes with the tendency of the last two decades toward Americanization.[54]

In playing with a shifting series of identifications between Israelis and Palestinians, Palestinians and Indians, and Indians and Jews, Semel casts her novel as a fable about Israeli history, even as she also sees it as offering an alternative vision of an "identity that could have been": a territorially distinct yet distinctly *American* Jewishness.

Prompted by the interviewer to elaborate on what Israelis "can learn" from this episode of American Jewish history, Semel responds:

> As for Israelis, I hope that they will learn to feel compassion for their neighbors, and understand that we were not the only victims in history! This is the reason that the story of genocide of the Indian nations and the injustice done to them by the appropriation of the land of their forefathers is told in the voice of Little Dove. Without a doubt, I tried to present in her voice an echo of the feelings of the injustice done to the Palestinians, because Zionism tried to ignore them when it arrived in the land of Israel and in its naiveté and in its enthusiasm believed that they would be swept up into our grand project. Little Dove asks Noah to recognize that he did not arrive in an empty land, and directs him to see the ghosts of the island, and their ancient heritage.[55]

Similar connections seem to have inspired poet Rachel Tzvia Back, an American-Israeli originally from Buffalo, New York—the site of Noah's Ararat—who published a collection titled *The Buffalo Poems* in response to the second intifada. Throughout Back's poems, the figure of the vanishing buffalo metonymically links Indians and Palestinians.[56] For Semel and Back, the once "utopian" and now increasingly strained fiction of Jewish-Indian encounter only seems possible through objects or symbols (like the vanishing buffalo) or through alternative, fantasized histories.

Michael Chabon's novel *The Yiddish Policemen's Union* (2007) does not mention Noah by name but imagines an alternative history, as does Semel, where the state of Israel does not exist and a "temporary" refuge for Jews has been established elsewhere: in Semel's novel, Noah's Ararat, and in Chabon's novel, Sitka, Alaska.[57] In Chabon's novel, Israel survived for only a few months before its destruction. As the novel opens in the present day, Sitka is only a few months away from "Reversion," at which moment Alaska will be returned to "Alaskans," and 60 percent or more of Sitka's Jews will be forced out.

Because in Chabon's novel, like Semel's, a temporary haven for Jewish refugees from genocide has resulted in the displacement of the region's original inhabitants, the strained relations between Jews and indigenous peoples that figure so centrally in *The Yiddish Policemen's Union* have been read as gestures to the very real and present conflict in Israel between Jews and Palestinians. Chabon himself, however, attributes the genesis of the novel to his accidental discovery of a 1958 "guide for travelers" called *Say It in Yiddish*, authored by Uriel Weinrich, then a Yiddish linguist at Columbia University, and his wife Beatrice Weinrich, a folklorist. Chabon described his reactions to *Say It in Yiddish*, which was still in print when he bought it in 1993, in a piece he wrote for *Civilization* in 1997. He calls the book "probably the saddest book that I own" and asks: "As for the country in which I'd do well to have a copy of *Say It in Yiddish* in my pocket, naturally I've never been there either. I don't think anyone ever has. . . . At what time in the history of the world was there a place of the kind that the Weinreichs imply, a place where not only the doctors and waiters and trolley conductors spoke Yiddish but also the airline clerks, travel agents, ferry captains and casino employees?"[58]

Shandler, in his discussion of the controversy among Yiddishists that erupted over "Guidebook to a Land of Ghosts," notes that *Say It in Yiddish* was part of a Dover series that included *Say It in Swahili, Say It in Indonesian*, and even *Say It in Hebrew*.[59] Dover's founder and president commissioned the book from the Weinreichs, with the justification that in the 1950s there were still "substantial"

Yiddish-speaking communities in cities like Paris, Montreal, Buenos Aires, and Mexico City, as well as in Israel. But in addition, he regarded the guidebook as a "symbolic gesture of his devotion to a language that he had learned as a child."[60] Shandler reads the guidebook as an exercise in imagining a "homeland for Yiddish," with all its implications of "indigenousness, territoriality, even sovereignty."[61] These and other invocations of an imagined "Yiddishland," Shandler continues, are efforts "endow this language with the symbolic value of a native, sovereign territory."[62]

Chabon himself, in "Guidebook to a Land of Ghosts," begins to imagine the sovereign Yiddish homeland that he would later bring to life in his 2007 novel. Chabon's piece was accompanied by cartoons by Ben Katchor, which depict urbanscapes entirely labeled in Yiddish, conjuring the Yiddishland of *Say It in Yiddish* and Chabon's imagination:

> Call it the State of Yisroel: a postwar Jewish homeland created during a time of moral emergency, located presumably, but not necessarily, in Palestine; it could be in Alaska or on Madagascar. . . . This Yisroel—or maybe it would be called Alyeska—is a kind of Jewish Sweden, social-democratic, resource-rich, prosperous, organizationally and temperamentally more akin to its immediate neighbor Canada, than to its freewheeling benefactor farther south. Perhaps, indeed, there has been some conflict, in the years since independence, between the United States and Alyeska. . . . Perhaps not all of the native peoples were happy with the outcome of Roosevelt's humanitarian policies and the treaty of 1948. (None of the empty places of the world is ever empty enough. If they had sent Jews to Antarctica, the penguins, one feels, would now be setting off bombs.)[63]

Chabon's Sitka, as his final lines in this quote might indicate, is a failed national experiment; its Jews and their language are not at all at home. They are not American citizens, nor can they hope to gain American citizenship. The Jews' bids for separate statehood or for "permanent status" as a federal district, marked by incursions into and violent skirmishes over "Indianer-Lands" (Tlingit territories, though this term, like much of Chabon's "Yiddish," is a Yinglish invention) have failed. Alaska will become "native, sovereign territory," not for Yiddish, but for the Tlingit. As Sarah Philips Casteel writes of the novel, "Chabon's appropriation of the North . . . serves to situate his Alaskan Jews as peripheral to the nation. Instead of their northern experience bolstering the Alaskan Jews' claim to citizenship, it augers the collapse of their dream of territorial belonging."[64] By the end of the novel, Chabon's protagonist Meyer Landsman, in an ironic counterpoint to his own name, rejects any dream of territoriality: "My homeland is in my hat. It's in my ex-wife's tote bag" (368).

Two characters in the novel, Hertz Shemets and his half-Tlingit, half-Jewish son, Berko Shemets, serve as particularly significant sites for Chabon's meditations concerning Native and Jewish collisions. Hertz Shemets is a refugee from Lodz who arrived in Sitka in 1941 with the "first wave" of "Galitzer settlers." He eventually works for the U.S. government, running the region's counterintelligence program. Hertz's study of Tlingit culture and his trips into the "Indianer-Lands" are a cover for his government work informing on Jewish and Native "reds," but at the same time he "was drawn to the Indian way of life" (42). He has a child with a Tlingit woman: "When she was killed during the so-called Synagogue Riots, her half-Jew son, an object of torment and scorn among the Raven Moiety, appealed for rescue to the father he barely knew" (42). If Hertz "goes native," even as, it turns out, he is funneling funds from U.S. government into a clandestine Jewish independence movement, his son Berko "goes Jewish": "Now Ber Shemets, as he came in time to style himself, lives like a Jew, wears a skullcap and four-corner like a Jew. He reasons as a Jew, worships as a Jew, fathers and loves his wife and serves the public as a Jew. He spins theory with his hands, keeps kosher, and sports a penis cut (his father saw to it before abandoning the infant Bear) on the bias. But to look at, he's pure Tlingit" (45).

In Casteel's discussion, Hertz represents "an alternative configuration of Jewish-Tlingit relations, one of contact and mixture rather than separation—but one that is also troublingly exploitative."[65] It turns out that Hertz himself is in fact responsible for instigating the Synagogue Riots that killed Berko's mother. For Berko, on the other hand, "performing Jewishness becomes a path to belonging," even though he experiences a double exclusion.[66] As a mixed-race character, "Berko performs his Jewish and his Tlingit identities, alternating between them as the circumstances demand."[67] This emphasis on the performative aspects of identity, Casteel argues, emerges in response to "historical and material circumstances that severely curtail both the Jews' and the Tlingit's possibilities for belonging."[68] Further, "Chabon's ironization of territorial belonging and controversial attempt to imagine a post-Holocaust world without Israel" coincides with Daniel and Jonathan Boyarin's "diasporic critique of autochnothy." The "lesson of diaspora," the Boyarins argue, is "that peoples and lands are not naturally and organically connected."[69]

The plot uncovered by Landsman—that the evangelical Christian U.S. government is helping fundamentalist Jews blow up the Dome of the Rock and rebuild the Temple in order to seize Palestine for the Jews—anachronistically associates Zionism with Hasidism and with religious extremism. Many readers of the novel have focused on the implicit critique of Zionism embedded within the explicit satire of religious fundamentalism. Ruth Wisse criticizes the novel for what she reads as its anti-Zionist politics: "Chabon's mock-Yiddish reinforces the sentimental stereotype of the Jew as harmless refugee, one who does not threaten the peace of the world, or the peace of the Jews themselves, unless and until he fatally conspires to resettle the land of Israel. A feisty character in the novel is described as fighting like a salmon—'that aquatic Zionist, forever dreaming of its fatal home.' Messages—in this case, beware the Zionists bearing death—hardly come clearer than this."[70] Chabon thus returns, Amelia Glaser writes, "to an age-old debate between Yiddishism and Zionism. In the end, his hypothetical continuation of Yiddish culture is not so much a nostalgic, herring-scented, shtetl utopia as it is a means of voicing a strong political affirmation of diaspora nationalism."[71] D. G. Myers writes critically that in the novel's ideological perspective, "Zionism represents a betrayal of Jewish history and exile is the proper Jewish condition."[72]

If Alaska's Jews are not Americans in Chabon's novel, it is also important to say that America is not America. Chabon imagines an evangelical Christian nation in which, one speculates, even its Jewish citizens ("Mexicans," in the mock-Yiddish parlance of the novel) do not feel at home. Chabon begins "Imaginary Homelands," an essay in which he revisits the controversy over "Guidebook to the Land of Ghosts," with this: "I write from the place I live: in exile."[73] Further, he has said elsewhere that "because Yiddish was the language of exile," and because he does not speak it, "I was exiled from exile itself."[74] Chabon has "confessed," writes Myers, "his own nostalgia for exile."[75] Chabon writes of America in "Imaginary Homelands" that

> strangeness is a universal condition among Americans, if not in fact a prerequisite for citizenship. At any rate it is impossible to live intelligently as a member of a minority group in a nation that was founded every bit as firmly on enslavement and butchery as on ideals of liberty and brotherhood and not feel, at least every once in a while, that you can no more take for granted the continued tolerance of your existence here than you ought take the prosperity or freedom you enjoy. I guess every American Jew has a moment at which he or she feels the bottom drop out. (171)[76]

For Chabon, American Jews feel "at home" in America only at the expense of those who have been dispossessed; Native assertions of territorial belonging and struggles for sovereignty are thus fundamentally incompatible, in the logic of the novel, with those of Jews. Perhaps it is not Chabon's ambivalence about Israel as a Jewish "homeland" that prompted *The Yiddish Policemen's Union* ("I loved it," Chabon writes of his visit to Israel, "but God knows I didn't feel I had come home" [174]) as much as his ambivalence about feeling at home in America, a place he believes he *should* not feel at home. Chabon writes that what led to the writing of *The Yiddish Policemen's Union* was the resolution that "I would build myself a home in my imagination as my wife and I were making a home in the world." Landsman too, at the end of the novel, "has no home, no future, no fate but Bina. The land that he and she were promised was bounded only by the fringes of their wedding canopy" (411). Landsman, like his creator, resists, even as he cannot escape, collective or tribal identities altogether.

Epilogue

In the mid-1990s, a delegation of rabbis visited Arizona for a "spiritual gathering" with Navajos.[1] Photographer Frédéric Brenner's image of this meeting appears in his photography collection titled *Diaspora: Homelands in Exile*. Brenner's photograph was taken from a car window. On the left, a group of Jewish men (with some women) gather by the side of the desert road. They are wrapped in prayer shawls, carrying a Torah. On the right, seen only in the car's rearview mirror, stand the group of Navajos. As writer Tvsi Blanchard comments of the photograph: "The Jews are looking at the Navajos who are looking at the Jews while we, the viewers, are looking at a photo of the Jews and a mirror image of the Navajos" (2:101).[2] According to Jacques Derrida, who joins several others in writing about both the gathering and its image, the event was the idea of a rabbi from Oregon: "Would this idea have occurred to a rabbi from another country?" he asks (2:101).

One participant, Rabbi Yitzhak Husbands-Hankin, writes of the gathering:

> I have long sensed a profound weave of connection between Native Americans and the Jewish people. Ancient Hebrew tribes deemed their land sacred. Driven into exile, we, their descendants, never abandoned the idea of returning home. . . . Unlike the exile that carried us far from home, the suffering that Native Americans bear was brought upon them by travelers from other nations who came into their ancestral home with genocidal force. (2:100)

Husbands-Hankin continues, "We saw each other in the mirror of time, and recognized our bond with one another, with creation, and with the Creator of all humanity" (2:100). Here, in a telling example of the negotiations between tribalism and universalism that characterize Jewish engagement with Indians, Husbands-Hankin invokes "humanity" in the service of his own tribal ethos. And just as the Navajos are only glimpsed as reflections in the photograph, their voices are also absent in the recollection of the event, as other (Jewish) voices debate Jewish-Native likeness or unlikeness and the gathering's utility or inutility.[3] In a similar fashion, I am painfully aware of how yet again, with very few exceptions, indigenous Americans have served throughout these discussions as represented objects, rather than as speaking subjects. Like the gathering in Arizona, I see that in intervening in a history of representation and mediation, this account might have run the risk of reproducing it.

A simultaneous exercise in Jewish-Indian tribal and universal identification, Elaine Heumann Gurian's essay "A Jew among the Indians: How Working Outside of One's Own Culture Works" (1991) began as a paper delivered in New York City at the Jewish Museum Association meeting. Gurian begins by invoking shared Jewish-Indian "tribal" identities, imagining how she might introduce herself at an "Indian pow wow": "My name is Elaine Heumann Gurian. I am a member of the tribe of Israel, and I will speak to you in my native language—Hebrew. In that language, my name is Mara-Tov bat Hanach vie [sic] Hannah, and I will sing to you the prayer of joy at our gathering—the Shehecheyanu." She continues: "My position on staff [of the National Museum of the American Indian (NMAI)] offers me an opportunity to view the forma-tion of an ethnically focused museum from a particular vantage point—that of the insider/outsider. As a person deeply attached to my ethnicity, I feel I can connect to other groups in a sympathetic way. Yet I'm clear that I am not of these people. I am also not a 'wannabe.'"[4] She then moves from a discussion of the NMAI planning process (the museum had not yet been built) into her concerns for Jewish museums. She wonders how to present histories free from "romance," with multiple perspectives and with a sense of how dynamic people, traditions, and cultures really are. She worries about using artifacts in ways that might be deemed offensive. She has concerns about which voices are designated as authoritative and authentic. She worries about alienating or confusing the visitor who is an "outsider" to the culture on display. She worries about overly rigid notions of identity boundaries between insiders and outsiders. She has concerns that "pride and self-esteem" in one's own history can "breed intolerance for others." And finally, she worries: "Are we emphasizing the commonalities among all of us enough?"[5] Like Rabbi Husbands-Hankin, Gurian's meditation on her tribal identity, articulated in terms of Indianness, leads her in fact to an assertion of a liberal universalism: "the commonalities among all of us."

This emphasis on the "commonalities among all of us" is a language that a U.S. context makes uniquely possible. By way of contrast, the Mexico of my grandparents and parents did not easily assimilate Jews and Jewishness into its national culture. In a Latin American context, neither the Sephardi (Iberian) Jews nor the Ashkenazi (western and eastern European) Jews who joined them later were comfortably European or clearly nonwhite. Any mention of Jews is noticeably absent in the hierarchy of race-mixture between African, Indian, and Spaniard through which New Spain consolidated a distinct colonial identity, as well as in the emergence of an independent Mexico, where *mestizaje* was valorized and celebrated as the new national model of identity and culture. The discussions in this book are thus generated by an awareness of two national cultures in which I consider the relationship between Jewishness and Indianness to be at the crux of national identity. I am at once aware of a Mexican national ethos that assimilated indigenousness as it marked Jewishness as both invisible and alien and a U.S. national ethos that, particularly in the second half of the twentieth century, has insisted on precisely the inverse.

I had three grandfathers, and let me say right away that none of them was an Indian (and neither were either of my grandmothers). My father's father was a Jew from Kovel, in Ukraine. He left Ukraine in 1929 as a teenager and joined his two brothers in Mexico City. They spoke only Yiddish when they arrived. They were among the lucky ones: the rest of the family—their mother, brother, sisters, brothers-in-law, nieces and nephews, untold cousins, the rest of the town's Jewish inhabitants, in fact—perished at the hands of the Einsatzgruppen, the shooting squads of Nazis and their local collaborators in the East. In Mexico City, my grandfather married my grandmother, a Jew from Poland whose family all managed to get Mexican visas in the late 1920s, when it had become impossible to enter the United States. One of my family's most heartbreaking possessions is the last postcard my grandfather received from his sister in Kovel in 1939, reporting the birth of a new baby and describing the situation in Ukraine, laconically, as "not good."

My other grandfather, the one I never knew, was from Cuba, and not a Jew. He was an artist, a political cartoonist, who had fled Batista's regime and arrived in Mexico City, where he met my mother's mother, a Polish Jewish immigrant of the Bundist variety, very pretty, and an actress. For a time they moved to Los Angeles, where my grandmother tried to make it in Hollywood (she had been in a couple of Mexican films). But after a few years, my grandmother, with a young son in tow and pregnant with my mother, left her husband and went back to

Mexico City. He would go on to another life: he lived in exile for several more years, went back to Cuba to join Castro's cabinet, and then disillusioned with Castro went into exile again, this time in Puerto Rico; he had another family. But this grandfather is shrouded in mystery. My mother did not know anything about him, nor did she care to; any information I have is from my uncle.

My grandmother, I think, had a taste for bohemians and radicals, intellectuals and artists. Her second husband was from Spain. He was from a wealthy, Catholic, liberal, Republican family in Valencia; they owned a newspaper. Franco and the civil war destroyed them. Their property and money were confiscated; one brother was kidnapped and made to fight in Franco's army. My grandfather, who was in medical school before the civil war, finally fled from Spain with his mother and other brothers (through France, where according to family lore he was imprisoned in a Nazi concentration camp). Like many other refugees from the Spanish civil war, my grandfather and his family eventually arrived in Mexico City, where he met my grandmother, an eccentric divorcée with two small children. He did not like to speak of his family's experiences during the war. He was a newspaperman in Mexico City for six decades, and he also published two books of poetry and two novels. The last novel he wrote was a fictionalized version of Francisco Coronado's quest for Quibiria, the "legendary city of gold," in 1540.[6]

As my grandparents, exiles all, demonstrate, the terrible, violent convulsions in the years leading up to the Second World War produced refugees the world over; Jews certainly do not hold a monopoly on experiences of exile and dispossession in the twentieth century even if they developed some of the most elaborate aesthetic responses to them. It is my grandfather's last novel above all that suggests to me the complex imaginative maneuvers that it is possible for traumatized immigrants to make and that has served, in a sense, as a model for the other narratives I have examined in this study. I read his novel, about the Spanish conquistador whose first name he shared, and his fruitless quest for treasure in Mexico, as a fascinating response to my grandfather's own experience of displacement, loss, and exile. Out of his own history he spun a fable about both conquest and failure. Was this his expression of both his identification with Spain and his hatred of its descent into fascism? Most fascinatingly, it turns out that my grandfather's last name, Fe, was a common one among converted Jews in Inquisition Spain. Such a complicated series of associations and displacements, then, makes it possible for me to call his novel a crypto-Jewish meditation on colonial and countercolonial identities. Into whom, I wonder, did my grandfather write himself? The soldiers, adventurers, and priests Spain had dispatched to the New World? The new Christians and secretly practicing Jews who came with them, desperate to escape the long arm of the Inquisition but also correctly estimating the potential profit of emerging new markets? Or the indigenous peoples whom European contact would change forever?

This is all to say that the arguments of this book did not emerge out of my own fascination, nor identification, with Native America—such urges are, as they should be at this point, deeply suspect to me in any case. I have been struck by certain convergences of critical vocabularies across Native and Jewish studies scholarship: for instance, that of cultural and national autonomy and sovereignty; problems of identity, authenticity, and definition; homeland, diaspora, and transnationalism; linguistic and cultural rupture and creative renewal and revival. However, my purpose was not to argue parallels or similarities or a "special" relationship between Jewish and Native peoples, histories, and identities but rather to lay bare the processes through which such relationships have been and still are imaginatively produced, invoked, and contested.

Notes

Introduction

1. This eighteen-minute 2005 film, which has won awards at multiple film festivals, "weaves together archival footage, graphics, animation, Barbie dioramas, and slam poetry to take audiences on an electric ride through the complex history of both the Barbie doll and the Jewish people—from Biblical times to present day." Throughout, the film plays with this "tribal" discourse to explore the transformations of Jewish identity that took place in modernity. See http://tribethefilm.com.

2. Gerald Vizenor, *The Heirs of Columbus* (Middletown, CT: Wesleyan University Press, 1991), 9 (hereafter cited in text).

3. Arnold Krupat, *The Turn to the Native: Studies in Criticism and Culture* (Lincoln: University of Nebraska Press, 1996), 58 (hereafter cited in text).

4. Vizenor, *Heirs of Columbus,* 71.

5. Alan R. Velie, "The Indian Historical Novel," in *Native American Writers: Modern Critical Views,* ed. Harold Bloom (Philadelphia: Chelsea House, 1998), 204–5.

6. Chadwick Allen, "Blood (and) Memory," *American Literature* 71, no. 1 (1999): 93–94.

7. Ibid., 110, 95.

8. Sigmund Freud, *Moses and Monotheism,* trans. Katherine Jones (1939; repr., New York: Vintage, 1967). Freud writes, for instance, that the "preference which through two thousand years the Jews have given to spiritual endeavour has, of course, had its effect: it has helped to build a dike against brutality and the inclination to

violence which are usually found where athletic development becomes the ideal of the people" (147).

9. Ibid., 127. For this reading of Freud I am indebted to Peter Gay, *A Godless Jew: Freud, Atheism, and the Making of Psychoanalysis* (New Haven: Yale University Press, 1989), and Yosef Hayim Yerushalmi, *Freud's Moses: Judaism Terminable and Interminable* (New Haven: Yale University Press, 1991). I am also grateful to Eliza Slavet for conversations about her work on Freud, Jewishness, and "blood memory."

10. There is indeed much scholarship devoted to Franz Boas, his Jewishness (or rather the source of his liberalism in a German-Jewish embrace of humanist Enlightenment ideals and rejection of "tribalism"), and his complex situation in regards to race. On the one hand, he was at the turn of the century uncritical of and enthusiastically participated in ethnic displays and re-creations, even, infamously, bringing a group of Eskimos to the New York Museum of Natural History to live in full view of visitors; all but two eventually died (see Shari Huhndorf, *Going Native: Indians in the American Cultural Imagination* [Ithaca, NY: Cornell University Press, 2001]). He became, however, highly critical of eugenics and of race theory, arguing in his 1931 address to the American Association for the Advancement of Science, "Race and Progress," that racial intermingling has not been proved to cause any degeneracy, that racial "antipathies" are a product of social conditioning, and finally issuing the following challenge: "No matter how weak the case for racial purity may be, we understand its social appeal in our society. While the biological reasons that are adduced may not be relevant, a stratification of society in social groups that are racial in character will always lead to racial discrimination. As in all other sharp social groupings the individual is not judged as an individual but as a member of his class. We may be reasonably certain that whenever members of different races form a single social group with strong bonds, racial prejudice and racial antagonisms will come to lose their importance. They may even disappear entirely. As long as we insist on a stratification in racial layers, we shall pay the penalty in the form of interracial struggle. Will it be better for us to continue as we have been doing, or shall we try to recognize the conditions that lead to the fundamental antagonisms that trouble us?" (Boas, *Race, Language, and Culture* [New York: Free Press, 1940], 17).

11. Allen, "Blood (and) Memory," 96.

12. Vizenor's trickster aesthetic has itself been read as an indigenous and Euro-inspired hybrid. Here I think of Claude Lévi-Strauss, another Jewish anthropologist, whose well-known analysis of tricksters in Native North American myth as "mediating" figures can perhaps be read more profitably as reflective of his own desires and anxieties vis-à-vis his Jewishness. Lévi-Strauss both does and does not think of Jewishness as a "blood" identity: "I know myself to be Jewish, and the ancientness

of the blood, as they used to say, suits me" (qtd. in Jeffrey D. Feldman, "The Jewish Roots and Routes of Anthropology," *Anthropological Quarterly* 77, no. 1 [2001]: 114). For further discussion of Lévi-Strauss and Jewishness, see Feldman, "Jewish Roots and Routes," 107–25.

13. Penelope Myrtle Kelsey, *Tribal Theory in Native American Literature* (Lincoln: University of Nebraska Press, 2008), 9.

14. Qtd. in Krupat, *Turn to the Native*, 90.

15. Qtd. in ibid., 102.

16. One of the earliest and most well known studies on white representations of Indians is Robert F. Berkhofer Jr., *The White Man's Indian: Images of the American Indian from Columbus to the Present* (New York: Knopf, 1978). Also see Roy Harvey Pearce, *Savagism and Civilization: A Study of the Indian and the American Mind* (Berkeley: University of California Press, 1988); Helen Carr, *Inventing the American Primitive: Politics, Gender, and the Representation of Native American Literary Traditions, 1789–1936* (New York: New York University Press, 1996); Leah Dilworth, *Imagining Indians in the Southwest: Persistent Visions of a Primitive Past* (Washington, DC: Smithsonian Institution Press, 1996); Philip J. Deloria, *Playing Indian* (New Haven: Yale University Press, 1998); Jill Lepore, *The Name of War: King Philip's War and the Origins of American Identity* (New York: Knopf, 1998); Joshua David Bellin, *The Demon of the Continent: Indians and the Shaping of American Literature* (Philadelphia: University of Pennsylvania Press, 2001); and Shari M. Huhndorf, *Going Native: Indians in the American Cultural Imagination* (Ithaca, NY: Cornell University Press, 2001).

17. Count Mole, "Napoleon's Instructions to the Assembly of Jewish Notables (July 29, 1806)," in *The Jew in the Modern World: A Documentary History*, ed. Paul Mendes-Flohr and Jehuda Reinharz, 2nd ed. (Oxford: Oxford University Press, 1995), 125.

18. Wendy Brown, *Regulating Aversion: Tolerance in the Age of Identity and Empire* (Princeton: Princeton University Press, 2006), 53; qtd. in Laura Levitt, "Impossible Assimilations, American Liberalism, and Jewish Difference: Revisiting Jewish Secularism," *American Quarterly* 59, no. 3 (2007): 807.

19. Mendes-Flohr and Reinharz, *Jew in the Modern World,* 115 (italics added). On the other side of the Atlantic, Indians would be extended the rights of American citizenship as individual Christians but not recognized as members of sovereign nations.

20. Yuri Slezkine, *The Jewish Century* (Princeton: Princeton University Press, 2004), 1.

21. Ibid., 2.

22. Wendy Brown cited in Levitt, "Impossible Assimilations," 807.

23. Ibid., 809.

24. Slezkine, *Jewish Century,* 2.

25. Stephen Whitfield, *In Search of American Jewish Culture* (Hanover, NH: Brandeis University Press, 1999), 10.

26. See in particular Werner Sollors, *Beyond Ethnicity: Consent and Descent in American Culture* (Oxford: Oxford University Press, 1987), as well as Sollors, ed., *The Invention of Ethnicity* (Oxford: Oxford University Press, 1989), xv. See also Frank Shuffleton, ed., *A Mixed Race: Ethnicity in Early America* (Oxford: Oxford University Press, 1993).

27. David Biale, "Confessions of an Historian of Jewish Culture," *Jewish Social Studies* 1 (Fall 1994): 43; qtd. in Whitfield, *American Jewish Culture,* 11.

28. See, for example, Michael Rogin, *Blackface, White Noise: Jewish Immigrants in the Hollywood Melting Pot* (Berkeley: University of California Press, 1996); Emily Miller Budick, *Blacks and Jews in Literary Conversation* (Cambridge: Cambridge University Press, 1998); and Jonathan Freedman, *Klezmer America: Jewishness, Ethnicity, Modernity* (New York: Columbia University Press, 2007).

29. This observation is part of the discussion of anthropology's unacknowledged "Jewish problem," in Feldman, "Jewish Roots and Routes," 115.

30. See Julia Reinhard Lupton, "Othello Circumcised: Shakespeare and the Pauline Discourse of Nations," *Representations* 57 (Winter 1997): 73–89. Lupton argues that "the play fashions the Muslim in the image of the Jew" (73).

31. Lupton explains: "Looking from Venice west and far to the south, toward pagan Africa and the New World, Othello would appear darker skinned, barbarian, and perhaps more capable of a full conversion because of his religious innocence. Looking east, toward Arabia and Turkey, and to the northern parts of Africa, Othello would become a Muslim-turned-Christian, probably lighter skinned than his Gentile version, inheritor of a monotheistic civilization already marked by frequent contacts with Christian Europe and hence more likely to go renegade" (ibid., 74).

32. Judith Laikin Elkin, *Imagining Idolatry: Missionaries, Indians, and Jews* (Newport: Touro National Heritage Trust of Newport, 1992), 28. Elkin cites sermons in Spanish and Quechua as well as various compilations of the laws of the Indies in which these slips occur.

33. Several ideas had been in circulation since Columbus that had attempted to link the New World Indians to the European-scriptural world—claiming they were descendants of Adam and Eve, or of Satan, for instance. It was not until the mid-seventeenth century that Indians were connected specifically with the ten lost tribes of Israel. See Richard H. Popkin, "The Rise and Fall of the Jewish Indian Theory," in *Menasseh ben Israel and His World,* ed. Yosef Kaplan, Henry Mechoulan, and Richard H. Popkin (New York: E. J. Brill, 1989), 63–66. Jonathan Sarna locates the beginnings of the ten-tribist theories even earlier, in the 1567 publication of Johanne Fredericus

Lumnius's *De Extremo Dei Judicio et Indorum vocatione* (Sarna, *Jacksonian Jew: The Two Worlds of Mordecai Noah* [New York: Holmes and Meier, 1981], 135).

34. Edward Winslow was certainly convinced, "especially," he writes, "considering the juncture of time wherein God hath opened [the Indians'] hearts to entertain the gospel, being so nigh the very years in which many eminent and learned divines have from Scripture grounds . . . foretold the conversion of the Jews" (Winslow, *The Glorious Progress of the Gospel among the Indians in New England. Manifested by Three Letters under the Hand of the Famous Instrument of the Lord, John Eliot* [London, 1649], 73). See also Popkin, "Rise and Fall."

35. European charges of cannibalism among indigenous peoples, for instance, could be read as another variation of the medieval charge against Jews of cannibalistically baking Christian blood into their Passover matzot. As Stephen Greenblatt observes, Catholic charges of idolatry and cannibalism among Indians mirrored and refracted Catholic practices, including iconography and taking communion. See Greenblatt, *Marvelous Possessions: The Wonder of the New World* (Chicago: University of Chicago Press, 1991), 119–39. Judith Elkin is particularly interested in Catholic charges of idolatry against Indians and Jews; both, as "New Christians," were vulnerable to Church persecution, especially as developing laws of *limpieza de sangre* effectively transformed what had been religious categories into racial, and inherited, ones. She writes: "The conjunction of . . . Christian triumphalism, greed, commercial rivalry, millenarianism, and fear of a foreign enemy, all came together to create a congenial atmosphere for what in later centuries would be called a pogrom" (Elkin, "Imagining Idolatry," 24).

36. Henry Mechoulan and Gerard Nahon demonstrate, however, in their introduction to the reprinted English edition of *The Hope of Israel* (originally translated by Moses Wall, a friend of Milton), that ben Israel, though he acknowledged that a lost tribe may have been found, was reluctant to affirm that all New World Indians were in actuality Jews but said, rather, that Jews were to be found among them. See Menassah ben Israel, *The Hope of Israel: The English Translation by Moses Wall, 1652,* ed. Henry Mechoulan and Gerard Nahon (Oxford: Oxford University Press, 1987).

37. Other well-known English texts in this debate include Thomas Thorowgood's *Jews in America, or, Probabilities That Those Indians Are of That Race,* in which he reproduces the famous first chapter of ben Israel's text (1650), and Hamon L'Estrange's rebuttal, in *Americans no Jewes* (1652).

38. Ben Israel, *Hope of Israel,* 62 (hereafter cited in text; all quotes are from the English version of *Hope of Israel*).

39. Ibid., ix–xi.

40. Ibid., 69. See the discussion of the *relacion* of Montezinos, including information about the historical Montezinos (68–76).

41. Ibid.

42. For another discussion of Montezinos's adventures in Brazil, see Ronald Sanders, *Lost Tribes and Promised Lands: The Origins of American Racism* (Boston: Little, Brown, 1978), 363–65. For the original text, see ben Israel, *Hope of Israel.* The most definitive and extensive treatment of Montezinos's *relacion* as a countercolonial text is in Jonathan Schorsch's *The Christian Atlantic: Judeoconversos, Afroiberians, and Amerindians in the Seventeenth-Century Iberian World* (Boston: Brill, forthcoming).

43. Mechoulan and Nahan address the facticity of Montezinos's account. They note that a descendant of Montezinos, Elisabeth Levi de Montezinos, located documents of the Inquisition that confirm that Montezinos was indeed jailed by the Inquisition in Cartagena from September 3, 1639, to February 19, 1641, that he refused to confess to religious offenses, and that the tribunal released him for "want of evidence showing that he was indeed the individual against whom there were testimonies which would have allowed them to charge him with Judaism" (Ben Israel, *Hope of Israel,* 74).

44. The conflicted literary encounter between Native peoples and Jewish immigrants to Latin America, such as those dramatized most notably in two contemporary Jewish-authored novels, Isaac Goldembarg's *The Fragmented Life of Don Jacobo Lerner* (Peru) and Moacyr Scliar's *The Centaur in the Garden* (Brazil), offer opportunities for poignant reflection on the limits of Jewish assimilation into Latin America.

45. See Irving Howe and Kenneth Libo, eds., *We Lived There Too: Their Own Words, Pioneer Jews, and the Westward Movement of America, 1630–1930* (New York: St. Martin's Press, 1985); as well as M. L. Marks, *Jews among the Indians: Tales of Adventure and Conflict in the Old West* (Chicago: Benison Books, 1992). As Howe and Libo note, many of these Jewish "Indian traders" later, with the creation of the Bureau of Indian Affairs, became Indian agents. Because the history of Jewish merchants in the Americas often begs the question of their involvement in the slave trade, I feel obliged to direct the interested reader to Howe and Libo as well as Jonathan Schorsch, *Jews and Blacks in the Early Modern World* (Cambridge: Cambridge University Press, 2003).

46. See "Far vos der foygl fibi bet shtendik oyf regn: an indianer legende," *Grininke Beymelekh* 2, no. 11 (1928): 21; "Der ershter kurbn fun a kleynem indianer," *Grininke Beymelekh* 7, nos. 19–20 (1933): 129–30; "Di indianer fun tsofn-Amerike," *Grininke Beymelekh* 7, nos. 17–18 (1933): 127–28; "Di indianer in di tropishe gebitn fun drom-Amerike," *Grininke Beymelekh* 8, no. 1 (1934): 131; "Kinder un shney," *Grininke Beymelekh* 11, no. 18 (1937): 208.

47. "Ethnographic" or descriptive articles included Heinrikh Deligdish, "Di Indianer in Meksike," *Tshernovitser bleter* 4, no. 124 (1932): 2–3, and no. 125 (1932): 2; and Avraham Taytlboym, "Tseremoniale tents bay di amerikaner indianer," *Literarishe bleter* 35 (August 28, 1936): 554–55, and 36 (September 4, 1936): 572–73.

More politically slanted articles—that is, protesting the ill treatment of American Indians—included A. Almi, "Tsvishn indianer," *Der moment* 10, no. 253 (1919): 5–6; Helene Khatzkels, "Di far).aynikte shtotn fun tsofn-amerike: dos lebn fun di negers un indianer," *Der khaver* 2, no. 4 (14) (1931): 161–70, and 5 (15) (1931): 231–41; and Khayim Shoshkes, "Bay di oys-shtarbene indianer: ayndrukn fun a rayze iber kanade in 1937," *Haynt* 30, no. 195 (1937): 6. Creative pieces included Yakov Glants, "Meksikaner Motivn," *Vakhnshrift far literature, kunst un kultur* 4, no. 17 (166) (1934): 6–7; and Shia Tenenboym, "Der letster indianer," *Literarishe bleter* 14, no. 34 (1937): 544–45. All translations from these sources are my own.

48. A. Almi, "Tsvishn indianer," 5 (hereafter cited in text).

49. The mythical lost tribes of Israel were often thought to be in Asia and were referred to as "red Jews" beginning in the Middle Ages. This coincidence of language certainly facilitated the identification of Jews with Indians.

50. For other iterations of this argument, see Walter Benn Michaels, *Our America: Nativism, Modernism, and Pluralism* (Durham: Duke University Press, 1995), and Alan Trachtenberg, *Shades of Hiawatha: Staging Indians, Making Americans, 1880–1930* (New York: Hill and Wang, 2004).

51. I am also indebted to an emerging chorus of scholars focusing on Jewish representations of Indians, Stephen Katz and Michael Weingrad, in particular. Both have forthcoming books on Hebrew literature and Native Americans (see Stephen Katz, *Red, Black, and Jew: New Frontiers in Hebrew Literature* [Austin: University of Texas Press, 2009]).

52. Michael Rogin, *Blackface, White Noise: Jewish Immigrants in the Hollywood Melting Pot* (Berkeley: University of California Press, 1996), 68. Also see Rogin's discussion of redface and *Whoopee!* (150–56).

53. Ted Merwin, *In Their Own Image: New York Jews and Jazz Age Popular Culture* (New Brunswick, NJ: Rutgers University Press, 2006), 6.

54. Karen Brodkin, *How Jews Became White Folks and What That Says about Race in America* (New Brunswick, NJ: Rutgers University Press, 1998).

55. Josh Kun, "Bagels, Bongos, and Yiddishe Mambos, or, the Other History of Jews in America," *Shofar: An Interdisciplinary Journal of Jewish Studies* 23, no. 4 (2005): 50–68. In this discussion of Jewish-Latin interchange in the 1940s through the 1960s, Kun argues that "Jews were drawn to Latin music neither to demonstrate their whiteness, nor to pretend to be Latin, but rather to find new ways of being Jewish" (50).

56. David Biale, "The Melting Pot and Beyond: Jews and the Politics of American Identity," in *Insider/Outsider: American Jews and Multiculturalism*, ed. David Biale, Michael Galchinsky, and Susannah Heschel (Berkeley: University of California Press, 1998), 27.

57. As Philip J. Deloria has written in another context, "For many Indian people, integration into the rights and equalities of American citizenship has as often looked more like assimilation *to* a repressive social order than a brand of liberation in which an American political structure built around citizenship offers refuge from institutionalized social and cultural oppression" (Deloria, "American Indians, American Studies, and the ASA," *American Quarterly* 55, no. 4 [2003]: 672).

58. Vizenor is an exception. Another writer worth mentioning is David Treuer, who is Ojibwe and Jewish. His forthcoming novel, *Neverland,* promises to feature an aging Jewish American novelist and his affair with a young Native girl. In an earlier novel, *The Hiawatha,* one of his characters has an affair with Vera, the daughter of Polish-Jewish refugees. Here, it is the Jewish immigrant who helps her Ojibwe lover feel more "American": "He is in love with her strangeness. The Polish and Yiddish words so different, so unbelievably thick and consonant. When she talks about her parents, or life at home, he feels thin, his language smooth and plain. With her he feels strangely American" (Treuer, *The Hiawatha* [New York: Picador, 1999], 236). Native American literatures, broadly and generally speaking, do not, with a few key exceptions, explicitly concern themselves with Jews, but tend to look inward, driven by the more urgent project of indigenous recovery and cultural autonomy.

59. Jonathan Boyarin, "Europe's Indian, America's Jew: Modiano and Vizenor," in *Storm from Paradise: The Politics of Jewish Memory* (Minneapolis: University of Minnesota Press, 1992), reprinted with permission in *Boundary 2* 19, no. 3 (1992): 197–211. Boyarin's longer work, titled *The Unconverted Self: Jews, Indians, and the Identity of Christian Europe,* is forthcoming. See Ward Churchill, *Indians Are Us?* (Monroe, ME: Common Courage Press, 1994), and Churchill, *A Little Matter of Genocide: Holocaust and Denial in the Americas, 1492 to the Present* (San Francisco: City Lights Books, 1997).

60. I borrow Michael Hughey's definition of tribalism as a "group-based" challenge to the "individualistic focus" of Western liberalism. See Hughey, *New Tribalisms: The Resurgence of Race and Ethnicity* (New York: New York University Press, 1998), 1.

Chapter 1

1. Ben Katchor, *The Jew of New York: A Historical Romance* (New York: Pantheon Books, 1998), 49 (hereafter cited in text).

2. Jennifer Glaser, "An Imaginary Ararat: Jewish Bodies and Jewish Homelands in Ben Katchor's *The Jew of New York*," *MELUS* 32, no. 3 (2007): 165–66.

3. As Michael Weingrad notes in a discussion of Mordecai Manuel Noah's afterlife

in English, Hebrew, and Yiddish literature, "It would seem that, so long as the meaning of the Jewish state, of America and its promise for the Jews, and of Jewish identity itself are in question, Noah will from time to time break out of his frame, rediscovered and reimagined for new times and contexts by new writers" (Weingrad, "Messiah, American Style: Mordecai Manuel Noah and the American Refuge," *AJS Review* 31, no. 1 [2007]: 75–108). Among the many texts discussed by Weingrad, one that in particular must be mentioned in the context of this study is a 1928 play by Harry Sackler about Noah's Ararat, performed first in Yiddish in 1929 under the title *Major Noah* and translated by the author into Hebrew with the new title, borrowed from Shmuel Niger's review, *Messiah—American Style* (90). Weingrad writes that Sackler "links Noah's proto-Zionism with an American combination of initiative, bluff, will, and dynamism. . . . [The] United States—rather than nineteenth-century nationalism—is the true model for the idea of a Jewish State" (91). The state as a refuge for American Indians as well as Jews is crucial in the play, as it was in Noah's vision. In the dedicatory ceremony for Ararat as represented in Sackler's play, Noah gathers together a Jew ("symbol of the people of Israel"), an Indian ("symbol of freedom"), and a Christian ("symbol and model of what Christianity strives to be") in a "holy covenant," which takes place under a Jewish prayer shawl and is officiated by the Reverend Addison Searle of the Episcopal Church of Buffalo (92).

4. Glaser, "Imaginary Ararat," 167.

5. Israel Zangwill, "Noah's Ark," in *Ghetto Tragedies* (Philadelphia: Jewish Publication Society, 1899), 79–123 (hereafter cited in text). The story is discussed at length in Weingrad, "Messiah, American Style," 86–87.

6. Qtd. in ibid., 87. Weingrad writes, "Zangwill's anguished consideration of the possible demise of the Jewish people links the Jews with the figure of the Indian, an oft-repeated comparison in American Hebrew literature. . . . Appropriately, then, Peloni dies according to the classic fashion of romantic image of the doomed Indian, throwing himself over the Falls" (87).

7. James Fenimore Cooper, *The Last of the Mohicans* (1826; repr., New York: Penguin Books, 1986), 350.

8. Henry Wadsworth Longfellow, "The Jewish Cemetery at Newport," in *The Heath Anthology of American Literature*, vol. B, *Early Nineteenth Century*, ed. Paul Lauter, 5th ed. (Boston: Houghton Mifflin, 2008), 2901–2.

9. See Arthur Hertzberg, *The Jews in America: Four Centuries of an Uneasy Encounter* (New York: Columbia University Press, 1997), 50–77.

10. Herman Melville, *Pierre, or the Ambiguities* (1852; repr., New York: Penguin Books, 1996), 6 (hereafter cited in text).

11. Qtd. in Hertzberg, *Jews in America*, 92–93.

12. Richard Moody, ed., *Dramas from the American Theatre, 1762–1909* (Cleveland: World Publishing, 1966), 124.

13. John Higham defines nativism as "intense opposition to an internal minority on the grounds of its foreign (i.e., 'un-American') connections," opposition that, though it can vary widely in intensity and target, expresses in all cases "the connecting, energizing force of modern nationalism" (Higham, *Strangers in the Land: Patterns of American Nativism, 1860–1925* (1955; repr., New Brunswick, NJ: Rutgers University Press, 1988), 4.

14. "Zion Near Buffalo: The Career of Mordecai M. Noah," *The American Hebrew,* December 25, 1908, 204.

15. It is significant for Weingrad, and for many of the authors he discusses, that Noah by the end of his life argued for Jewish migration to Palestine. Noah's Zionism thus anticipates and preempts Theodor Herzl, who also moved between advocating a Jewish homeland in Palestine and a Jewish territory in Uganda, and also dramatizes the ambivalent place of America as a temporary stopping point for Hebrew authors. Like Noah, Herzl was a playwright who mined the theatrical possibilities of politics. Weingrad suggests that referencing Noah and Ararat are frequently opportunities for authors to meditate upon Herzl and Israel.

16. See Noah's account of the dedication ceremonies in the *Buffalo Patriot-Extra,* September 17, 1825; as well as the *New York National Advocate,* September 1, 1825; the *New York Herald,* October 27, 1842; and the *New York American,* September 21, 1825.

17. For works on Noah, see Isaac Goldberg, *Major Noah: American-Jewish Pioneer* (Philadelphia: Jewish Publication Society of America, 1936); Jonathan Sarna, *Jacksonian Jew: The Two Worlds of Mordecai Noah* (New York: Holmes and Meier, 1981); Abraham J. Karp, *Mordecai Manuel Noah, the First American Jew* (New York: Yeshiva University Museum, 1987); and *The Selected Writings of Mordecai Noah,* ed. Michael Schuldiner and Daniel J. Kleinfeld (Westport, CT: Greenwood Press, 1999).

18. Noah, *Selected Writings,* 77–104.

19. Ibid., 91–92. Also see J. Hector St. John de Crèvecoeur, *Letters from an American Farmer* (New York: Penguin Books, 1986).

20. Edward Watts, *Writing and Postcolonialism in the Early Republic* (Charlottesville: University of Virginia Press, 1998), 20.

21. The play was celebrated as a work of "American authorship, and dealing with American subject matter" (Moody, *Dramas,* 121).

22. Noah, *Selected Writings,* 13.

23. Moody, *Dramas,* 122.

24. Noah was operating in a context: playwrights of the early republic such as William Dunlap, Royall Tyler, and James Barker (author of *The Indian Princess* in 1808,

the first staging of the Pocahontas myth and the first American play to feature Native characters) saw drama as a nation-building project. Craig Kleinman writes, however, that "once viewed from a Jewish dialogical angle, the play can also be read as potentially subversive, in part because of its mass popularity, and because it is a performance which not only plays off but carnivalizes the multiple b/orders that limit those deemed Other, such as Noah, an outspoken Jewish writer" (Kleinman, "Pigging the Nation, Staging the Jew," *American Transcendental Quarterly* 10, no. 3 [1996]: 201–2).

25. See Winifred Morgan, *An American Icon: Brother Jonathan and American Identity* (Newark: University of Delaware Press, 1988). Morgan writes: "As a popular media construct, the Brother Jonathan figure supposedly represented the ordinary American. But since Jonathan was constructed by people who did not consider themselves 'ordinary,' the figure may tell us more about the producers of and myths about the ordinary American than about the ordinary American himself" (preface, n.p.).

26. The text of *She Would Be a Soldier* is reprinted in Noah, *Selected Writings*, 25–64 (hereafter cited in text). As Michael Schuldiner points out, Noah did not miss the opportunity to allude to certain partisan battles he himself was involved in. During the War of 1812, Massachusetts and Connecticut, dominated by Federalist, anti-Madison politicians, had refused to commit their state militias, citing constitutional privilege. At the battle of Queenstown, New York State militiamen had refused to fight, again claiming constitutional privilege. Noah, a loyal Democratic-Republican, purposefully used the stock stage Yankee—whose innocent punning in other plays often served as a sly, subversive, and thoroughly democratic force—to lambaste his political enemies and question their, and Jerry Mayflower's, patriotism (in Noah, *Selected Writings*, 22).

27. Morgan, *American Icon*, 46–47.

28. Moody, *Dramas*, 121.

29. Kleinman, "Pigging the Nation," 206.

30. This paradoxical reading of the American Indian as quintessential patriot is not unique to Noah, even if Noah offers a radical expression of it. Consider Washington Irving's contemporaneous *Sketch Book* essays that deal with the American Indian: in "Traits of the Indian Character" Irving compares Native American resistance to white colonization to the brave Roman senators when the Gauls destroyed Rome; in "Philip of Pokanoket," Irving "rehabilitates" King Philip in nationalistic terms as a "patriot attached to his native soil." See Sally L. Jones, "Edwin Forrest and Mythic Re-creations of the Native," in *Dressing in Feathers: The Construction of the Indian in American Popular Culture*, ed. S. Elizabeth Bird (Boulder, CO: Westview Press, 1996). Also consider Catherine Maria Sedgewick's *Hope Leslie* (1827) in which the Pequod Magawisca makes a powerful and persuasive case for her liberty, echoing the language of the Declaration of Independence.

31. Kleinman argues that the play's many border crossings—cross-dressing, masquerade, spying, acting—highlight the "fragility of identity in the national regime," and thereby suggest an "openness to resignification and recontextualization" in what it meant to be a Jew in early-nineteenth-century America (Kleinman, "Pigging the Nation," 215). The peace signaled in the play's abrupt ending is in Kleinman's argument not a celebratory affirmation of American nationalism but a "carnivalization of the national moment" (214). This moment of carnival, however, in Kleinman's discussion, still presumes an element of consensus, as the "happiness and laughter of the stage characters, many of whom are country folk, are designed to leak into the audience's response" (214).

32. "A Memoir of the Theatre," in Noah, *Selected Writings*, 65.

33. Jonathan Sarna writes: "In short, all over the western world, reformers came to view colonies—especially, but not exclusively, American frontier colonies—as the best solution to the problems posed by minority, deviant, and oppressed groups. Rather than attempting to create an equitable pluralistic state, they proposed to create insulated communities where each individual group could flourish on its own" (Sarna, *Jacksonian Jew*, 62).

34. Mordecai Manuel Noah, *Discourse on the Evidences of the American Indians Being the Descendents of the Ten Lost Tribes of Israel* (New York: James Van Norden, 1837) (hereafter cited in text).

35. Sarna, *Jacksonian Jew*, 61.

36. *The American Hebrew*, December 25, 1908, 205.

37. Sarna, *Jacksonian Jew*, 62.

38. Noah did not forget to mark New York State's important role in this narrative; in his proclamation he states: "The asylum referred to is in the state of New York, the greatest state in the American confederacy . . . one hundred and fifty thousand militia, armed and equipped, a constitution founded upon an equality of rights; having no test oaths, and recognizing no religious distinction, and seven thousand free schools and colleges affording the blessings of education to Four Hundred Thousand children. Such is the great and increasing State to which the emigration of the Jews is directed" (Noah, *Selected Writings*, 108).

39. Sarna, *Jacksonian Jew*, 73.

40. Noah, *Selected Writings*, 107.

41. Sarna, *Jacksonian Jew*, 74.

42. "Ararat Proclamation and Speech," in Noah, *Selected Writings*, 114.

43. Priscilla Wald writes: "Alternative Declarations that borrowed the language and sought to capture the spirit of Thomas Jefferson's document were plentiful in the first half of the nineteenth century, representing, for example, workingmen and trade unionists, antimonopolists and industrialists, nonrenters and nonproducers, and,

perhaps the most widely remembered, advocates of the rights of women" (Wald, *Constituting Americans: Cultural Anxiety and Narrative Form* [Durham: Duke University Press, 1995], 48).

44. Quotes are from the *New York Evening Star for the Country,* April 7, 1835, 2:1, and the *New York Evening Star,* October 1, 1835.

45. James Gordon Bennett in the *New York Herald,* September 16, 1842, 2:1; qtd. in Sarna, *Jacksonian Jew,* 107.

46. William Apess, *A Son of the Forest and Other Writings,* ed. Barry O'Connell (Amherst: University of Massachusetts Press, 1997), 10. Also see Sandra Gustafson on the similarities in rhetoric between Ralph Waldo Emerson, Apess, Joseph Smith, and Noah, in "Nations of Israelites: Prophecy and Cultural Autonomy in the Writings of William Apess," *Religion and Literature* 26, no. 1 (1994): "Foregrounding the priority of American Indians on the continent, and bringing natives within the common discourse of Hebrew identity derived from the Puritans, Noah, Smith, and Apess redefined that discourse to legitimize cultural autonomy for a variety of non-Puritan ethnic or ethnically modeled traditions within America" (35–36).

47. William Apess, "An Indian's Looking Glass for the White Man," in *Heath Anthology of American Literature,* vol. B, 1463–64.

48. Bertram Wallace Korn, introduction to *Incidents of Travel and Adventure in the Far West,* by Solomon Nunes de Carvalho (Philadelphia: Jewish Publication Society, 1954), 23–27.

49. Carvalho's daguerreotypes became the property of Fremont, who had several artists make engravings from the plates. These engravings later appeared in Fremont's *Memoirs of My Life, 1813–90*—for example, an engraving of a Cheyenne woman and another of the view of the Huerfano Butte. Paintings such as James Hamilton's *Buffaloes Escaping from a Prairie Fire* were probably worked from Carvalho's plates, since Carvalho describes making these pictures in his narrative. The plates themselves, however, have disappeared (Joan Sturhahn, "Solomon N. Carvalho's Lost Daguerreotypes," in *Solomon Nunes de Carvalho: Painter, Photographer, and Prophet in Nineteenth-Century America* [Baltimore: Jewish Historical Society of Maryland, 1989]. An exhibition catalog).

50. From the Brady-Handy Collection, now in the Library of Congress. See Sturhahn, "Carvalho's Lost Daguerreotypes," 39. Both Sturhahn and Korn speculate that Carvalho's plates were mixed up with Brady's collection (Brady had developed many of the plates in his studio) and still "repose, unmarked and unknown, among the thousands of Brady items in the National Archives in Washington, where someday a researcher may experience the joy of discovery" (Korn, intro. to *Incidents of Travel,* 40).

51. *Incidents of Travel* was originally published by Derby and Jackson in 1856. All

quotes are from the latest reprint edition: Solomon Nunes de Carvalho, *Incidents of Travel and Adventure in the Far West* (Lincoln: University of Nebraska Press, 2004) (hereafter cited in text).

52. For details of Carvalho's involvement in Jewish religious and cultural life before and after the expedition, see Korn, intro. to *Incidents of Travel*, 28–33.

53. Egloffstien was also apparently Jewish, though that fact is never mentioned by Carvalho (see M. L. Marks, *Jews among the Indians: Tales of Adventure and Conflict in the Old West* [Chicago: Benison Books, 1992], 127–51). Carvalho writes that stopping to make pictures on the trail, he found himself "frequently with my friend Egloffstien, who generally remained with me to make barometrical observations" (81), and Carvalho and Egloffstien were the members of the party who were forced to leave the expedition at Salt Lake City because of ill health.

54. Later Carvalho notes, when describing the preparation of a fallen horse, that although the Indians would save the blood of the animal in the camp kettle, he "never partook" of the blood. He does not say explicitly that blood is proscribed by Jewish dietary law (189).

55. Korn, intro. to *Incidents of Travel*, 34. At the first meeting of the society on July 2, 1854, the following motion was passed: "Resolved, unanimously, That the thanks of this meeting be tendered to Mr. S. N. Carvalho for his valuable services in organizing this Society, and that he be elected an honorary member; also, that these proceedings be published in the Occident" (35).

56. Richard Slotkin, *Gunfighter Nation: The Myth of the Frontier in Twentieth-Century America* (New York: Atheneum, 1992), 61.

57. See ibid., 63ff.

58. Arthur Kopit and John Lahr, "*Indians*: A Dialogue," in Kopit, *Indians* (New York: Bantam, 1971), 49.

59. Glenda Riley, "'Buffalo Bill' Cody and Annie Oakley: Romancing the West," in *Western Lives: A Biographical History of the American West,* ed. Richard W. Etulain (Albuquerque: University of New Mexico Press, 2004), 265.

60. For a broad introduction to the history of Yiddish theater, see Nahma Sandrow, *Vagabond Stars: A World History of Yiddish Theatre* (Syracuse: Syracuse University Press, 1995).

61. See Mark Slobin, "From Vilna to Vaudeville: Minikes and 'Among the Indians' (1895)," in "Jewish Theater," special issue, *The Drama Review: TDR* 24, no. 3 (1980): 17–26 (hereafter cited in text). I am indebted to Slobin's translation of the playlet as well as his brief introduction.

62. Indeed, Brooks's own "Jewish Western with a black hero," *Blazing Saddles*, ends when the characters, embroiled in a huge brawl, break through the fake building fronts of the set and spill over into the movie lot. The film as fiction is revealed. I

borrow Sanford Pinsker's description of its most famous scene: "As a wagonload of Blacks move across the prairie, a group of Indians (headed by Mel Brooks, in redface) investigate the intruders. When Brooks realizes who they are, he looks befuddled, then aghast . . . then shouts his way into celluloid immortality: '*Schvartzers?*' It is a page out of Leslie Fiedler's *Love and Death in the American Novel*: black and white interchange; and, at bottom, all men—even Indians—are secretly Jews" (Pinsker, "Mel Brooks and the Cinema of Exhaustion," in *From Hester Street to Hollywood: The Jewish American Stage and Screen*, ed. Sarah Blacher Cohen [Bloomington: University of Indiana Press, 1983], 249–50).

63. See Don Russell, *The Lives and Legends of Buffalo Bill* (Norman: University of Oklahoma Press, 1960), 305–6.

64. "I'm a Yiddish Cowboy (Tough Guy Levi)," Tin Pan Alley lyric by Edgar Leslie, Al Piantadosi, and Halsey K. Mohr (1907). The sheet music is in the Harris Collection at Brown University, and the lyrics are reprinted in Harley Erdman, *Staging the Jew: The Performance of an American Ethnicity, 1860–1920* (New Brunswick, NJ: Rutgers University Press, 1997), 169.

65. Ibid., 141.

66. "Big Chief Dynamite," words by Jeff T. Branen, music by Al Piantadosi (Chicago: Al Piantadosi, 1909). The song was featured by Harry Koler in *Girls from Happyland Co.* Also see "Big Chief Mose," words by Jack Freedman, music by Ed Dangel, published by Evans, Dangel Music Publishing, Boston. The chorus reads, in part: "Big Chief Mose, Big Chief Mose / An Indian chief with a Yiddish nose / Like a real "Red Man" he paints his face / and wears his blanket trimmed with lace / But he's a dandy just the same / He even went and changed his name / It used to be as long as his nose / But now it's just plain Big Chief Mose" (undated).

67. J. Fuchs, "Nahum Blanberg, Indian Chief," *American Hebrew*, May 28, 1909, 82 (hereafter cited in text).

68. Philip Cowen, "Nahum Blanberg, Indian Chief," *American Hebrew*, June 11, 1909, 143 (hereafter cited in text).

69. Also see Marks, *Jews among the Indians*, as well as Gordon Bronitsky's many publications on Jews of the Southwest and on Solomon Bibo. Gordon Bronitsky, "Solomon Bibo: Jew and Indian at Acoma Pueblo," *New Mexico Magazine* (August 1990).

70. J. Fuchs, "Nahum Blanberg: How a Jew Became an Indian Chief" *American Israelite*, July 28, 1910, 1.

71. "Vi azoy a yid iz govern a hoyptman fun vilde indianer," *Undzer Lebn* 4, no. 213 (25) (1910): 2–3 (hereafter cited in text). All translations from this narrative are my own.

72. Michael Rogin writes: "The Indian/Jewish confusion proleptically ridicules Hollywood for eliminating Jewish characters from movies—for Sam Goldwyn explaining, 'A Jew

can't play a Jew. It wouldn't look right on screen'—such that the only Jews in from of the camera at Harry Cohn's Columbia Pictures were said to be playing Indians" (Rogin, *Blackface, White Noise: Jewish Immigrants in the Hollywood Melting Pot* [Berkeley: University of California Press, 1996], 154).

73. For a discussion of *Whoopee!* see ibid., 150–56. Rogin includes a photograph of Paul Whiteman's orchestra in Indian costume. Peter Antelyes delivered a paper titled "Jewish Indians and the Columbia Complex" at the Next Turn in American Literary Studies, Harvard University, May 14, 2002, in which he drew upon Rogin's arguments in his more extended analysis of Jewish redface, most particularly of a Fanny Brice performance in which she sang "I'm an Indian" dressed as a squaw. For a discussion of both *Whoopee!* and *Girl Crazy,* see Andrea Most, "'Big Chief Izzie Horowitz': Theatricality and Jewish Identity in the Wild West," *American Jewish History* 87, no. 4 (1999): 313–41; as well as Most, *Making Americans: Jews and the Broadway Musical* (Cambridge: Harvard University Press, 2004). For a sweeping and very critical account of the representation of Indians in popular musical entertainments throughout the twentieth century, including both *Whoopee!* and *Girl Crazy* (among many other musicals, many of which were written by Jews though did not feature Jewish characters), see Jace Weaver (Cherokee), "Ethnic Cleansing, Homestyle," *Wicazo Sa Review* 10, no. 1 (1994): 27–39. For a discussion of "Hebrew comedy" and sheet music covers from the Lester S. Levy Collection at Johns Hopkins University, see "Yonkle Doodle Dandy," introduction by Jody Rosen, in *Guilt and Pleasure* No. 2. Also worth mentioning are Mickey Katz's Yiddishized versions of cowboy ballads as in "Shleppin' My Baby Back Home," "Yiddish Mule Train," "Borshtriders in the Sky," and "Haim Afn Range." In the Katz version of "I'm an Old Cowhand," Katz sings about "Apatchke Indians." But as Josh Kun points out, "It is significant, I think, that this is Katz's only Yiddishization of Native Americans . . . when Katz went West he always went as a cowboy-dialogizing the symbol of Anglo-American masculinity instead of identifying with its victims" (Kun, "The Yiddish Are Coming: Mickey Katz, Anti-Semitism, and the Sound of Jewish Difference," *American Jewish History* 87, no. 4 [1999]: 370).

74. Rogin, *Blackface, White Noise,* 150.

75. Ibid., 151.

76. Most, "Izzie Horowitz," 319.

77. Ibid., 325.

78. Ibid., 319.

79. Rogin, *Blackface, White Noise,* 151.

80. Most, "Izzie Horowitz," 321.

81. Ibid., 331.

82. Ibid., 332. Jace Weaver's take on this scene is rather different. He reads this moment

as a sinister recasting of the lost tribes myth: "it . . . bespoke of an in-built prejudice that no people could attain any degree of civilization, even language, unless they came from the same stock as Europeans. By having Gieber speak to Natives in Yiddish, this ancient bit of racism is re-cast" (Weaver, "Ethnic Cleansing," 31).

83. Most, "Izzie Horowitz," 339.

84. Ibid., 340.

85. Rogin, *Blackface, White Noise,* 150–51.

86. Ibid., 154.

87. My thanks to Jonathan Freedman for introducing me to this film. See http://aparchive. com, Universal Newsreels, 1949: Part 13, Story no. X02324, December 12, 1949.

Chapter 2

1. Michael North argues, alternatively, that "the story . . . of becoming modern by acting black was to be retold over and over in the next decade" (North, *The Dialect of Modernism: Race, Language, and Twentieth-Century Literature* [Oxford: Oxford University Press, 1994], 8). He also writes: "That the modern covets the primitive—perhaps even created it—is another frequently acknowledged fact" (preface, n.p.). See also Marianna Torgovnick, *Gone Primitive: Savage Intellects, Modern Lives* (Chicago: University of Chicago Press, 1990), for an account of primitivist modernism, though Native Americans are not discussed.

2. Mary Antin, *The Promised Land* (1912; repr., New York: Penguin, 1997), 3 (hereafter cited in text).

3. Barbara Kirshenblatt-Gimblett quotes a paper delivered at the 1893 Chicago World's Fair, titled "Mission Work among the Unenlightened Jews," which characterized immigrants in London and New York as "half-dressed, pale-skinned natives in our own towns" and remarked that "Borrioboola Gha has been supplanted by 'Whitechapel,' 'Mulberry Bend,' and the nearest district tenements" (Kirshenblatt-Gimblett, *Destination Culture: Tourism, Museums, and Heritage* [Berkeley: University of California Press, 1998], 52). A review of Abraham Cahan's novel *The Rise of David Levinsky* (1917) calls the novel a critique of Jewish immigrant society, which the reviewer describes as "pushing" and "primitive" ("Americans in the Making," *The New Republic,* February 2, 1918, 32).

4. Susan Hegeman, *Patterns for America: Modernism and the Concept of Culture* (Princeton: Princeton University Press, 1999), 8.

5. Oliver La Farge, ed., *Introduction to American Indian Art* (Glorieta, NM: Rio Grande Press, 1985), 15. Originally published New York: Exposition of Indian Tribal Arts, 1931.

6. Here I agree with Hegeman, who writes: "My claim is exceptionalist to the extent that I believe that modernism did take on specific forms in the United States between 1900 and 1950, brought about by, among other things, thoroughly ideological views about the existence, and nature, of a uniquely American 'culture'" (Hegeman, *Patterns for America*, 20). For other writers who either assert or assume the unique nature of American modernism, see C. Barry Chabot, *Writers for the Nation: American Literary Modernism* (Tuscaloosa: University of Alabama Press, 1997); North, *Dialect of Modernism;* and Rita Barnard, *The Great Depression and the Culture of Abundance* (Cambridge: Cambridge University Press, 1995); as well as Werner Sollors's arguments concerning "ethnic modernism" in chapter 8 of *Beyond Ethnicity: Consent and Descent in American Culture* (Oxford: Oxford University Press, 1986). For an example of the opposite point of view, see Hugh Kenner, who writes that "the movement was by tacit definition international" (Kenner, *A Homemade World: The American Modernist Writers* [New York: Knopf, 1975], xii).

7. For studies that give a sense of the contentious, polyphonic culture of the eighteenth-century United States, see Christopher Looby, *Voicing America: Language, Literary Form, and the Origins of the United States* (Chicago: University of Chicago Press, 1996); Larzer Ziff, *Writing in the New Nation: Prose, Print, and Politics in the Early United States* (New Haven: Yale University Press, 1991); Michael Warner, *The Letters of the Republic: Publication and the Public Sphere in Eighteenth-Century America* (Cambridge: Harvard University Press, 1990); and Edward Watts, *Writing and Postcolonialism in the Early Republic* (Charlottesville: University of Virginia Press, 1998).

8. Alan Trachtenberg, *Shades of Hiawatha: Staging Indians, Making Americans, 1880–1930* (New York: Hill and Wang, 2004), xxii.

9. See Walter Benn Michaels, *Our America: Nativism, Modernism, and Pluralism* (Durham: Duke University Press, 1995), 32, 44–45.

10. Ibid., 106.

11. Philip Rahv, *Image and Idea: Fourteen Essays on Literary Themes* (New York: New Directions, 1949), 1.

12. Ibid., 5.

13. Ibid. Rahv's discomfort with the "redskins" may be accounted for by the fact that he wrote this essay at a moment in which he had distanced himself from Marxism, replacing it, in the late 1930s, with a "quasi-Trotskyism." Alan Wald reads this essay as emerging from Rahv's, and the New York Intellectuals' emergent ideology in the late 1930s and 1940s that critiqued Marxism in favor of "a new variant of middle-class individualism." See Alan Wald, *The New York Intellectuals: The Rise and Decline of the Anti-Stalinist Left from the 1930s to the 1980s* (Chapel Hill: University of North Carolina Press, 1987), 230.

14. Khaym Zhitlovski, "Vegn dem vert fun iberzetsungen," in *The Song of Hiawatha*, by Henry Wadsworth Longfellow, translated into Yiddish by Yehoash (New York: Yehoash Publication Society, 1910), xxii–xxiv.

15. I am indebted to Alan Trachtenberg for pointing out Leyb's poem to me, as well as for his remarks concerning Yehoash's translation of Longfellow, delivered at Yiddish on the American Scene, UCLA, October 2000. See also his article based on that paper, "'*Babe in the Yiddish Woods*': Dos Lied fun Hiavat'a" (*Judaism* 50, no. 3 [2001]: 331–40), and his *Shades of Hiawatha*, which features a chapter on the "Yiddish Hiawatha." Trachtenberg in fact suggests the ways in which Yehoash's translation also functions both as a critique of Longfellow and a reassertion of the poem's Jewish origins. Longfellow's final passage about the misguided Jews is excised in the Yiddish version. And further: "The familiar story," writes Trachtenberg, "is that Longfellow adapted the eight-syllable unrhymed trochaic meter from a German translation of the so-called national epic of Finland, the *Kalevala*, a nineteenth-century concoction like *Hiawatha* itself, one of many invented traditions feeding insurgent nationalisms of the times. He may also have encountered the unrhymed trochaic tetrameter measure in Heine's *Romanzero* (1851), especially in the famous 'Prinzessin Sabbat' in the section of 'Hebräischen Melodien.' Was it in fact a Jewish poem that asserts itself in the 'measure' Longfellow noted in his diary in 1854 that he had 'hit upon' as the 'right and only one' for his 'Indian Edda'?" (Trachtenberg, "Yiddish *Hiawatha*," *Judaism* 50, no. 3 [2001]), 337.

16. For discussions of Yiddish literature in America that communicate this richness and variety, see Irving Howe, *World of Our Fathers* (New York: Harcourt Brace Jovanovitch, 1976); Judd Teller, *Strangers and Natives: The Evolution of the American Jew from 1921 to the Present* (New York: Delacorte Press, 1968); and Ruth R. Wisse, *A Little Love in Big Manhattan* (Cambridge: Harvard University Press, 1988).

17. See, for instance, Janet Hadda, "Di hashpoe fun amerike af der yidisher literature," *Yivo-Bleter* 44 (1973): 250–51; Teller, *Strangers and Natives*; and Wisse, *A Little Love*. For more on the generations of Yiddish poetry in the United States, including the "sweatshop" poets and the radical modernist group In Zikh as well as the Yunge, see Howe, *World of Our Fathers*, and Benjamin Harshav and Barbara Harshav, eds., *American Yiddish Poetry: A Bilingual Anthology* (Berkeley: University of California Press), 1986.

18. In this respect, the Yiddish engagement with American Indians diverged from that of Hebrew poets. The Hebrew *Hiawatha* was a major influence on at least one Hebrew Indian epic. Benjamin Silkiner published his epic Hebrew poem *Mul ohel T'murah* (Before Timorah's Tent) in 1910, the same year that Yehoash's translation of *Hiawatha* appeared. Two other Hebrew Indian epics, by Ephraim Lissitsky and Israel Efros, soon followed: Lissitsky's poem, *Medurot Doakhot* (Fading Flames),

inspired by *Hiawatha,* was published in 1937 (he later published another volume of poetry about blacks in America, titled *In the Tents of the Ethiopians*). Efros published his two book-length poems, *Vigvamim Shotkim* (Silent Wigwams) and *Zahav* (Gold, about the California gold rush), in 1933 and 1942, respectively. But, as Michael Weingrad argues, these poems represented in many ways a "personal and ideological alienation from America," and moreover, demonstrated the ways in which these poets were "not only uncomfortable with modernity, they were also uncomfortable with modernism," (Weingrad, "Lost Tribes: The Indian in American Hebrew Poetry," *Prooftexts* 24, no. 3 [2004]: 294). Weingrad's discussion is an excellent overview of the figure of the Indian in American Hebrew poetry. See also Stephen Katz's *Red, Black, and Jew: New Frontiers in Hebrew Literature* (Austin: University of Texas Press, 2009) for a discussion of representations of Native and African Americans in Hebrew literature. Also see Ruth Arazi, "The American Indian in American Hebrew Poetry" (PhD diss., Hebrew text, New York University, 1987), and *Hebrew in America: Perspectives and Prospects,* ed. Alan Mintz (Detroit: Wayne State University Press, 1993).

19. For a thorough account, see Ellen Williams, *Harriet Monroe and the Poetry Renaissance: The First Ten Years of* Poetry, *1912–22* (Urbana: University of Illinois Press, 1977). Also see *The Letters of Ezra Pound, 1907–41,* ed. D. D. Paige (New York: Harcourt, Brace, 1950).

20. Pound sent six of Tagore's poems to *Poetry,* where they were published in 1912. Tagore became one of *Poetry*'s great triumphs, as he was awarded the Nobel Prize the following year.

21. I am indebted here to Helen Carr's excellent discussion of *Poetry* magazine in *Inventing the American Primitive: Politics, Gender, and the Representation of Native American Literary Traditions, 1789–1936* (New York: New York University Press, 1996), 222–26. For her complete discussion of anthropological and literary modernism's turn to the Native American, see 197–256.

22. Ezra Pound, "A Pact," *Poetry* 2 (April–September 1913): 12.

23. Alice Corbin Henderson, "A Perfect Return," *Poetry* 1 (October 1912–March 1913): 87–91.

24. Margaret Anderson, *My Thirty Years War: An Autobiography by Margaret Anderson* (New York: Covici, Friede, 1930), 36.

25. Williams, *Harriet Monroe,* 77.

26. Ibid., 78 (italics added).

27. See Williams, *Harriet Monroe,* for a fuller explication of Pound's break with *Poetry,* which effectively occurred in 1917 but did not become explicit until two years later (205).

28. Pound, *Letters,* 157.

29. Williams, *Harriet Monroe*, 228–29.

30. Alice Corbin Henderson, "Too Far from Paris," *Poetry* 4 (June 1914): 109–11.

31. Harriet Monroe, "Editorial Comment," *Poetry* 9 (February 1917): 251.

32. Translated in Harshav and Harshav, *American Yiddish Poetry*, 797. The Inzikhistn as a movement are thoroughly documented in this collection.

33. Bodenheim, however, began increasingly to argue with Monroe, writing to her in 1916, "You were among the first to print the 'new poetry' in this country, but it would have eventually have gathered impetus, even if you had not noticed it. . . . You have done little for the less popular 'new poets' beyond printing their excellent poetry now and then. Your favors have been reserved for those 'new poets' whose work has won at least budding popularity" (reprinted in Williams, *Harriet Monroe*, 196).

34. Florence Kiper Frank, "The Jew as Jewish Artist," *Poetry* 22 (July 1923): 209–11.

35. See Leonard Prager, "Walt Whitman in Yiddish," *Walt Whitman Review* 1, no. 3 (1983): 22–35.

36. As Ruth Wisse writes, "The handsome volumes of *Shriftn*, filled with stories and poems about America and carrying the portraits and poems of Walt Whitman as if he were its patron saint, impressed Jewish literary circles in Europe. It was now clear that, in addition to their commercially successful theater and press, the American immigrant community had generated a literary movement that was free of the shtetl, the insularity that had characterized Yiddish literature in its early phase" (Wisse, *A Little Love*, 56). I am extremely indebted in this discussion to Wisse's work on the Yunge, in *A Little Love* and in her articles "Di Yunge: Immigrants or Exiles?" *Prooftexts* 1 (1981): 43–61, and "Di Yunge and the Problem of Jewish Aestheticism," *Jewish Social Studies* 38 (Summer–Fall 1976): 265–76.

37. Editorial (unsigned), *Di yugend* 2 (January 1908): 1–2; translated in part by Wisse in "Di Yunge: Immigrants or Exiles?" 44.

38. See Wisse, *A Little Love*, 246n17.

39. Reuben Eisland, "Di Yunge," *Shriftn* 1 (1912): 3.

40. David Ignatov Archives, YIVO Institute for Jewish Research, New York, New York.

41. Wisse, *A Little Love*, 13–14. Wisse does note, however, that "everyone who wrote about the period produced a slightly different roster of its members" (247n28).

42. Eisland, "Di Yunge," 20.

43. Andre Lefevere, *Translation, Rewriting, and the Manipulation of Literary Fame* (London: New Routledge, 1992), 50.

44. Tejaswini Niranjana, *Siting Translation: History, Poststructuralism, and the Colonial Context* (Berkeley: University of California Press, 1992), 3.

45. Lawrence Venuti, *Scandals of Translation: Towards an Ethics of Difference* (London: Routledge, 1998), 76 (hereafter cited in text).

46. Qtd. in ibid., 76.

47. Walt Whitman, *Leaves of Grass,* ed. Sculley Bradley and Harold W. Blodgett (New York: Norton, 1973), 137n.

48. Ibid.

49. Ibid., 336–37.

50. See George Cronyn, ed., *Path on the Rainbow* (New York: Boni and Liveright, 1918), ix.

51. Mary Austin, introduction to ibid., xvi (hereafter cited in text).

52. Mary Austin, *The American Rhythm* (New York: Harcourt Brace, 1923), 42. The role of the American environment is of premier importance in Austin's analysis of innate rhythm: "A primitive state of mind is, as nearly as I can make out, a state of acute, happy awareness. Streams of impressions of perennial freshness flow across the threshold of sense, distinct, unconfused, delicately registering, unselected" (28). Austin praises Amy Lowell, Carl Sandburg, Vachel Lindsay, and Edgar Lee Masters (all of whom immigrant Jewish writers were keenly aware of) for "exhibiting a disposition to derive their impulses from the gestures and experiences enforced by the American environment [and in this way display] . . . an extraordinary, unpremeditated likeness . . . to our own aboriginals" (45–46).

53. Ibid., 19.

54. Ibid., 31.

55. Mary Austin, "New York: Dictator of American Criticism," *The Nation* 111 (1920); reprinted in *The Selected Essays of Mary Austin,* ed. Reuben Ellis (Carbondale: Southern Illinois University Press, 1996), 57–58. Helen Carr writes: "Mary Austin was a contradictory figure: in some ways she was extraordinarily open for her day to the possibilities of value not just in Native-American art but in their thought; in other respects she was quite racist, deeply anti-semitic, and suspicious of Black Americans and their culture" (Carr, *Inventing,* 221).

56. Austin, *American Rhythm,* 38.

57. Karen S. Langlois, "Marketing the American Indian: Mary Austin and the Business of Writing," in *A Living of Words: American Women in Print Culture,* ed. Susan Albertine (Knoxville: University of Tennessee Press, 1995), 151–68.

58. Mary Austin, *American Rhythm,* 37–41; qtd. in ibid., 161, italics added.

59. Louis Untermeyer, review of *Path on the Rainbow,* ed. George Cronyn, *The Dial,* March 8, 1919, 240.

60. Mary Austin, letter to the editor, *The Dial,* May 31, 1919, 570. For a discussion of the reception of *Path on the Rainbow* and *The American Rhythm,* see Michael Castro, *Interpreting the Indian: Twentieth-Century Poets and the Native American* (Albuquerque: University of New Mexico Press, 1983), 42–45.

61. Alice Corbin Henderson, review of *Path on the Rainbow,* ed. George Cronyn, *Poetry* 14 (April 1919): 45–46.

62. Harriet Monroe, "Comment: The Southern Number," *Poetry* 20 (April 1922): 31.
63. Kling mayn loyb-lid shtarker, brayter!
     Ikh bin groys, nito kin tsveyter.
     Ikh geveltik iber lender,
     Iber felker, iber rasn.
     Mayn geshtalt ven ikh farender
     Fleytsn far mir mentshn masn,
     Mentshn shtromen vi di taykhn
     Mayns a shmeykhl tsu erblikn—
     Ver vet vagn mikh oysveykhn?!
     Shoyfros blozn, glokn klingn
     Ven ikh gey di velt batsvingn . . .
     Mentshn, geter, knekht un har
     Faln koyrim far dem nar . . .

     Sound, my song of praise, stronger, wider!
     I am great, there is no other.
     I rule over lands,
     people, races.
     Multitudes flood toward me
     When I change my shape
     People stream like rivers
     Towards me, to glimpse a smile—
     Who will dare avoid me
     When I take over the world?!
     Shofars blow, bells sound
     When I overwhelm the world . . .
     People, gods, slave and lord
     Grovel before the fool . . . (All translations in this section are mine.)
64. H. Leyvik, "Di Yunge," *Shriftn* 4 (1919): 33.
65. Ikh lig in hamak
     Durkh tsvaygn shaynt heys arayn di zun
     Ikh farmakh mayne oygn
     Un zeh a bloye khinezishe shrift
     Af a goldenem blat.
     Likhtig bloye khinezishe oysyes
     Finkln aruf un arop,
     Vi kleyne fantastishe fenster,
     Af a vant fun goldenem turem

Ikh farshtey nit di shrift
Nor epes fardrikt mayn hartz,
Ikh dermon zikh:
"Ikh lib dikh, ikh lib dikh,"
Azoy lez ikh di bloye
Khinezishe shrift. (Tselia Dropkin, "The Hammock," *Shriftn* 5 [Fall 1919]: 18)

66. For a consideration of Jewish themes in Max Weber's work, including a full translation of "Hannukah Lights," see Matthew Baigell, "Max Weber's Jewish Paintings," *American Jewish History* 88, no. 3 (2000): 341–60.

67. Mayn gayst shpilt,
Mayn neshome zingt,
Mayn hartz bentsht,
Varem zi kumt,
Zi kumt,
Zi kumt tsu mir. (19)

68. Yidelekh, briderlekh, kha-kha-kha!
Tantsn mir, shpringn mir, kha-kha-kha!
Heybn mir hentelekh, va-va-va!
Pleskn tsu, pleskn tsu, pa-pa-pa!
Briderlekh, yidelekh, kha-kha-kha!
Nokhamol. nokhamol, kha-kha-kha! (9)

69. Cronyn, *Path on the Rainbow,* 129.

70. Harriet Monroe, "Editorial Comment," *Poetry* 9 (February 1917): 251.

71. In an interesting reversal of the trajectory described in this chapter, the Egyptian poetry translated by Shtiker included some of the same verse that Pound would translate thirty-five years later in his *Love Poems of Ancient Egypt* (1961).

72. From Ignatov's *Opgerisene bleter,* excerpted in *Yiddish Literature in America, 1870–2000,* vol. 1, ed. Emanuel S. Goldsmith (New York: Congress for Jewish Culture, 1999), 335, my translation.

73. *Der Hammer: komunistisher khoydesh-zhurnal* 3, no. 7 (1928): 1–2.

74. Ibid., 57. The original Yiddish reads: "Mit zayne lider geyt der indianer afn 'stezshkele funem regnboygn' tsum land fun 'oyfgang-yingl.'" I read this last phrase as a somewhat comical mistranslation: rising sun/son.

Chapter 3

1. For more on Whitman and Native Americans, see Ed Folsom, *Walt Whitman's Native Representations* (Cambridge: Cambridge University Press, 1994), 55–98.

2. See Jamil Khader, "Transnationalizing Aztlan: Rudolfo Anaya's *Heart of Aztlan* and U.S. Proletarian Literature," *MELUS* 27, no. 1 (2002): 84. Khader compares Anaya's novel with Olsen's, reading both in the context of 1970s and radical politics of that moment, namely, the Chicano and feminist movements.

3. See Alan Wald, *Writing from the Left: New Essays on Radical Culture and Politics* (London: Verso, 1994), for suggestions on neglected texts from the Left that foreground representations of the Native American struggle. Some examples Wald lists are Robert Gessner, *Broken Arrow* (1933); Robert Cantwell, *The Land of Plenty* (1934); and Howard Fast, *The Last Frontier* (1944). Wald also notes, "there is a significant use of Native American Indian cultures in the radical modernist poetry of Norman McLeod and Thomas McGrath." He also urges recognition of the achievements of the nearly forgotten John Sanford (80).

4. Wald, for instance, lists the following: Maxwell Bodenheim, *Ninth Avenue* (1925); Laura Caspary, *The White Girl* (1929); Guy Endore, *Babouk* (1934); Len Zinburg, *Walk Hard, Talk Loud* (1940); Benjamin Appel, *The Dark Stain* (1943); Howard Fast, *Freedom Road* (1944); David Alman, *The Hourglass* (1947); Earl Conrad, *Rock Bottom* (1954); and Earl Conrad, *Gulf Stream North* (1954). See Wald's introduction to *The People from Heaven*, by John Sanford (1943; repr., Urbana: University of Illinois Press, 1995), xxxiv. Radical Yiddish poets composed many more poems concerning antiblack racism than anti-Native racism. See the translated poems in *Proletpen: America's Rebel Yiddish Poets,* ed. Amelia Glaser and David Weintraub (Madison: University of Wisconsin Press, 2005).

5. Harold Cruse, for instance, argues that "all attempts by Jewish-American Communists to write about African Americans are, in fact, expressions of Jewish chauvinism" (qtd. in Wald, intro. to *People from Heaven*, xxxiii). See Cruse, *Crisis of the Negro Intellectual* (New York: William Morrow, 1967).

6. Michael Gold, *Jews without Money* (New York: Horace Liveright, 1930), 180 (hereafter cited in text).

7. Qtd. in Rita Barnard, *The Great Depression and the Culture of Abundance: Kenneth Fearing, Nathanael West, and Mass Culture in the 1930s* (Cambridge: Cambridge University Press, 1995), 158. Olsen's parents were socialist Russian Jews who left Russia after the failure of the 1905 revolution, in which they were participants. They settled on a farm near Omaha, Nebraska, and eventually relocated to Omaha, where Olsen's father, Samuel Lerner, worked both as a peddler and in a confectionary. Samuel and Ida Lerner were founding members of the first Omaha Workmen's Circle (a Yiddishist socialist organization) and were active in Omaha socialist party activities. Olsen broke with her parents' socialist politics when she became a member of the Young Communist League in the early 1930s. She was briefly jailed in 1932 for distributing leaflets to packinghouse workers in Kansas City. In 1933, while she

was pregnant and in Minnesota, she began drafting sections of *Yonnondio,* which survived only in drafts and fragments until she returned to the work in the 1970s. She and her husband continued their activities in the Communist Party for many years (see Linda Ray Pratt's introduction to *Yonnondio: From the Thirties,* by Tillie Olsen [Lincoln: University of Nebraska Press, 2004]).

8. Michael Gold, "A Report from the Dakotas," *Daily Worker,* September 2, 1933; reprinted in *Mike Gold: A Literary Anthology,* ed. Michael Folsom (New York: International Publishers, 1972), 215. Folsom explains: "One of the ways Gold invented to meet his daily assignment as a columnist was to furbish up in the form of prose-poetry letters which rank-and-file party workers sent in to the *Daily Worker* describing their activities" (215).

9. Indeed, I follow many scholars on the literatures of the Left in thinking this a somewhat false boundary. The literary cultures of the 1920s and 1930s should be read as continuous with one another, rather than as distinct "stages." Some of the most exemplary texts of the 1930s, such as *Jews without Money,* can be more accurately read as emerging out of a 1920s literary and political aesthetic. Pieces of *Jews without Money,* published in book form in 1930, had been published in radical journals throughout the 1920s.

10. I am particularly indebted to Rita Barnard's discussion of West's *A Cool Million,* of which she writes, "*A Cool Million,* which critics usually dismiss as a tasteless and inaccurate satire on the rise of American fascism, can then . . . be read profitably as a satire on the commodification of American culture" (Barnard, *Great Depression,* 149). Barnard dedicates a good portion of her Nathanael West section in *The Great Depression and the Culture of Abundance* to *A Cool Million,* writing that critical interpretation of his work has tended to cast it "as a battle between art and the cheap clichés and disorders of mass culture, a battle from which art emerges victorious. . . . This kind of interpretation has necessitated the exclusion or slighting of certain interesting aspects of West's work, such as the irredeemably (and deliberately) trashy satire *A Cool Million* and the overtly revolutionary poem 'Burn the Cities'—both of which critics have generally preferred to see as aberrations" (11). Other scholars who have considered *A Cool Million* with a similar degree of seriousness are Jonathan Veitch in *American Superrealism: Nathanael West and the Politics of Representation in the 1930s* (Madison: University of Wisconsin Press, 1997); Susan Hegeman, who in *Patterns for America: Modernism and the Concept of Culture* (Princeton: Princeton University Press, 1999) offers a sustained reading of *A Cool Million,* Jewish Indians, and mass culture; and, as early as 1971, T. R. Steiner in "West's Lemuel and the American Dream," *Southern Review* 4, vol. 7 (1971), reprinted in Harold Bloom, ed., *Nathanael West: Modern Critical Views* (New York: Chelsea House, 1986).

11. For discussions of West as a Jewish writer, see Bloom, *Nathanael West*, and Ben Siegel, ed., *Nathanael West: Critical Essays* (New York: G. K. Hall, 1994), 32.

12. Nathanael West, *Novels and Other Writings*, ed. Sacvan Bercovitch (New York: Library of America, 1997), 793. West was so involved in this dilemma that he also wrote to F. Scott Fitzgerald, repeating verbatim: "Somehow or other I seem to have slipped in between all the 'schools'" (791).

13. Qtd. in Jay Martin, *Nathanael West: The Art of His Life* (New York: Farrar, Straus, and Giroux, 1970), 80. John Sanford, in his five-volume autobiography, recounts the following conversation with West during the summer they spent together in Warrensburg, New York, writing their novels:

> On the way later, you [Sanford] said, "I'm afraid some of your best friends are Christians."
> "What's that supposed to mean?"
> "You don't care much for the Jews."
> "I'm a Jew myself!"
> "That's what the guide says in *Balso*."
> "He was speaking as a character, not as the author." (Sanford, *Scenes from the Life of an American Jew*, 5 vols. [Santa Rosa: Black Sparrow Press, 1986], 2:119)

14. Waldo Frank, *Our America* (New York: Boni and Liveright, 1919), 79 (hereafter cited in text).

15. In a later chapter, "New York," Frank discusses Alfred Stieglitz and other New York Jews whom he sees as taking up "the ancient destiny where the degenerate Jew whom we have observed had let it fall. He is the prophet. And his ways are near to the old ways of his people.... Stieglitz is primarily the Jewish mystic.... A true Jew" (186). Other Jewish moderns whose spirituality Frank praises include James Oppenheim, Paul Rosenfeld, and Leo Ornstein, of whose music Frank says, "Since there is no good American music save that that of the Indians and Negroes, his music is as American as any" (187). Later, Frank would become increasingly attracted to African American life and culture, using eroticized black female figures in his short fiction, enlisting his friend Jean Toomer to take him on a Southern tour (where they both "passed" as black Northerners), and writing the novel *Holiday*, about interracial desire and lynching. He and Toomer wrangled in their correspondence over the essentiality of race. Daniel Itzkovitz suggests that Frank's alternating "fetishization" of Toomer's African American ancestry and his own anxious fantasy, during his visit to the south, that he was "with" the "Negro," indeed, "was a Negro," was a reflection of his own "racial panic." Itzkovitz writes, "his was clearly an identity under siege" (Itzkovitz, "Passing Like Me," *South Atlantic Quarterly* 98, nos. 1–2 [1999]: 35–36). Mary

Austin did not share Frank's romantic views on black life (in fact, quite the opposite), but she writes of Indians: "A primitive state of mind is, as nearly as I can make out, a state of acute, happy awareness. Streams of impressions of perennial freshness flow across the threshold of sense, distinct, unconfused, delicately registering, unselected" (Austin, *The American Rhythm* [New York: Harcourt Brace, 1923], 28).

16. Oliver La Farge, ed., *Introduction to American Indian Art* (1931; repr., Glorieta, NM: Rio Grande Press, 1985), 15.

17. Walter Benn Michaels reads Willa Cather's 1925 novel *The Professor's House* in similar terms, in the opposition the novel sets up between Tom Outland, a "descendant" of a lost Indian tribe who is engaged to the Professor's daughter, and the Jew Louie Marsellus, who marries her after Tom's death: "The point, then, of identifying as a Jew the 'stranger' who wants to marry into your family is to identify as American the family he wants to marry into" (Michaels, *Our America: Nativism, Modernism and Pluralism* [Durham: Duke University Press, 1995], 8).

18. Hegeman, *Patterns for America*, 107.

19. Mabel Dodge Luhan, *Movers and Shakers* (New York: Harcourt, Brace, 1936), 534; cited in ibid., 108.

20. Waldo Frank, *Memoirs,* ed. Alan Trachtenberg (Amherst: University of Massachusetts Press, 1973), 99, italics in the original; cited in Hegeman, *Patterns for America*, 105.

21. Barbara Kirshenblatt-Gimblett, *Destination Culture: Tourism, Museums, and Heritage* (Berkeley: University of California Press, 1998), 20–21.

22. James S. Wamsley, *American Ingenuity: Henry Ford Museum and Greenfield Village* (New York: Harry N. Abrams, 1985), 19–23.

23. Susan Hegeman writes that although the United States was more modernized as a whole than was Europe, America did not experience its modernity "in a uniquely uniform fashion. Indeed, it could well be that the very things that made the United States more advanced compared to other nations also heightened the experience of difference *among* Americans in different regions, where modernization was differently experienced" (Hegeman, *Patterns for America*, 22).

24. Wamsley, *American Ingenuity,* 27.

25. Ford's tribute to Edison often verged into the fetishistic. Max F. Schultz writes that "in Greenfield Village, Henry Ford's monument to Americana, there is an ash heap meticulously encased and labeled as having come from behind Thomas Edison's Menlo Park laboratory. Gazing at this dump pile, one can never be quite sure of the degree of fetish worship and, contrariwise, of sly humor that it represents" (Shultz, "Nathanael West's Desperate Detachment," in Bloom, *Nathanael West,* 83).

26. *A Guide Book for Williamsburg, Virginia* (An Official Publication of Colonial Williamsburg, 1936), 22.

27. According to a late-eighteenth-century census, about half of the town's population

were enslaved or free African Americans. It was not until the 1970s, however, under pressure from several advocacy groups, that Colonial Williamsburg began to employ black actors to represent their experiences. The lives of women and the working class were also not part of the Colonial Williamsburg reenactments until the 1970s. In the mid-1990s Colonial Williamsburg caused a controversy with its reenactment of a slave auction. See Kirshenblatt-Gimblett, *Destination Culture,* 173. Also see Anders Greenspan, *Creating Colonial Williamsburg* (Washington, DC: Smithsonian Institution Press, 2002).

28. Robert W. Rydell, *World of Fairs: The Century-of-Progress Expositions* (Chicago: University of Chicago Press, 1993), 74. Also see William B. Rhoads, "The Colonial Revival and the Americanization of Immigrants," in *The Colonial Revival in America,* ed. Alan Axelrod (New York: Norton, 1985), 341–61.

29. Kirshenblatt-Gimblett, *Destination Culture,* 51, 54.

30. Cited in Rydell, *World of Fairs,* 15.

31. Robert Rydell writes: "Beginning with the 1893 Chicago World's Columbian Exposition, every American international fair held through World War I included ethnological villages sanctioned by prominent anthropologists who occasionally organized university summer school courses around these displays" (ibid., 21).

32. Burton Benedict writes, "During nearly 150 years of world's fairs, ethnic stereotypes gradually altered, moving from manifestations of Euro-American superiority and imperialism toward expressions of new nationalisms in new nations" (Benedict, "Rituals of Representation: Ethnic Stereotypes and Colonized Peoples at World's Fairs," in *Fair Representations: World's Fairs and the Modern World,* ed. Robert Rydell and Nancy Gwinn [Amsterdam: VU University Press, 1994], 28).

33. Rydell, *World of Fairs,* 22.

34. Rydell describes the "Mayan-moderne" and "mishmash" of "Asian" styles that characterized the structures built for the 1939 San Francisco Golden Gate Exposition, which aimed explicitly at a vision of a new "Empire of the West" (ibid., 85–86).

35. Martin, *Nathanael West,* 235. See also Barnard, *Great Depression,* 149–54.

36. Rita Barnard writes that on his way to the schoolbook exhibit, which she guesses to be the exhibition by Ginn and Company of educational books from the sixteenth through the nineteenth centuries displayed in a colonial schoolroom in the Hall of Social Science, West would have had to pass a series of dioramas presenting "progress in the life of the family" (ibid., 150). Barnard focuses on this particular exhibit's cheerful notions of historical progress and family improvement and the way in which these are attacked in *A Cool Million.* Barnard also describes the "inanimate" section of S. Snodgrasse's "Chamber of American Horrors" as a "surrealistically distorted version of the kind of thing one might have encountered in the medical exhibitions at the Century of Progress's Hall of Science or he displays of new commodities and

new production processes (suggesting a strange 'combination of Hollywood and Houdini,' as one visitor complained) in the various manufacturers' pavilions" (151).

37. Kirshenblatt-Gimblett, *Destination Culture,* 128.

38. Rydell, *World of Fairs,* 22.

39. Qtd. in ibid.

40. Kirshenblatt-Gimblett, *Destination Culture,* 79.

41. Ibid., 80–81; see the chapter "Exhibiting Jews," 79–128.

42. Qtd. in ibid., 121. Also see Meyer Weisgal's autobiography, *Meyer Weisgal . . . So Far: An Autobiography* (New York: Random House, 1971), 106–7, italics added.

43. Weisgal and newspapers reported record-breaking attendance at the pageant. See the *Chicago Daily News,* July 5, 1933.

44. See Walter Roth, *Looking Backward: Stories from Chicago's Jewish Past* (Chicago: Academy Chicago Publishers, 2002).

45. Rydell, *World of Fairs,* 55.

46. Isador Lewi qtd. in Kirshenblatt-Gimblett, *Destination Culture,* 97.

47. Ibid., 105.

48. Rydell, *World of Fairs,* 21. Aram A. Yengoyan also writes: "Anthropologists had a keen interest in shaping the cultural and scientific side of these early exhibitions. Not only were displays an expression of progress, but in some cases the universities conceived these non-literate peoples as laboratories in which anthropological research could be conducted" (Yengoyan, "Culture, Ideology, and World's Fairs," in Rydell and Gwinn, *Fair Representations,* 75).

49. Edward Curtis's elegiac, deliberately composed, sepia photographs, published between 1907 and 1930, featured as a key image a line of Navajo horsemen disappearing into a canyon. Although Curtis condemned conventional studio portraits of Native Americans as inauthentic, he nevertheless brought with him into the field an inventory of props such as masks and feather headdresses, which would resurface in photographs of different tribes. For Curtis, as for other romantics, "real" Indians were only those who remained "ethnographically pristine and uncontaminated by Whites" (Alison Griffiths, "Native-American Representation in Early Cinema," in *Dressing in Feathers: The Construction of the Indian in American Popular Culture,* ed. S. Elizabeth Bird [Boulder, CO: Westview Press, 1996], 88).

50. Marcel Mauss, the French sociologist, nephew and student of Emile Durkheim, wrote extensively on the potlatch in his 1925 *Essai sur le don, forme archaïque de l'échange.* He refers to earlier work on the subject by Pere Lambert, Franz Boas, "Mayne, Dawson, Krause, etc" (Mauss, *The Gift: Forms and Functions of Exchange in Archaic Societies,* trans. Ian Cunnison [New York: Norton, 1967], 31–37). Jonathan Veitch argues a connection between West and Georges Bataille, who used the term *potlatch* to describe a phenomenon in which the pressures

of class struggle transform traditional modes of nonproductive expenditure (the building of monuments, games, spectacles, and so on) into "an immense travail of recklessness, discharge, and upheaval": in other words, the potlatch of revolution (Veitch, *American Superrealism,* 129).

51. La Farge, *American Indian Art,* 14–15.

52. Ibid., 15.

53. On the other hand, for a late-twentieth-century Native critique of Marxism, see Ward Churchill, ed., *Marxism and Native Americans* (Boston: South End Press, 1999).

54. See Hegeman, *Patterns for America,* 126–57.

55. As Hegeman notes, West eventually would "create a nightmare negation of Frank's vision, in which he would satirize Frank's cultural typologies and his optimism about cultural change, but even suggest some sinister political implications of Frank's vision of transformation through a lyrical cultural nationalism" (ibid., 148).

56. For an excellent discussion of the biographical context of the writing of *A Cool Million,* including West's growing political disillusionment, see "The Black Hole of Calcoolidge," in Martin, *Nathanael West,* 219–41.

57. One-fifth of the novel is copied, with little alteration, from Alger's books. See Douglas H. Shepard, "Nathanael West Rewrites Horatio Alger, Jr.," *Satire Newsletter* (Fall 1965): 13–28; Gary Scharnhorst, "From Rags to Patches, or *A Cool Million* as Alter-Alger," *Ball State University Forum* 21 (1980): 58–65. West called the novel "my Horatio Alger book" (letter to Edmund Wilson, July 25, 1933; reprinted in West, *Novels and Other Writings,* 780).

58. Nathanael West, *A Cool Million and The Dream Life of Balso Snell: Two Novels* (New York: Farrar, Straus, and Giroux, 1963) (hereafter cited in text).

59. By invoking the nom de plume that the real Samuel Clemens had tried out and then discarded in favor of Mark Twain, West affiliates his novel with Twain's satirical and politically pointed critiques of race, modernity, authoritarianism, and commercial culture in such novels as *The Adventures of Huckleberry Finn, Pudd'nhead Wilson,* and, especially, the dystopic *A Connecticut Yankee in King Arthur's Court.*

60. The conclusion of the novel describes the "youth of America" singing the "Lemuel Pitkin Song," just as German schoolchildren sang the "Horst Wessel Lied" in commemoration of a young Nazi storm trooper who was killed in a political street brawl in 1930 and subsequently declared a "saint" by the Nazis.

61. Martin, *Nathanael West,* 193. In *A Cool Million,* Lem opens the newspaper to the headline: "'PRESIDENT CLOSES BANKS FOR GOOD,' he read one night. He sighed profoundly. Not because he had again lost the few dollars he had saved, which he had, but because it made him think of Mr. Whipple and the Rat River National Bank. He spent the rest of the night wondering what had become of his old friend"

(174).

62. West, *Novels and Other Writings,* 781.

63. The three volumes of the revived *Contact* were reprinted in 1967 by Kraus Reprint Corporation, New York.

64. Martin, *Nathanael West,* 147. Also see West's letter to William Carlos Williams, April 1932, reprinted in West, *Novels and Other Writings,* 775.

65. The pieces included Nathan Asch, "Mary"; Erskine Caldwell, "Over the Green Mountains"; Robert McAlmon, "Mexican Interval"; Julian Shapiro, "The Fire at the Catholic Church"; and Charles Reznikoff, "My Country 'Tis of Thee."

66. Williams not only identifies all Americans as Indians in his 1925 "history" *In the American Grain* (New York: A&C Boni, 1925)—"I do believe the average American to be an Indian, but an Indian robbed of his world" (128)—he also explicitly asserts his desire to "lift dead Indians tenderly from their graves, to steal from them—as if it must be clinging even to their corpses—some authenticity, that which" (74).

67. West, *Novels and Other Writings,* 772–73.

68. West's Jewishness, Steiner argues, "begins to be seen in the intertwining of native American and Christian (and New Testament) with Jewish (and Old Testament) strains." Each character has a Hebrew name, Steiner notes: Nathan Whipple, Levi Underdown, Ephraim Pierce, Jake Raven, and Israel Satinpenny. West's point, Steiner observes, is that "the American mythic landscape is about and for Jews if they attend to it closely enough" (Steiner, "West's Lemuel," 105).

69. Martin, *Nathanael West,* 281. Rita Barnard devotes a few pages of her discussion to West's interest in the fate of Native Americans, to which, she notes, "his critics have paid surprisingly little attention" (Barnard, *Great Depression,* 157). I am indebted to her discussion on pages 157–61.

70. Martin, *Nathanael West,* 281.

71. Martin argues that the inspiration for Whipple's Leather Shirts was William Dudley Pelley's fascist organization, the Silver Shirts, profiled by John Spivak for *The New Masses* in 1934. According to Pelley's 1933 account, he died for seven minutes one night in April 1928, during which he learned from an "Oracle" of an international Jewish conspiracy and of his own mission to return America to Americans in the form of a giant corporation, with Pelley himself as president and with only "100 per cent Americans" as stockholders. The Oracle also told him that when "a certain young house-painter comes to the head of the German people" he should take this as a sign of his time to launch his Christian militia. The organization soon numbered seventy-five thousand, with members in forty-six of the forty-eight states (Martin, *Nathanael West,* 233–34).

72. In Spivak's interview with one of Pelley's lieutenants, Eugene R. Chase, Chase admits the opportunistic economic motives behind his use of anti-Semitic rhetoric, saying:

"'You got to give them something to get mad about. It's business. What the hell! The official shirtmaker for the Silver Legion is a Jew. Look—' He points out an advertisement in the Silver Ranger: 'Milton's Toggery: Official Shirt Maker for the Silver Legion'" (ibid.).

73. Ibid., 122.

74. The novel's epigraph, billed as an "old saying" was indeed a saying at Brown, West's alma mater: "John D. Rockefeller would give a cool million to have a stomach like yours." Whether that stomach would go inside Rockefeller, or inside a museum or exhibit funded by him, is perhaps the source of the satire (ibid., 227).

75. In 1920 Ford's *Dearborn Independent* published a series of articles on the *Protocols of the Elders of Zion*, a document that was said to present proof of the Jews' desire to take over the world. The collected articles were published in 1921 as *The International Jew: The World's Foremost Problem.*

76. Martin writes that "in making his white slavers and Wu Fong speak Italian, [West] alludes also to Big Jim Colosimo's famous Chicago operation, overseen by John Torrio" (Martin, *Nathanael West,* 240n).

77. Ibid., 247.

78. Ibid., 248.

79. Ibid.

80. Ibid., 249.

81. Michaels writes, "Insofar as the family becomes the site of national identity, nationality becomes an effect of racial identity" (Michaels, *Our America,* 8). In 1920 the Kansas Free Fair featured a Fitter Families for Future Firesides contest, the object of which, in the words of eugenicist Dr. Florence Brown Sherbon, was "the stimulation of a feeling of family and racial consciousness and responsibility" (qtd. in Rydell, *World of Fairs,* 49). Fitter Families exhibits became a staple of expositions and world fairs throughout the two decades following, and even the New York World Fair of 1940 featured a "typical American family" display, informed by eugenicist principles and underwritten in part by the Ford Motor Company, that proved to be one of the fair's most popular exhibits. Americans were invited to write essays explaining why they were "typical"; winners received a free trip to the fair and lived on the fairgrounds, in a curious incarnation of the ever-popular ethnographic village. The typical American family, unsurprisingly, was white and native-born: as the governor of Arkansas wrote in his letter to the family selected from his state, "you typify the best that this nation can produce, for Arkansas, by virtue of its high percentage of native-born population, is the most American state in the union" (ibid., 56–57).

82. Martin, *Nathanael West,* 214–15.

83. West, *Novels and Other Writings,* 404.

84. Nathanael West, *Day of the Locust,* in *Novels and Other Writings,* 374.

85. Barnard, *Great Depression*, 161.

86. Ibid.

87. Immediately after publishing *A Cool Million* in 1934, West applied for a Guggenheim Foundation grant for an apparently autobiographical project, modeled, West wrote, in part on Joyce's *Portrait of the Artist as a Young Man*. One of West's chapters is titled "Chapter Four; Business and the objectives involved. An attempt to love, and the difficulties encountered. The impossibility of experiencing a genuine emotion" (West, *Novels and Other Writings*, 465).

88. My thanks to Daniel Itzkovitz, who pointed out to me that "Vas you dere, Sharlie?" was the signature line of the Jewish radio comic Jack Pearl (born Jake Perlman), who became enormously popular in the early 1930s playing Baron Munchausen, an exaggerated German who would address this catchphrase to his sidekick, Charlie, when the latter expressed doubt about the baron's tall tales.

89. Martin, *Nathanael West*, 221.

90. Ibid., 345.

91. Ibid., 344.

92. Ibid., 346.

93. Ibid., 353.

94. Sanford, *Scenes*, 3:168.

95. Martin, *Nathanael West*, 392.

96. Yitskhok (Isaac) Raboy, *The Jewish Cowboy*, trans. Nathaniel Shapiro (Westfield, NJ: Tradition Books, 1989), 124, 127.

97. The novels discussed here were written before Fast officially joined the party, but during the period of his "sympathizing." Fast was a member of the Communist Party from 1944 until 1956. He left the party after Kruschev's revelations about Stalinist crimes and was especially disturbed by Stalin's purging of Yiddish intellectuals and writers in the late 1940s and 1950s. See Fast, *Being Red* (Boston: Houghton Mifflin, 1990), as well as Fast, *The Naked God: The Writer and the Communist Party* (New York: Frederick A. Praeger, 1957).

98. Sanford writes: "*The People from Heaven* was your first book to be published after his death, and though you hadn't been friends when he died, the dedication went to him by right. Had it not been for Nat West, for Pep, for Natchie Weinstein, you might never have written a line, you might only have gone one with the law, always wondering why your days were so dry, one like another" (Sanford, *Scenes*, 3:251).

99. Some examples, in addition to *The Last Frontier* and *The Romance of a People*, include *Haym Solomon: Son of Liberty* (1941), a novel for young readers about a Jewish immigrant who becomes a hero of the American Revolution; *The Unvanquished* (1942), about the Continental army's "most desperate moment"; *Citizen Tom Paine* (1943); *Freedom Road* (1944), about black Reconstruction in the South; and *My*

Glorious Brothers (1948), about the Maccabee uprising against the Greco-Syrian Empire. This last novel, written in the same year as the creation of the state of Israel and quickly translated into Hebrew, became a bestseller in the new nation. Fast writes in *Being Red* that "Morris Schappes, one of the party's experts on Jewish affairs, suggested that I be brought up for expulsion on charges of Jewish nationalism. When this came to the attention of Jack Statchel, a member of the party's National Committee, he threw up his hands in despair and told Schappes to forget it and said that any Jew who did not feel sentiments of Jewish nationalism in 1948 had lost his soul" (193–94).

100. Oliver La Farge, "Flight of the Cheyennes," *Saturday Review,* July 26, 1941, 5.

101. Howard Fast, *The Last Frontier* (New York: Press of the Reader's Club, 1941), 231.

102. Carl Van Doren, foreword to ibid., ix.

103. Fast attributes his title to Weisgal: "Acknowledgement is made to Meyer W. Weisgal for permission to use the title 'Romance of a People' which was produced by him as a pageant in 1933" (ibid., copyright page).

104. Howard Fast, *The Romance of a People,* with illustrations by Raffaello Busoni (New York: Hebrew Publishing, 1941).

105. Ibid., 216–18.

106. Fast, *Last Frontier,* 195–96.

107. Fast, *Romance of a People,* 4. See Fast, *Last Frontier,* 9–10, for a more extended description of the hills, fertile valley, and dry plains of the Cheyennes' homeland, strikingly reminiscent of how Fast describes the landscape of ancient Canaan.

108. Fast, *Romance of a People,* 139–40.

109. Ibid., 120.

110. Fast discusses his growing awareness that he could not tell the story from the Cheyenne point of view, because of the impossibility of accessing their language (Fast, *Being Red,* 71–72). *The Last Frontier,* like many of Fast's novels, was translated into Hebrew in 1952 by A. Birman (*Merhavyah: Sifriyat poalim: Hotsaat ha-Kibuts ha-artsi ha-shomer hatsa'ir*). The book jacket of the 1953 Blue Heron Press edition claims it was also translated into Yiddish, but I have not been able to locate an extant copy. *Spartacus,* another account of courageous resistance against the Roman Empire, was translated into Yiddish in 1955 by P. Kats (Buenos Aires: IKUF).

111. Fast, *Being Red,* 141–42.

112. The Adirondacks, in fact, served as the setting for a number of Sanford's stories, six of which were later published as *Adirondack Stories* (Santa Barbara: Capra Press, 1976), as well as for a novel set in Warrensburg that featured several of the same characters as *The People from Heaven,* called *Seventy Times Seven* (1939). Two sections of *The People from Heaven* were published in West's literary magazine *Contact* in the early 1930s: "The Fire at the Catholic Church" appeared in *Contact,*

and "Once in a Sedan and Twice Standing Up," rejected from the first issue of *Contact* by William Carlos Williams, finally appeared in the third issue, *Contact* 1, no. 3 (1932) (see Sanford, *Scenes*, vol. 2, for a discussion of this). Williams would later write of *The People from Heaven* in a letter to Harcourt Brace: "Sanford's *The People from Heaven* is the best thing he has ever written and in some ways the most important book of fiction published here in the last twenty years. . . . Sanford is in a tradition which is just getting up steam. His language is marvelous" (Sanford, *Scenes*, 3:255).

113. Wald, intro. to *People from Heaven*, xi.

114. Wald writes, "Undergirding the whole novel is a powerful examination of the historical roots of the ugly racism lying beneath the superficial harmony of a rural community" (ibid., xxiv). I am indebted to Wald's excellent discussion of the novel in his thorough introduction to the republished edition, part of his series of reissues of left-wing fiction, "The Radical Novel Reconsidered."

115. Ibid., xiv, xxv.

116. See Sanford, *Scenes*, 3:164–66.

117. Sanford, *People from Heaven*, 163–64.

118. Ibid., 230.

119. Sanford, *Scenes*, 3:202–3. Fast, in his memoir, also describes reprimands from the party for some of his writing. In one instance, he had written an article for the *Daily Worker* in which he described a group of "boys and girls, white and Negro": "The day after that I was called downtown to face three of the editors and to undergo a process the party called 'charges.' I was being brought up on charges of 'white chauvinism'" (Fast, *Being Red*, 141). It might be worth saying, however, that neither Fast nor Sanford made the changes recommended, and neither was expelled from the party. Both Fast and Sanford continued to write from a profoundly left-liberal position over their fifty-year careers.

120. Sanford, *Scenes*, 3:216.

121. Ibid., 3:233.

122. Ibid., 3:242.

123. Reviewers who praised the novel included Iris Barry in the *New York Herald Tribune* and Ted Robinson in the *Cleveland Plain Dealer*. Robinson called the novel "the most arresting piece of fiction of the week-perhaps of the entire season." Philip Van Doren Stern in "Sanford's Variorum" in the *Saturday Review* discussed the book's experimental form. Carl Sandburg in the *Chicago Times* wrote a particularly ambivalent review, saying, "It's a strange book. I like it. It disgusts me." Reviewers who condemned the book included Mark Schorer in the *New York Times* under the title "Assorted White Trash." In *The People's World*, a San Francisco Communist newspaper, a reviewer praised the novel for assailing bigotry but then criticized it

for failing to trace it to its "class origins." See Sanford, *Scenes,* 3:253–60.

124. Ibid., 3:261.

125. Ibid., 3:24.

126. Ibid., 3:284–85. Sanford eventually warns Riggs away from the party, saying that "if the red man turned pink," some "paleface committee of micks and hunkies would tell you what to think." But the real reason, Sanford finally confesses, is that the party believes homosexual members are a "risk," "open to pressure," and fearing exposure might "turn informer" (3:285–86).

Chapter 4

1. Allen Ginsberg, *Howl and Other Poems* (San Francisco: City Lights, 1956), 33–34.

2. See Steven Kellman, *Redemption: The Life of Henry Roth* (New York: Norton, 2005).

3. Ruth Wisse writes: "Roth's novel unwittingly reveals how little is left of the existential artist after he has freed himself from an implicit community. Child of a loveless family, Jew without Jewishness, American master without an ennobling myth of American culture, Roth and his hero have entered the emptied world that Jean Paul Sartre conceived in his philosophy, and it is not surprising that he expressed his existential selfhood the same way Sartre did, by abdicating his moral freedom in favor of the Communist ideal. At that point in his life, Roth might as well have called it sleep" (Wisse, "The Classic of Disinheritance," in *New Essays on* Call It Sleep, ed. Hana Wirth-Nesher [Cambridge: Cambridge University Press, 1996], 74). Joel Shatzky, in a letter to the *New York Times,* December 13, 1964, theorized that Roth's block had been caused by his beating at the hands of longshoremen during the course of his research for his second novel (see Hana Wirth-Nesher, "Henry Roth's and Philip Roth's Meta-Memoirs," *Prooftexts* 18, no. 3 [1998]: 266). Roth himself, as will become clear as this chapter continues, has at alternative moments suggested that his block was caused by all these things, as well as by his arrested emotional development.

4. Henry Roth, Letter to Maxwell Geismar, April 20, 1964; reprinted in Henry Roth, *Shifting Landscape: A Composite, 1925–1987,* ed. Mario Materassi (New York: St. Martin's Press, 1987), 109.

5. Henry Roth, "The Dun Dakotas," *Commentary* (August 1960), reprinted in Roth, *Shifting Landscape,* 107–9 (hereafter cited in text).

6. The only extant portion of that second novel is titled "If We Had Bacon" and was published in 1936 in a magazine called *Signatures: Works in Progress;* it is reprinted in Roth, *Shifting Landscape,* 21–44 (hereafter cited in text). Roth describes his desire

to "break away from an extension of the immigrant East Side Jewish child and do something from the American Middle West. . . . I broke away and was going to do the proletarian, right out of the American scene" (22). The second novel was to be about Roth's acquaintance Bill Clay, an illiterate, working-class "proletarian hero"; the preface to the novel was to be about the fictional Clay's father, a cavalry scout (Kellman, *Redemption*, 139, 165–68).

7. Roth, *Shifting Landscape*, 111.

8. The title of this section, "Bing! I'm an Innian," is taken from *Call It Sleep,* during a scene in which David plays with his neighbor, Yussie: "He lifted the clothes hanger, pulled back an imaginary string. 'Bing! I'm an Innian. If you don' have a bow 'n' arrer, I c'n kill yuh. Bang!' Another shaft flew. 'Right innee eye. W'yntcha wanna play?'" (Henry Roth, *Call It Sleep* [1934; repr., New York: Noonday, 1990], 81).

9. Werner Sollors, "'A World Somewhere, Somewhere Else': Language, Nostalgic Mournfulness, and Urban Immigrant Family Romance in *Call It Sleep*," in Wirth-Nesher, *New Essays*, 179n72.

10. Eda Lou Walton, ed., *The City Day: An Anthology of Recent American Poetry* (New York: Ronald Press Company, 1929), vii.

11. Bonnie Lyons, "An Interview with Henry Roth," *Shenandoah* 25, no. 1 (1973): 52. Also see Kellman, *Redemption*, especially chapter 3, "City Boy."

12. Lyons, "Interview with Henry Roth," 57.

13. Sollors, "A World Somewhere," 160–61.

14. Ibid., 180n81. The comment is reported by Marcus Klein in *Foreigners: The Making of American Literature, 1900–1940* (Chicago: University of Chicago Press, 1981), 193.

15. Roth notes: "Eliot's *Waste Land* had a devastating effect on me, I felt stunned by the vastness of its conception. I had been introduced to the work by Eda Lou Walton, a professor of literature at New York University. It was to her that I dedicated *Call It Sleep*. . . . I had already read Joyce as a freshman in college, and a copy of *Ulysses* which Eda Lou had brought me from France introduced me to an entirely new way of seeing things. I felt I could see doors swinging open on untried possibilities in literature" (David Bronsen, "A Conversation with Henry Roth," *Partisan Review* 36 [1969]: 270).

16. Eda Lou Walton, *Dawn Boy: Blackfoot and Navajo Songs* (New York: Dutton, 1926), vii–ix.

17. Walton, *City Day*, v.

18. Walton had given Roth a turquoise and silver Navajo ring as a gift, which he then later gave to his wife, Muriel. When Muriel died, he wore the ring. When Hana Wirth-Nesher visited Roth in New Mexico in the early 1980s, she remembers vividly that he had a photograph of the Lower East Side on his wall and a copy

of the *Jerusalem Post*, which he read every day, on the table and that he wore the ring, as well as a turquoise and silver bolo tie (visible in many photographs from his later years, it had clearly become a signature piece of jewelry for Roth). These were, Wirth-Nesher speculates, the touchstones of his daily life: his immigrant origins, his Zionism, and Walton's "gift" of Native materials (conversation with Hana Wirth-Nesher, July 2007).

19. Henry Roth, *A Diving Rock on the Hudson*, vol. 2 of *Mercy of a Rude Stream* (New York: St. Martin's Press, 1995), 359.

20. Roth's story of Zaru is clearly based on Ishi, the last surviving Yahi Indian, who had been "discovered" by Alfred Kroeber, Walton's dissertation advisor at Berkeley. Kroeber turned Ishi into a "museum exhibit," and Ishi died of tuberculosis in 1916, surviving his "collision with modernity" by no more than five years. Steven Kellman observes that "Roth, in effect, was Walton's Ishi—an interloping primitive she hoped to initiate, more gently and benignly, into the ways of civilization" (Kellman, *Redemption*, 96).

21. Roth, *Diving Rock,* 361–62.

22. Henry Roth, *Requiem for Harlem*, vol. 4 of *Mercy of a Rude Stream* (New York: St. Martin's Press, 1998), 237.

23. Roth, *Diving Rock,* 362.

24. David Greenhood, "Eda Lou Walton's Use of Her Native Scene," *New Mexico Quarterly* 33 (1963): 258, 262. For Walton's comment about Irish and Scottish poetry, see T. T. Waterman, "American Indian Poetry," *American Anthropologist* 27 (January–March 1925); cited in Greenhood, "Eda Lou Walton": "Modern Irish and Scottish poetry, like English songs . . . runs strongly to parallelism similar to that of the Navajo" (262). Roth himself made use of such "parallelistic repetitions" in *Call It Sleep,* using a technique of accumulation and variation with such images as crosses, darkness and light, and swords. See Sollors, "A World Somewhere," 144, 178n48. Walton's translations of Navajo chants, republished in the *Multilingual Anthology of American Literature* alongside a more literal translation, give a vivid picture of the ways in which she read a modernist aesthetic project onto the Indian chant she translated (Marc Shell and Werner Sollors, eds., *Multilingual Anthology of American Literature* [New York: New York University Press, 2000]).

25. Greenhood, "Eva Lou Walton," 255.

26. Lyons, "Interview with Henry Roth," 60.

27. See Sollors, "A World Somewhere," 173n48, 174n50, 177n64. Sollors notes Roth's adaptation of Walton's arguments concerning "accumulative imagery" and quotes Marya Zaturensky's poem "Nostalgia" ("That field so green, so green / In the sun's graying gold") and compares the technique of Cummings's "Chansons Innocentes I" with that of the novel's final passages.

28. Walton, *City Day*, 26.
29. Ibid., 29.
30. Ibid., 30.
31. Roth, *Call It Sleep*, 14 (hereafter cited in text).
32. Walton, *City Day*, 32.
33. The two descriptions are "And light, unleashed, terrific light bellowed out of iron lips" (253) and "Terrific rams of darkness collided" (419).
34. See Brian McHale, "Henry Roth in Nighttown, or, Containing *Ulysses*," in Wirth-Nesher, *New Essays*, for a thorough discussion of the novel's quotations and references to *Ulysses*, as well as for a précis of Joycean criticism of the novel.
35. Walton, *City Day*, 35.
36. Ibid., 69.
37. "Cortege for Rosenbloom" reads:

> Now, the wry Rosenbloom is dead
> And his finical carriers tread
> On a hundred legs, the tread
> Of the dead.
> Rosenbloom is dead. (Walton, *City Day*, 36)

In *Call It Sleep*, David witnesses a funeral:

> Two men came out, laboring under the front-end of a huge black box, then two more at the other end. Red-faced, they trod carefully down the steps, advanced toward the carriage, rested one end of the box on the carriage floor.
> That was—! Yes! That was! He suddenly understood. Mama said— Inside! Yes! Man! Inside! His flesh went cold with terror. (61)

38. For a discussion that introduces the term "family romance" into a discussion of *Call It Sleep*, see Sollors, "A World Somewhere." Also consider Walter Benn Michaels, *Our America: Nativism, Modernism, and Pluralism* (Durham: Duke University Press, 1995), for his arguments concerning kinship metaphors as the reigning logic in the formation of national identities: "The significance of the family is that it was in terms of familial relations (as opposed, say, to economic relations or regional or even generational relations) that the new structures of identity were articulated. *America, a Family Matter* was the title of Charles W. Gould's nativist polemic of 1922" (6).
39. Sollors has pointed out the echoes here of Walton's relationship with Roth (Sollors, "A World Somewhere," 181n81). He also highlights the line "She told him awestruck how he was all three, / Boy, and sensualist, and tender lover" (Eda Lou Walton,

Jane Matthew and Other Poems [New York: Brewer, Warren, and Putnam, 1931], 38 [hereafter cited in text]).

40. Sollors writes, "There may also be an allusion in the story of Ludwig the organist [in *Call It Sleep*] to Walton's poems evoking the Organ Mountains of New Mexico" (Sollors, "A World Somewhere," 181n81). I would add that the symbolic importance of crosses in *Call It Sleep* could be an allusion to "Las Cruces" in this poem (which in Spanish means crossings, junctions, or crisscrosses).

41. Maxwell Geisman, introduction to *Call It Sleep,* by Henry Roth (Paterson, NJ: Pageant Books, 1960), xliii.

42. Marc Shell, *The End of Kinship: 'Measure for Measure,' Incest, and the Ideal of Universal Siblinghood* (Baltimore: Johns Hopkins University Press, 1988), 21.

43. Ibid.

44. Vine Deloria Jr. writes in a 1979 introduction to *Black Elk Speaks* (Lincoln: University of Nebraska Press, 1979): "In the 1960s interest began to focus on Indians and some of the spiritual realities they seemed to represent. Regardless of the other literature in the field, the scholarly dissertations with inflections and nuances, *Black Elk Speaks* clearly dominated the literature dealing with Indian religions" (xii). Michael E. Staub dates the revival of *Black Elk Speaks* a bit later; after its 1932 publication, "the book was soon out of print; it was the early 1970s before *Black Elk Speaks* 'exploded into surprising popularity'" (Staub, *Voices of Persuasion: Politics of Representation in 1930s America* [Cambridge: Cambridge University Press, 1994], 55). Staub quotes from John G. Neihardt, "Preface: The Book That Would Not Die," in *Black Elk Speaks* (New York: Pocket, 1972), xiii.

45. *Black Elk Speaks: Being the Life Story of a Holy Man of the Oglala Sioux,* as told through John G. Neihardt (Lincoln: University of Nebraska Press, 1932, 1961, 1979, 1988), 25.

46. Isaiah 6:1–3 (*The New English Bible: Oxford Study Edition* [Oxford: Oxford University Press, 1976]).

47. "Then I asked, How long, O Lord? And he answered, Until cities fall in ruins and are deserted, houses are left without people, and the land goes to ruin and lies waste" (Isaiah 6:11).

48. That tragedy is the massacre at Wounded Knee.

49. Alan Velie, "The Indian Historical Novel," in *Native American Writers: Modern Critical Views,* ed. Harold Bloom (Philadelphia: Chelsea House, 1998), 197.

50. See Sollors, "A World Somewhere," 172n42.

51. Michael Castro, *Interpreting the Indian: Twentieth-Century Poets and the Native American* (Albuquerque: University of New Mexico Press, 1983), xi–xii.

52. Leslie A. Fiedler, *Return of the Vanishing American* (New York: Stein and Day, 1968), 12 (hereafter cited in text). In addition, the 1960s saw a rash of "revisionist"

Western films, such as John Ford's *Cheyenne Autumn* (1964), based on Fast's *The Last Frontier*, and Arthur Penn's *Little Big Man* (1970), based on Thomas Berger's 1964 novel, which, in seeking to correct earlier representations of Native Americans in Westerns, often invoked comparisons with the Holocaust or the Vietnam War experience. See Leslie A. Fiedler, "The Demon of the Continent," in *The Pretend Indians: Images of Native Americans in the Movies*, ed. Gretchen M. Bataille and Charles L. P. Silet (Ames: Iowa State University Press, 1980).

53. Fiedler, *Return*, 37.

54. John G. Cawelti, *Adventure, Mystery, and Romance: Formula Stories as Art and Popular Culture* (Chicago: University of Chicago Press, 1976); Fiedler, *Return*.

55. Cawelti, *Adventure*, 258.

56. Arthur Kopit and John Lahr, "*Indians*: A Dialogue," in Kopit, *Indians* (New York: Bantam, 1971), 4.

57. Arthur Kopit, *Indians* (London: Methuen, 1970), scene 13, p. 71 (hereafter cited in text).

58. Kopit and Lahr, "Dialogue," 41.

59. Ibid., 23, 36; quotes are reproduced in John Bush Jones, "Impersonation and Authenticity: The Theatre as Metaphor in Kopit's *Indians*," *Quarterly Journal of Speech* 59 (1973): 443–51.

60. N. Scott Momaday, "Bring on the Indians," *New York Review of Books*, April 8, 1971, 39.

61. Momaday writes, "Even with the little perspective we have at this moment in time, it is obvious that the decade of the Sixties was a period of profound change in America. It would be difficult, I think, to point to anything like it in our previous experience. The cumulative effect of a hopeless war in Asia, of revolution at home, of repeated assassinations, and of an almost incredible venture into space has perhaps left us more anxious and exhausted than we know. I believe that the American of the Seventies, whatever his individual or racial experience might be, is obliged of necessity to conceive a new idea of himself. In general, this is what has happened—and is happening—to the Indian" (ibid.).

62. Ibid. It is worth noting that another famous Jewish radical, Abraham Polonsky, son of Russian Jewish immigrants and a Hollywood director blacklisted in the McCarthy period for his unrepentant communism, directed both *Tell Them Willie Boy Is Here* (1969), about a Native American fugitive from the law, and *Romance of a Horse Thief* (1971), based on a Yiddish novella by Joseph Opatoshu, within a very few years of each other. The links between Native and Jewish nationalist discourse in the late 1960s will be addressed in my last chapter.

63. Duane Niatum, Simon J. Ortiz, Roberta Hill, and James Welch all began to publish in the 1960s. In 1969 the Pulitzer Prize went to N. Scott Momaday's *House Made*

of Dawn (see Arnold Krupat, *The Voice in the Margin* [Berkeley: University of California Press, 1989], 122). Other poets who showed interest in Native texts were Robert Bly, Robert Creeley, Edward Dorn, Richard Hugo, Galway Kinnell, W. S. Merwin, Rochelle Owens, William Stafford, David Wagoner, James Wright, and Louis Simpson (ibid., 120n10). Gary Snyder's *Myths and Texts* appeared in 1960; Kenneth Rexroth's essays "The Poet as Translator" and "American Indian Songs" were published in 1961 (ibid., 118).

64. The story appeared in *Summering: A Book of Short Stories* (New York: Henry Holt, 1966). It was reprinted in Joyce Antler, ed., *America and I: Short Stories by American Jewish Women Writers* (Boston: Beacon Press, 1990), 178–89 (quotes are taken from the Beacon Press edition, hereafter cited in text).

65. Jerome Rothenberg, *Poland/1931* (New York: New Directions, 1974), 143. My thanks to Ranen Omer-Sherman for sending me this reference.

66. Fiedler, *Return*, 70, 173.

67. Leslie A. Fiedler, "Henry Roth's Neglected Masterpiece," *Commentary* 30 (August 1960): 103.

68. Ibid., 105, 106–7.

69. Fiedler, *Return*, 186.

70. William Freedman, "Henry Roth in Jerusalem: An Interview," *The Literary Review: An International Journal of Contemporary Writing* 23 (1979): 8–9 (hereafter cited in text).

71. Kellman, *Redemption*, 169.

72. Henry Roth Papers, American Jewish Historical Society, Newton, MA, and New York, NY, Journal 1967 (Box 14, Folder 11), 107–8.

73. Ibid., 117. I read the word "perhaps" in "perhaps that should be the goal of any pro-Israeli Marxist" as key in Roth's increasingly strained sense of himself as a proper Marxist. Roth's papers show that he joined the Left organization Committee on New Alternatives in the Middle East in 1970–71, and in 1974 joined AIPAC (American Israel Public Affairs Committee), a more conservative Israel lobbying organization. In 1976 Roth advocated the release of Eldridge Cleaver, leader of the militant African American group the Black Panthers, who had become a born-again Christian and a vigorous champion of Israel (see Kellman, *Redemption*, 264, as well as correspondence between Roth and Cleaver in Roth Papers, Box 1, Folders 31, 32). In 1978 he considered contributing to an edited collection of pieces by Edward Alexander and Robert Loewenberg (a book that does not seem to have been published, at least in this proposed form) to be about, in Alexander's words, "a fundamental incompatibility between Jewish religion, peoplehood, and nationality on the one hand, and leftism (more loosely, liberalism) in its various guises on the other. We wish in our book to present a coherent collection which visibly establishes the

existence of a Jewish intellectual position that is both independent of and opposed to liberalism" (letter to Roth from Edward Alexander, January 2 1978, Roth Papers, Box 1, Folder 1).

74. In the early twenty-first century Israel continues to fulfill this imagined religious destiny. On a television appearance during the second intifada, Oral Roberts, looking positively gleeful, described the Israeli-Palestinian conflict as a sign that the end of days was at hand: "This is all foretold in Scripture," he said, affirming that America's interest in Israel is a deeply religious as well as political one, steered by explicitly messianic thinking. See also *Time* magazine's cover story of July 1, 2002, which describes a millenarian renaissance in the United States that has gone mainstream. The magazine's timeline explicitly marks Israel's 1967 war and the capture of East Jerusalem (which includes the Old City, with the Western Wall/Al Aqsa Mosque/Church of the Holy Sepulchre site) as a sign of the impending apocalypse.

75. Steven S. Schwarzschild, "On the Theology of Jewish Survival," *CCAR Journal* (October 1968): 2–21; reprinted in Michael Staub, ed., *The Jewish 1960s: An American Sourcebook* (Waltham, MA: Brandeis University Press, 2004).

76. Roth, *Shifting Landscape*, 134.

77. Ibid., 244.

78. Ibid., 150.

79. Ibid., 244.

80. Ibid., 245.

81. Ibid., 247–48.

82. Henry Roth, *From Bondage*, vol. 3 of *Mercy of a Rude Stream* (New York: Picador, 1997), 67.

83. Roth, *Diving Rock*, 116.

84. Jonathan Rosen, "Lost and Found: Remembering Henry Roth," *New York Times*, December 10, 1995, 47.

85. Roth, *Shifting Landscape*, 228.

86. Roth recalls: "I was taken from a neighborhood that had been home for me and put in a highly hostile environment. That produced a shock from which I have perhaps never recovered. . . . *Call It Sleep* is set in the East Side, but it violates the truth about what the East Side was like back then. Ninth Street was only a fragmentary model for what I was doing. In reality, I took the violent environment of Harlem—where we lived from 1914–28—and projected it back onto the East Side. It became a montage of milieus, in which I was taking elements of one neighborhood and grafting them onto another. This technique must have grown out of the rage I had been living with all those fourteen years. I was alienated—to use that old hack of a word—and my novel became a picture in metaphors of what had happened to me" (Bronsen, "Conversation with Henry Roth," 266–67).

87. Roth, *Shifting Landscape,* 230.
88. Bronsen, "Conversation with Henry Roth," 279.
89. Roth, *Shifting Landscape,* 228–29.
90. Vizenor studied with Walton in 1956 and later became a professor at her alma mater, the University of California. According to Kellman, Vizenor believed Walton had changed his life: "She made me believe I could write" (qtd. in Kellman, *Redemption,* 228). Kellman speculates that in Vizenor Walton saw "a future American Indian poet like the ones she had collected in *Dawn Boy* thirty years earlier" (228).
91. The *Oxford English Dictionary* attributes the first use of the term "postmodern," applied to literature, to, as it happens, Leslie Fiedler in *The Partisan Review* 32, no. 508 (1965).
92. Jeffrey J. Folks, "Henry Roth's National and Personal Narratives of Captivity," *Papers on Language and Literature: A Quarterly Journal for Scholars and Critics of Language and Literature* (Southern Illinois University, Edwardsville) 35, no. 3 (1999): 292. Hana Wirth-Nesher considers *Mercy* postmodern because it is a "self-conscious" work "absorbed in the telling, in the strategies of unmasking and of evading that incorporate postmodern metacommentaries on [its] own telling" (Wirth-Nesher, "Meta-Memoirs," 272).
93. See, for instance, Henry Roth, *A Star Shines over Mt. Morris Park,* vol. 1 of *Mercy of a Rude Stream* (New York: Picador, 1995), 198–213.
94. Wirth-Nesher, "Meta-Memoirs," 265–66.
95. Roth, *A Star Shines,* 68–72; originally published in the *New Yorker,* March 23, 1940; reprinted in Roth, *Shifting Landscape,* 62–66.
96. One such moment occurs toward the beginning of the first volume, just after an eight-year-old Ira and his parents have moved to Harlem from the Lower East Side. The "young Irish matron from upstairs" accuses Ira, falsely, of pushing her son to the sidewalk. Ira's father is sent into a fury:

> Ira never could recall afterward with what rod he was chastised, whether with a stick or a stove poker. He was being sacrificed to avert more disastrous reprisal. He could only recall that he groveled, screaming, "Don't, Papa, please, Papa! No more!" . . . And now, Mom, apprised by her son's screaming as soon as she entered the lower hallway of the house, rushed up the stairs and into the kitchen.
>
> "Mama!" Never had her face seemed more heaven-sent than now, furious in his defense. (Roth, *A Star Shines,* 33)

A virtually identical scene takes place toward the beginning of *Call It Sleep,* when David is punished by his father for having inadvertently struck his playmate Yussie:

The chopping strokes of the clothes hanger flayed his wrists, his hands, his back, his breast. There was always a place for it to land no

matter where he ducked or writhed or groveled. He screamed, screamed, and still the blows fell.

"Please papa! Please! No more! No more! Darling papa! Darling papa!" he knew that in another moment, he would thrust his head beneath that reign of blows. Anguish! Anguish! He must escape!

The door was thrown open. With a wild cry, his mother rushed in, flung herself between them.

"Mama!" he screamed, clutching at her dress. "Mama!" (84)

97. Wirth-Nesher, "Meta-Memoirs," 272–73.
98. Roth, *A Star Shines,* 106.
99. Wirth-Nesher, "Meta-Memoirs," 272.
100. Folks, "Narratives of Captivity," 294–95.
101. Roth, *Diving Rock,* 364.
102. Ibid., 362.
103. Ibid., 360.
104. Ira wonders where to take his cousin Stella and decides upon Fox's Theater on Fourteenth Street, whose second balcony had "two toilets in the back. . . . Oh, what a villain! . . . Nah, he couldn't, wild Indian, he couldn't. But nobody could say that he didn't have injunity—enginuity" (Roth, *From Bondage,* 271).
105. Wirth-Nesher, "Meta-Memoirs," 268.

Chapter 5

1. *Jerusalem Post,* January 15, 2007, 2. The photograph is by Nasser Ishtayeh of AP.
2. See Emily Miller Budick, *Blacks and Jews in Literary Conversation* (Cambridge: Cambridge University Press, 1998), and Eric Sundquist, *Strangers in the Land: Blacks, Jews, Post-Holocaust America* (Cambridge: Cambridge University Press, 2005).
3. Budick, *Blacks and Jews,* 208.
4. Edward Linenthal, *Preserving Memory: The Struggle to Create America's Holocaust Museum* (New York: Columbia University Press, 1995, 2001), 3.
5. Shmuel Dayksel, "My Indian Mother," in *The New Country: Stories from the Yiddish about Life in America,* ed. Henry Goodman (New York: YKUF, 1961), 496.
6. Sh. Dayksel, *Indianishe dertseylungen* (New York: Farlag Sh. Dayksel bukh komitet, 1959) (hereafter cited in text). Other English translations besides "My Indian Mother"

are my own.

7. Sh. Dayksel, "Indianishe mayselekh," *Der Hammer* (July 1928): 20–22.

8. *New Yorkish and Other American Yiddish Stories,* trans. and ed., Max Rosenfeld (Philadelphia: Sholom Aleichem Club and the Congress of Secular Jewish Organizations, 1995), 191–200 (hereafter cited in text).

9. This wasn't Tenenboym's first Indian-themed story; "Der letster indianer" (The last Indian) appeared in *Literarishe bleter* 14, no. 34 (1937): 544–45. The earlier piece describes the last surviving Indian of an unspecified tribe, written in an impressionistic, lyrical style. "The Last Indian" thus also suggests Tenenboym's linking of Indians and Jews around shared experiences of violence and devastation.

10. Katz writes: "The last secular Yiddish masters . . . are disappearing daily" (Dovid Katz, *Words on Fire: The Unfinished Story of Yiddish* [New York: Basic Books, 2004], 349). Just for example, my husband's grandmother, a survivor of Terezin, used to call herself "the last of the Mohicans." When a student of mine interviewed her grandmother for a film on immigrant Yiddish culture, she too called herself "the last of the Mohicans."

11. Shlomo Kidron, "Malamud Explains Jewish Contribution to U.S. Writing," *Jerusalem Post Week-End Magazine,* April 1, 1968, 13; reprinted in Lawrence M. Lasher, ed., *Conversations with Bernard Malamud* (Jackson: University Press of Mississippi, 1991), 28–31.

12. Bernard Malamud, *The People and Uncollected Stories* (New York: Farrar, Straus, Giroux, 1989), xii (hereafter cited in text). In a late interview, Malamud, when asked if his newest book represented a new direction in his work, responded, "No question about it. It's one of the things that has me on tenterhooks about whether I can make it come off" (interview with Joel Salzberg [1986] in Lasher, *Conversations,* 143).

13. Janna Malamud Smith, *My Father Is a Book* (New York: Houghton Mifflin, 2006), 248.

14. Ibid., 249. Max Malamud was Bernard's father, an immigrant grocer. Malamud's mother, like Ginsberg's, was mentally ill for much of Malamud's childhood. Malamud's parents spoke Yiddish at home, and Janna Malamud Smith speculates that her father's curious gift for language was a result of having learned his second language late, in school: "I imagine the second language might have met the Yiddish, rock against flint, and sparked this energetic pidgin discord. Part of the mastery of the craft for him must have been in turning the hybrid possibilities to his purpose, fusing them with his sensibility" (ibid., 248). The stroke, she writes, ended this knack, returning him, I might suggest, to a kind of "elemental" Yiddish style, which in *The People* turns out to be highly compatible with the simple, vivid, poetic language attributed by modernists to Indians.

15. Pirjo Ahokas, "A Jewish Peddler as an Indian Chief: The Revisionist Western and

Bernard Malamud's *The People*," *Yiddish* 9, nos. 3–4 (1994).

16. Robert Penn Warren, *Chief Joseph of the Nez Perce: Who Called Themselves the Nimipu, "The Real People"* (New York: Random House, 1983), 55.

17. Christopher Clausen, "Exploration of America," in *New Expansive Poetry,* ed. R. S. Gwynn (Ashland, OR: Story Line Press, 1999), 241.

18. Alan Cheuse and Nicholas Delbanco, eds., *Talking Horse: Bernard Malamud on Life and Work* (New York: Columbia University Press, 1996), 150.

19. Evelyn Avery (1990), in Lasher, *Conversations,* 151.

20. An interview exchange: "What set off *The Tenants?*" "Jews and blacks, the period of the troubles in New York City; the teachers strike, the rise of black activism, the mix-up of cause and effect. I thought I'd say a word." "Why the three endings?" "Because one wouldn't do" (interview with Daniel Stern [1975], in ibid., 66).

21. Sherman Alexie, "Inside Dachau," in *The Summer of Black Widows* (Brooklyn: Hanging Loose Press, 1996), 117–22 (hereafter cited in text). For a history of the growing centrality of the Holocaust in both American Jewish memory and American politics and culture, see Peter Novick, *The Holocaust in American Life* (Boston: Houghton Mifflin, 1999). Also see "The Museum of Tolerance," another poem in Alexie's collection. The Museum of Tolerance, another Holocaust memorial museum, opened in Los Angeles in 1993.

22. Sherman Alexie, "What You Pawn I Will Redeem," *The New Yorker* 79, no. 9 (2003) (hereafter cited in text).

23. Elaine Heumann Gurian, "A Blurring of the Boundaries, 1994," in *Civilizing the Museum: The Collected Writings of Elaine Heumann Gurian* (New York: Routledge, 2006), 176. My thanks to Vanessa Ochs for introducing me to Gurian's work.

24. Jonathan Boyarin spoke to a sentiment commonly expressed in the years before the NMAI opened: "How, then, could or should Native Americans react to the fact that there is a U.S. Holocaust Museum but no U.S. Memorial to the Slaughtered Native Americans—especially if they want to avoid offending Jews in the process of expressing any opinion whatsoever?" (Boyarin, "Europe's Indian, America's Jew: Modiano and Vizenor," in *Storm from Paradise: The Politics of Jewish Memory* [Minneapolis: University of Minnesota Press, 1992]; reprinted with permission in *Boundary 2* 19, no. 3 [1992]: 207). In 2003 a letter from Carolina C. Butler of Scottsdale, Arizona, was published in *USA Today*: "Our government planned and built the United States Holocaust Memorial Museum in Washington to tell the tragic story of the Jewish people in Europe. On Wednesday, a ceremony marked this museum's 10th anniversary. But where is the Holocaust museum to tell the tragic stories of the Native Americans? They fared worse. We have lost entire tribes, cultures, histories, languages, religions, songs, dances, stories and more. A national memorial museum is needed" (May 1, 2003, 12a). Also see Linenthal, *Preserving Memory,* 63–72.

25. Michael Bernard-Donals, "Conflations of Memory, or What They Saw at the Holocaust Museum after 9/11," *CR: The New Centennial Review* 5, no. 2 (2005): 88–89.

26. Qtd. in Linenthal, *Preserving Memory,* 45.

27. Michael Berenbaum, "The Nativization of the Holocaust," *Judaism: A Quarterly Journal of Jewish Life and Thought* (1986); also see Berenbaum, *After Tragedy and Triumph: Modern Jewish Thought and the American Experience* (Cambridge: Cambridge University Press, 1990). The museum has also been criticized for this: "Jewish identity is . . . exhibited as a thing of the past, dead or dying. It only emerges from the exhibition in an American guise. In other words, Jews and other victims are exhibited only in death or through a total identification with the nation-state that rescued them" (Rick Crownshaw, "Photography and Memory in Holocaust Museums," *Mortality* 12, no. 2 [2007]: 178).

28. Lilian Friedberg, "Dare to Compare: Americanizing the Holocaust," *American Indian Quarterly* 24, no. 354 (2000). Friedberg also mentions a history of German and German-Jewish interest in American Indians. That list includes Karl May's western adventure novels, Franz Kafka, Else Lasker-Schuler, George Tabori, and Raphael Seligman. Also see Seth Wolitz, "From Parody to Redemption: George Tabori's Weisman und Rotgesicht," in *Verkorperte Geschichtsentwurfe: George Taboris Theaterarbeit,* ed. Peter Hoyng (Tubingen: Francke Verlag, 1998), 151–76; and Raphael Seligman, *Mit beschrankter Hoffnung: Juden, Deutsche und Israelis* (Hamburg: Hoffman und Campe, 1991), cited in Sander Gilman, *Jews in Today's German Culture* (Bloomington: Indiana University Press, 1995), 19.

29. Tiffany Midge, "After Viewing the Holocaust Museum's Room of Shoes and a Gallery of Plains' Indian Moccasins, Washington D.C.," *Cold Mountain Review* 34, no. 1 (2005): 18–19. Reproduced in full with the permission of Tiffany Midge.

30. And what might the NMAI offer a Jewish visitor fresh from a visit to the USHMM? Michael Shurkin writes: "The NMAI is a revolt against entire academic disciplines as well as a joyous celebration of life by a beleaguered and often invisible people. Jews would do well to take note." (Shurkin, "Tribal Lessons: A Jewish Perspective on the National Museum of the American Indian," *Zeek,* http://zeek.net/art_0505.shtml.)

31. Philip Gourevitch, "Behold Now Behemoth," *Harper's Magazine,* July 1993.

32. Amy Lonetree writes, "the failure to tell these tragic stories alongside our stories of triumphant survival is wrong" (Lonetree, "Missed Opportunities," *American Indian Quarterly* 29, nos. 3–4 [2005]: 642).

33. Amanda Cobb, "The National Museum of the American Indian: Sharing the Gift," *American Indian Quarterly* 29, nos. 3–4 (2005): 367.

34. John Haworth notes that the 2000 census indicated that more than eighty-seven

thousand New Yorkers describe themselves as American Indians or Alaska Natives. He observes: "This surprising number makes New York home to the largest urban Indian population in the country" (Haworth, "New York in Indian Possession," in *Spirit of a Native Place: Building the National Museum of the American Indian*, ed. Duane Blue Spruce [Washington, DC: National Museum of the American Indian, Smithsonian Institution, in association with National Geographic, 2004], 146).

35. Jeffrey Shandler, "Heritage and Holocaust on Display: New York City's Museum of Jewish Heritage: A Living Memorial to the Holocaust," *Public Historian* 21, no. 1 (1999): 75.

36. Ibid. This compression of "heritage sites" includes Ellis Island Immigration Museum and the Statue of Liberty, the Irish Hunger Memorial Garden, the Skyscraper Museum, the African Burial Ground National Monument, the Vietnam War Veterans Memorial, the World Trade Center Site, and the Fraunces Tavern (billed as the oldest building in New York City).

37. The Customs House, built in 1907, is a lavish Beaux Arts building celebrating in the city's financial center America's ascendance as a world power. The building is surrounded by limestone sculptures representing the continents, including one of "America" that features a subservient Indian; inside, the imposing rotunda features murals celebrating exploration and conquest in the past and capitalism and the marketplace in the present. Housing the NMAI in this monument to American empire can be read as profoundly troubling or as potentially subversive. Interestingly, the argument against housing the MJH in the Customs House echoes what would later become a charge against having the NMAI there: "There is not anybody I know who is opposed to a museum of the Holocaust in New York City. [But for] an enormous neo-Renaissance palazzo-dedicated to a manifestation of power, money, and nothing but money-to be transformed into a museum of the Holocaust is displeasingly, offensively ironic" (Brendan Gill, *New York Times*, August 2, 1984; qtd. in Rochelle G. Saidel, *Never Too Late to Remember: The Politics behind New York City's Holocaust Museum* [New York: Holmes and Meier, 1996], 127). Also see Patricia Penn Hilden and Shari Huhndorf, "Performing 'Indian' in the National Museum of the American Indian," *Social Identities* 5, no. 2 (1999), for a sharp critique of the NMAI-NY when it opened.

38. *New Tribe New York* exhibition statement, Gerald McMaster (Plains Cree/Siksika Nation), Curator, and Sandra Starr, Assistant Curator. This language of "urban tribe" echoes sociologists in the 1970s and 1980s who discussed new "urban tribes" linked with one another not through kinship or family ties but through common interests.

39. From *New York New Tribe*.

40. *New York New Tribe* exhibition statement.

41. *Remix* exhibition statement, Joe Baker, Director for Community Engagement,

Herberger College of the Arts at Arizona State University.

42. As Jeffrey Shandler observes, such installations point to "the larger challenge of embodying traditional culture through objects" (Shandler, "Heritage and Holocaust," 83). He then notes: "An interesting comparison can be made to the display of artifacts in the National Museum of the American Indian (New York), where item labels offer differing commentaries on the same artifact from anthropologists, curators, and tribal members" (83n23).

43. Ibid., 86.

44. Ibid., 85.

45. Vine Deloria Jr., *Custer Died for Your Sins: An Indian Manifesto* (1969; repr., Norman: University of Oklahoma Press, 1988), 179. In the chapter "The Red and the Black," Deloria considers the sites of contention and cooperation between black civil rights and later power movements and American Indian groups, valorizing "tribalism and nationalism," using the Jewish example alongside the Native one.

46. Ira Gelnick and Jonathan Brandow, "Radical Zionist Manifesto," *Genesis 2*, 1:37 (1970); reprinted in Michael Staub, ed., *The Jewish 1960s: An American Sourcebook* (Waltham, MA: Brandeis University Press, 1991), 246–47.

47. See Michael Staub, *Torn at the Roots: The Crisis of Jewish Liberalism in Postwar America* (New York: Columbia University Press, 2004). The U.N. resolution condemning Zionism as racism was heavily supported by African, Arab, and Soviet bloc states and was clearly influenced by the historical anti-Zionist position of the Soviet Union. The resolution's major principles condemning Zionism had in fact been articulated by the United Nations in 1953, well before the 1967 war.

48. My thanks to Dr. Bronitsky for sending me information about his work.

49. Jamal Najjab, "Land Day Commemorated at National Museum of American Indian," *The Washington Report on Middle East Affairs* 27, no. 5 (2008): 53.

50. For an account of thematic and metaphorical similarities between Palestinian and Native American literature, see Ben White, "Dispossession, Soil, and Identity in Palestinian and Native American Literature," *Palestine-Israel Journal of Politics, Economics, and Culture* 12, nos. 2–3 (2005): 149. White discusses Darwish's poem "Speech of the Red Indian," about which he writes: "Darwish's eloquent rendition of the Native American voice, as a comparison to the Palestinian narrative, is just one example of contemporary Palestinian literature reaching for an understanding of the exile's relationship with the land through metaphor or analogy" (149).

51. See online Jewish culture journal *Zeek* for an excerpted translation of Semel's novel: http://jewcy.com/post/fiction_excerpt_nava_semels_israland. See also Adam Rovner, "Interview with Israeli Author Nava Semel," *Zeek*, May 1, 2008, http://jewcy.com/post/interview_israeli_author_nava_semel.

52. Nava Semel, *'I-yisra'el* (Tel Aviv: Yediot Ahronot Books, 2005). Semel's title (and

the name of Noah's state in the novel) is translated as "Isra-Island" but can also be understood to mean, as Michael Weingrad points out, "Not-Israel." The book jacket features several images of Indians: on the cover a young woman in two braids is photographed from the back, her head encircled by a band with a feather (she presumably is meant to recall the character of Little Dove in the novel, a young Native girl and last Native resident of her people's island, who accompanies Noah on his visit to Grand Island before his dedication ceremonies and eventually becomes his lover); on the book flaps are a pair of photographs: in the first a young man in robe and feathered headdress stands in front of a teepee, and in the second he has taken off his headdress to reveal a skullcap (the photograph is attributed to a well-known Israeli photographer, Moshe Shai). In the novel, Jewish and Native cultures have intertwined: the state flag of Isra-Island is a Star of David above elm leaves, and bar and bat mitzvah ceremonies imitate Native American vision quests (Weingrad, "Messiah, American Style: Mordecai Manuel Noah and the American Refuge," *AJS Review* 31, no. 1 [2007]: 105).

53. Talia Goldschmid, "Of Indians, Noah, and New Ararat," *Ha'Aretz,* September 16, 2005.

54. Rovner, "Interview with Nava Semel."

55. Ibid.

56. Rachel Tzvia Back, *The Buffalo Poems* (Sausalito, CA: Duration Press, 2003). My thanks to Adina Hoffman and Peter Cole for introducing me to Back's work.

57. Michael Chabon, *The Yiddish Policemen's Union* (New York: HarperCollins, 2007) (hereafter cited in text).

58. Michael Chabon, "Guidebook to a Land of Ghosts," *Civilization* 4, no. 3 (1997): 67–70.

59. Jeffrey Shandler, *Adventures in Yiddishland: Postvernacular Language and Culture* (Berkeley: University of California Press, 2006), 31.

60. Ibid., 32.

61. Ibid., 33.

62. Ibid., 34.

63. Chabon, "Guidebook," 67. For another discussion of Chabon, Shandler, and Katchor, see Jennifer Glaser, "An Imaginary Ararat: Jewish Bodies and Jewish Homelands in Ben Katchor's *The Jew of New York,*" *MELUS* 32, no. 3 (2007): 154–55.

64. See Sarah Philips Casteel's excellent discussion of the novel in "Jews among the Indians: The Fantasy of Indigenization in Mordechai Richler's and Michael Chabon's Northern Narratives" (forthcoming in *Contemporary Literature* 50, no. 4 [2009], quoted in manuscript, 20).

65. Ibid., 28.

66. Ibid., 29.

67. Ibid.
68. Ibid., 32.
69. Qtd. in ibid., 23.
70. Ruth Wisse, "Slap Shtik," *Commentary* (July/August 2007).
71. Amelia Glaser, "From Polylingual to Postvernacular: Imagining Yiddish in the Twenty-first Century," *Jewish Social Studies: History, Culture, Society* 14, no. 3 (2008): 159–60.
72. D. G. Myers, "Chabon's Imaginary Jews," *Sewanee Review* 116, no. 4 (2008): 587.
73. Michael Chabon, "Imaginary Homelands," in *Maps and Legends: Reading and Writing along the Borderlands* (San Francisco: McSweeney's Books, 2008), 169 (hereafter cited in text).
74. Qtd. in Myers, "Chabon's Imaginary Jews," 587.
75. Ibid.
76. In an instructive comparison, Henryk Grynberg, a Polish-Jewish writer who survived the war as a child, describes his poem "American Home" as an expression of gratitude to America, his foster country. In it, he equates America with "sky-scraper oaks" climbed by the wild ivy of "Indian souls" (recalling those Manhattan skyscrapers so famously built by Mohawk ironworkers in the early twentieth century):

> Built of silence and loneliness
> it floats through my nights and my days
> under sky-scraper oaks
> it opens its friendly arms
> when I manage to return from a journey
> and shelters me from cold glances
> hello home I love you I say
> when it rocks me like a mother
> for an eternal sleep
> under sky-scraper oaks
> still climbed by the wild ivy
> of Indian souls

Henryk Grynberg, "The Holocaust as Literary Experience," Monna and Otto Weinmann Lecture Series, May 12, 2004, United States Holocaust Memorial Museum Center for Advanced Holocaust Studies. The text of the paper is available online through the Center for Advanced Holocaust Studies, http://ushmm.org/research/center/publications/occasional/2004-08/paper.pdf.

Epilogue

1. My thanks to participant Rabbi Ephraim Eisen for his memories of the event, and to Aviva Ben-Ur for introducing me to Brenner's photograph, which appears in Frédéric Brenner, *Diaspora: Homelands in Exile*, 2 vols. (New York: HarperCollins, 2003), 1:220–21 (hereafter cited in text).

2. Brenner himself contributes to a Jewish-Native identification even as he alludes to a competition, as when he writes of another photograph in the collection, *Citizens Protesting Anti-Semitic Acts* (Billings, Montana, 1994): "It is very important for me to understand the significance of this anti-Semitic act within a Native American narrative. . . . Marjorie Bear Don't Walk, one of the leaders of the Billings Native American community, did not want to take part in the photograph at first. 'If the same problem had happened to us Indians,' she said, 'nobody would have stood up. There would have been no condemnation and no demonstration.' This is a photograph about Jews without Jews. In a way, the Native Americans are the Jews of this picture" (2:102).

3. Contra Rabbi Husbands-Hankin, Stanley Cavell asks ironically (as might Michael Chabon): "So the Jews in this picture wanted to learn from the Navajos about love of the land, and the Navajos from the Jews about how they survived for millennia in the condition of the Diaspora. Isn't it awfully late for such learning?" (2:101).

4. Elaine Heumann Gurian, *Civilizing the Museum: The Collected Writings of Elaine Heumann Gurian* (New York: Routledge, 2006), 189.

5. Ibid., 192–93.

6. Francisco Fe Alvarez, *En Busca de Quibiria: La Legendaria Ciudad de Oro* (Col del Valle, Mexico: Edamex, 1989).

Index

with 1967 war, 137–38, 141, 172,
227n73; *Mercy of a Rude Stream,*
118, 122–23, 127, 138, 142–45;
modernist aesthetic, 118; rediscovery
of Judaism through Spain and Israel,
139–40; relationship with Israel,
141–42; *Shifting Landscape,* 141;
"The Surveyor," 138–39; and T. S.
Eliot, 137, 140, 222n15; and Walton,
120–21, 123, 127, 223n20; writer's
block, 118, 144, 221n3; "The Wrong
Place," 139–40, 144; Zionism, 118,
136–37, 138. *See also Call It Sleep*
(Roth)
Rothenberg, Jerome: "Cokboy," 134;
Poland/1931, 134; *Shaking the
Pumpkin: Traditional Poetry of the
Indian North Americas,* 134; *Techni-
cians of the Sacred,* 134
Rozenfeld, Hersh, 85
Rydell, Robert W., 94, 97, 213n31

Said, Edward, 73
Sandburg, Carl, 62, 67; "Early Moon," 83
Sanford, John, 17, 108; *The People
from Heaven,* 88, 110, 111, 113–15,
219n112; and Riggs, 115–16,
221n126; *Scenes from the Life of an
American Jew,* 108, 115–16, 211n13,
218n98, 220n123, 221n126
Sapir, Edward, 60, 68
Saroyan, William, 62
Say It in Yiddish (Weinrich and Weinrich),
174–75
Schoolcraft, Henry Rowe, 63
Schwarzschild, Steven S., 138
Semel, Nava: *'I-yisra'el,* 172–73, 235n52
Sephardic immigrants to U.S., 13
Seven Arts, 65, 69

Shakespeare, William: *Othello,* 9, 188n31
Shandler, Jeffrey, 169, 170, 174–75
Shapiro, Lamed: "White Halla(h)," 80
Shell, Marc: *The End of Kinship,* 127
Shlain, Tiffany, 1
Shriftn, 17, 69–72; anthology of international verse, 76, 79, 83–84; cosmopolitan and internationalist, 70,
79–84, 84; final issue, 83–84; 1921
issue, 83; modernism, 64–65; and
Poetry: A Magazine of Verse, 64, 70;
primitivist woodcuts, 81; reenactment
of immigrant's journey from Europe
to America, 80; showcasing of art,
reviews, essays, and translations, 70,
79; translations of American Indian
chants, 75–76, 81, 83; translations
of American literature, 72–78; and
Whitman, 70, 80; Yiddish "interpretations" of Indian poetry, 82–83
Shtiker, Meyer, translation of Indian verse
for *Shriftn,* 76, 77–78, 83
Shvarts, Y. Y., 71, 72; *Kentucky,* 64, 74,
83; translation of "Salut au Monde,"
70, 74
Silko, Leslie Marmon, 4
Silver Shirts, 104, 216n71
Simon, Erasmus H., 32
Sitting Bull, 43, 132
Slezkine, Yuri, 7–8
Sloane, John, 98
Slobin, Mark, 44
Slotkin, Richard, 42
"slumming," 93–94
Smith, Janna Malamud, 159, 231n14
socialism, 8, 108, 171
Sollors, Werner, 8, 121, 224nn38, 39,
225n40
"The Song of the Sea," 170